The Daddy Track and The Single Father

by

GEOFFREY L. GREIF

Lexington Books

D.C. Heath and Company • Lexington, Massachusetts • Toronto

Library of Congress Cataloging-in-Publication Data

Greif, Geoffrey L.
The daddy track and the single father : coping with kids,
housework, a job, an ex-wife, a social life, and the courts /
Geoffrey Greif.
p.   cm.
Includes bibliographical references.
ISBN 0-669-19849-8 (alk. paper)
1. Single fathers—United States.   2. Custody of children—United
States.   I. Title.
HQ759.9f15.G69   1990
306.85′6—dc20
89-13611
CIP

Published simultaneously in Canada
Printed in the United States of America
Casebound International Standard Book Number: 0-669-19849-8
Library of Congress Catalog Card Number: 89-13611

The paper used in this publication meets
the minimum requirements of American National Standard
for Information Sciences—Permanence of Paper
for Printed Library Materials, ANSI Z39.48-1984.
♾™

Year and number of this printing:
90 91 92 8 7 6 5 4 3 2 1

Contents

Preface and Acknowledgments

THE DADDY TRACK AND THE SINGLE FATHER is meant to be both a descriptive and a self-help book. As such, the chapters describe what single fathers have experienced with housekeeping, childrearing, working, socializing, their ex-wives, and the court system. Their early lives and how they gained custody are also discussed. In-depth case studies and information from hundreds of interviews have been included, as have numerous suggestions for how to make single parenting successful. In addition, this book speaks to fathers in other single-parent situations. Chapters for joint custodians and widowers, also based on survey returns and interviews, round out the picture of those who father alone. It is believed that by understanding how others handle their lives, the reader will learn his situation is not unique and can become, if it is not already, a meaningful and enjoyable experience.

Based on my 1985 book, *Single Fathers*, and a new national survey completed in 1988 of over 1,100 separated and divorced single fathers, this book's purpose is twofold: to provide a thorough picture of this population as we enter the 1990s and to specifically help the father raising children alone on a full-time basis. It is rare that one gets to return to the scene of a crime, so to speak. Yet with this second survey of single fathers I have been able to do just that. Both surveys had samples of comparable size, which allows for some easy comparisons (see Appendix for a detailed discussion of the surveys). The opportunity to ask many of the same questions of fathers at two different points in the past decade has allowed me not only to wallow in data (perchance even to sink in it) but also to come to some tentative conclusions, given the limitations of the sample, about the changes this population is undergoing. There is good news and bad news.

In 1985 I predicted that the growth of this population would make life increasingly easy for the custodial father and his children. It is not clear that this has happened. In fact, statistical comparisons of the two groups show that the fathers in 1988: 1) were dating less; 2) were less socially satisfied; and 3) found balancing work and childrearing more difficult. Learning that single fathers were dating less and enjoying it less is not surprising, given the rise in concern about sexually transmitted diseases. The greater difficulty at work is more puzzling. Were there so few gains in the workplace during the 1980s? Is there a daddy track that hurts men who are raising their children alone? There may be. The fathers in 1988 were more apt to have been fired, to have quit, and to have experienced job-related changes because of their child-care responsibilities. In fact, as the stories of these fathers unfold in subsequent chapters, it may be that they are on a daddy track in a host of areas that extends far beyond just their life at work.

Comparisons between fathers in 1982 and 1988 raise another intriguing question. Were the 1988 fathers less unusual and more likely to have difficulty adapting? The earlier fathers had usually gained custody during the 1970s, when it was a much less common arrangement. They were perhaps more extraordinary because they contended with a less sympathetic court system and a society that was unaccustomed to this custodial arrangement. A very strong desire to parent alone as well as a higher-than-average income were two of their distinguishing characteristics. By the middle to late 1980s, this arrangement was more common. For example, from 1985 to 1987 in Baltimore County roughly 10 percent of custody decisions were going to the father and a higher percentage ended up as joint custody. Fewer than 10 years earlier, in 1978, in the same county, only 4 percent of the cases ended up with the father or in joint custody. The 1988 fathers were not the pioneers their predecessors were. They may not, as a group, have had the outstanding financial and personal characteristics that some of those pioneers had. As single fathers are now more common (there are about 1 million of them), this would be expected. What this new book supplies, then, is an up-to-date and realistic appraisal of the demands now facing many of these fathers.

Now for the good news. The 1988 fathers reported more satisfaction with their children's progress, held a higher opinion of the children's mother, and reported more amicable visitation arrangements. How to interpret this? It could be that as divorce becomes more institutionalized, children have fewer problems than their predecessors dealing with it. It could also be that as this custody arrangement becomes more common, relationships between the father and the noncustodial mother are less extraordinary. Increasingly mothers are becoming noncustodial for reasons that have little to do with their emotional stability or behavior. Money, the desire to get out of an unhappy marriage, the children's choosing to stay with the father in their own home, and career choices are more often considerations now. This may mean that these custody arrangements can be carried out under less acrimonious or upsetting circumstances. The public also knows more now about the importance of not putting children in the middle of parental conflict. These parents may be able to work together more easily than in previous times.

IMPRESSIONS

From my own interviews with the fathers and my debriefing the more than thirty students who also conducted interviews, two distinct types of custodial fathers emerge. The first is the father, who, when initially interviewed, says that things are going well for him and his children. This response is almost a reflex. As is typical of many men, the father adopts a stiff-upper-lip mentality as a way of dealing with his situation. The feeling is that parenting is a job that has to be undertaken and there is no need to complain about it. Not much insight is offered into the reasons for the divorce or for his getting custody. A deep understanding of the needs of the children is not forthcoming. It is as if this father has not given himself permission to think about these things, that he has decided that such thoughts will only distract him from the task of parenting. It is a defense, and, perhaps, a necessary one. His life is painted in shades of black and white with very little gray in-between. Yet as the interview unfolds, the father slowly opens up and begins to question his situation. He permits himself the luxury of considering the issues raised. His defenses start to fall. His own pain spills out, as does anger at his ex-wife. Raising children alone becomes a little less cut and dried. It also becomes more realistic.

The second type of father makes a very different initial impression. He expresses some frustration with his situation, describes the difficulties inherent in single parenting, and is very much aware of the gray areas that shade so many of life's tough decisions. He is able to go right to the heart of the single-parent issue. The children and he are struggling but surviving. He usually has sought the advice of other single parents, read a book or two, and perhaps even sought counseling for his children and himself. The optimism in his voice is palpable. He allows himself the necessary chuckle at his and his children's foibles. They become his war stories. Ultimately, he says, things are working out for the best. I believe him.

This book is not meant to be a scientific discourse on the topic of fathering alone. Peer-reviewed articles based on these surveys are included in the bibliography and can be acquired either from the professional journal where they were published or from the author. I have tried to make this information as accessible as possible to the fathers who need it. I hope this book will be helpful to the fathers who spend so much of their time, energy, thoughts, and love raising their children alone.

Many people have helped with this book in different ways over the years. The staff of Parents Without Partners and *The Single Parent* magazine have shown, over the last eight years, a consistent level of support and interest in the topic of single fathers. Their realization that more information is needed on this population has helped single parents learn a great deal more.

Lexington Books needs to be thanked for the safe harbor it has provided in bringing this book to print. Their eagerness to look again at these fathers has made the writing much easier for me. Thanks, Margaret and Steve.

Alfred Demaris, Ph.D., was instrumental in designing the questionnaire, in analyzing the data, and in helping me understand the finer points. A very fine statistician, sociologist, and theoretician, he has the knack for bringing excellence to everything he does. Our telephone calls between Baltimore and Bowling Green were, and continue to be, a great learning experience for me.

Risa Garon, LCSW, the coauthor of chapter 13, has been a pleasure to work with. Her expertise as director of the Children of Separation and Divorce Project, a clinical service at the Columbia, Maryland, Family Life Center for families experiencing separation, divorce, and remarriage, is easily recognized with the clear suggestions she provides the fathers.

Special thanks goes to the University of Maryland at Baltimore's Designated Research Initiative Fund, which provided partial funding so that the research could be undertaken. A host of University of Maryland School of Social Work and Community Planning students also need to be mentioned. Between September 1987 and December 1989, almost forty students helped gain a sample from the local court systems, coded returned questionnaires, and telephoned fathers throughout the United States. A few helped analyze the information gained from the interviews. The students were all inquisitive, industrious, humorous, and a pleasure to work with. Space forbids me from mentioning every one of you, but **Thanks Again!**

A special nod needs to be made to my parents, wife, and daughters. Their continued support in their own ways has made my career and writing a pleasure.

Finally, I wish to thank the fathers who participated in the research. It was your willingness to fill out the questionnaire, be interviewed, and share an important part of your life that has made this book possible. I dedicate the book to you and to other fathers raising their children alone.

1

Fathering Alone

FATHERING alone! The idea strikes terror in the hearts and minds of men who have never considered taking full-time responsibility for their children after the breakup of their marriage. If it does not strike terror, it at least makes most men uncomfortable. How could it not? Traditionally, mothers have been the ones to gain custody if the marriage falls apart. A father was supposed to visit the children and pay child support. Yet increasingly, the roles are reversing and it is Dad who is doing the childrearing alone. It is not an easy role to assume, though, particularly for fathers who grew up during a time when women were expected to be the primary caretakers. One father, raising his children alone, said he felt like a "freak."

If you have just gained custody, you may wonder how you and your children are ever going to survive. You may feel your hair graying even as you read this. If you have been a custodial father for a few years, you may wonder how you managed to have survived this long. You are probably filled with questions: How do I handle working and raising my children alone? Will I ever have time to myself? What about dating? Who is going to do the housework? How can I get along better with my children? What do I do with a daughter who is going through puberty? Will I ever be able to communicate civilly with my ex-wife again? Can she and I really continue to parent together even though the marriage is over? Will I have to spend an arm and a leg on lawyers if she drags me into court? Will my children and I ever get over the pain of the family's breakup?

Whatever the length of time you have been raising your children on your own (or if you are considering this custody arrangement), it is important to know you are not alone. About 1 million divorced and separated fathers in the United States are now raising almost 1.5 million children.[1] Another one hundred thousand widowers are raising their children and a larger number of fathers are involved in joint custody arrangements. Even more important for you to know is that these fathers are not only surviving but thriving. Fathering alone is an incredibly fulfilling experience for many of those whose stories fill this book.

These fathers have moved into what, until recently, has been a virtual no-man's land. When they were growing up, single fathers with custody were unheard of except in extreme family situations. Here they tell of their own struggles with this role. They tell of gaining custody, often with little preparation, of working to get their house in order, and of trying to fit together the emotional puzzle pieces of their own and their children's lives. While many are completely unprepared for this, others are well aware of the tasks before them. They speak of having a strong desire for single parenting. They have been intimately involved in their children's lives—assisting at the birth, changing diapers and feeding them as babies, and maintaining an active role throughout their early years. They have had time to prepare. For them, assuming custody is the most natural of steps.

Others feel emotionally prepared even though they may not have been overly involved with their children when they were younger. These men have begun to sense what their family means to them after years of toiling in the workplace. They want custody very much but may not have a clear idea of what is in store for them.

The experiences and wisdom of the separated and divorced fathers reported on in this book were gained from interviews and a survey of more than 1,100 of them (see appendix A for a description of the research). With the information they provide, and building on an earlier survey of another 1,136 fathers, a comprehensive profile is constructed that will help single fathers understand what life is like raising children alone. This information may help dispel some of the myths that have spread about these dads.

General conclusions about the fathers are presented in the

chapters that follow. Briefly, what we'll discuss is that housekeeping, after an initial few months, does not pose a problem for these fathers. The relationships they establish with their children are quite positive, with the fathers expressing a great deal of satisfaction and pride in how their children progress. Balancing the demands of work and childrearing is much more problematic, with some fathers even being fired or having to quit because of being a single parent. Socializing also is difficult for the fathers, as is establishing a consistent relationship with their ex-wives. Finally, the court process and child support determinations appear to be unpredictable, leaving many fathers bewildered and worried about the possibility of future court appearances.

The difficulties fathers experience are not surprising. The trials of single parenting are well-documented, especially from the mother's perspective. Women have been grappling with similar problems for years and have had to do it with less income than many fathers. Mothers also have had less social support and less praise. Because people expect the mother to be the parent with custody, they tend to give her less assistance when the marriage ends. No one rushes to her aid. Yet in the hands of a father, single parenting in some ways is quite different. When a father gains custody, people think, as one man put it, it is noble. The father is often praised for being so caring and for staying involved with his children. As the praise is being heaped on his shoulders, certain benefits come his way. He may receive offers of help with child care, cooking, cleaning, and shopping. For many fathers, this attention is greatly needed and appreciated.

At the same time, offers of assistance and attention can have their down side. He may get the feeling that people want to help him because they think fathers are incompetent to parent alone. The offers of help that are intended to ease the way may be insulting. These reactions from others can add to the father's own confusion about how he should act.

Pats on the back and offers of assistance are not universally forthcoming, of course. Some men get ignored when they have custody. The community of mothers that exists does not always provide a haven for them. The mothers may sympathize with the ex-wife or not know how to relate to a man in the father's position. As a result, some dads feel discriminated against by a world that assumes a mother is the only competent parent. School-teachers wait to start conferences until the mother arrives. Notes are sent home from school addressed to Mom. Child-oriented magazines and television advertisements pretend fathers do not exist.

If you have custody you no doubt have experienced some of these reactions. People may have acted surprised when they heard you have custody. They may have tried to bring the conversation around to asking about your ex-wife. They may have praised, yet doubted, you. Your children may also have experienced some of this scrutiny because you are raising them. Your family may be feeling buffeted by people's reactions to your parenting alone; you are never quite sure how the next person you meet will react.

Historically, it was not always that way. We do not have to look too far back to a period when fathering alone was a frequent occurrence.

A Historical Look at Custody

Before this century, a father was much more likely to be the parent raising the children alone, for two reasons. First, the high mortality rate associated with childbirth plunged many fathers, particularly in rural areas with less developed medical facilities, into widowerhood.[2] Second, fathers had social status, whereas mothers—and women in general—had little. Men had always been the dominant sex and there was no reason for them not to raise their children if the marriage ended. But by the mid-1800s, profound changes were afoot. These would initially increase the father's economic power, while eventually eroding his control over his children. During that period, the Industrial Revolution began pulling men away from the farm and into the factory and the urban economic system. No longer were they around the house teaching sons and daughters crafts, hunting, and farm work. As men developed skills in the workplace their economic power over women grew. Women who had worked on the farm or at home had few salable skills or property they could easily market to support a family. In cases of contested divorce, the mother would not win because she had little chance of supporting herself. The mother's social status was so much lower than the father's that even when she did have custody, the courts usually absolved the father of paying child support.[3] The status of children was no better. They were seen as second-class citizens and the property of the father.

With the close of the nineteenth century came further evolution. In an era of progressivism, the legal position of children began to improve. They gained rights of their own. Women's status also improved. The father's departure from the home for the workplace had resulted in the mother's gaining primacy with the children. She became the nurturer and caretaker of an increasingly valued part of the family while the father was away.[4] With the suffragette movement in the early 1900s, and other gains, including women's wholesale participation in the workforce during the First World War, her status was further enhanced. Help for the mother seeking custody came from another front. Modern psychology from Freud began characterizing the mother's involvement as vital during the child's socalled tender years, the period between birth and four years old.

This changing view of the mother affected the way parents made decisions about custody when a marriage ended. A father who was trying to prove his mettle away from home in the workplace would be loathe to assume the care of children, particularly when the mother's role was acknowledged to be so important. The courts tended to agree. Only in clear cases of maternal instability or immorality did a father have a chance of gaining custody.

The result has been the supremacy of women in gaining and maintaining custody. This supremacy has eroded only in the last decade. The reasons for this decline are many and stem largely from the women's movement. The women's movement has provided women more options for how they wish to pursue their lives. They can more easily define themselves in roles other than that of mother. Opportunities that did not exist in the workplace now do. Women who twenty years ago felt bound to an unhappy marriage by a lack of economic freedom can consider leaving. Society has forged ahead with improved methods of transportation and communication. More is known of other cities and ways of life. The ease with which a marriage can be legally dissolved has been enhanced. As a result, divorce is more common. With more divorces come more chances for men to be sole custodians. When there is a dispute, the courts are using more sex-neutral criteria to decide on custody. Finally, fathers are showing a greater interest in nurturing. The pendulum that had swung in favor of the mother has now swung back to a more middling position, one that results in fathers being more likely to gain custody of their children.

These changes have meant a great increase in the number of fathers with custody. Between 1980 and 1987, for example, their ranks grew by more than 50 percent, to just under 1 million. By comparison, the number of single mothers increased by only 16 percent.[5]

The Daddy Track

What emerges from the fathers' own descriptions is that there is a daddy track, a set of complex and often competing demands and roles that they are faced with when taking primary responsibility for their children. While some married fathers are on the daddy track, it seems to be particularly apt to consider single fathers raising their children in this way as they are the most affected by these issues. They are treated differently and they act differently because they are single fathers. For some, as mentioned, this treatment works to their advantage; for others it is problematical.

The phrase daddy track is adapted from the work of Felice Schwartz whose article on working mothers rekindled the use of the term mommy track to refer to women whose career progression was jeopardized if they were mothers.[6] Daddy track is being used here to apply not only to what happens to single fathers at work but also to refer to what happens to them socially, in the court system, with their children, and with regard to their feelings about themselves. It is not a phrase that is being used to imply that these fathers have a heavier burden than single mothers. In most cases, they do not. Yet these fathers do face many challenges. Their situation needs recognition.

Illustrative of the daddy track is the father who told me he felt like a freak raising his children alone, the man who quit his job because of his child care demands, the father who has difficulty finding a sitter for his children because teenage girls are afraid to be alone with a man in his house late at night, and the dad who had trouble getting custody and child support because the courts had never considered a father having custody. Using the term daddy track is meant to frame these fathers' experiences by recognizing them, spelling them out, and, hopefully, normalizing them so that they will find parenting easier.

As fathers move into these roles they are greatly misunderstood. Myths develop about how they gained custody, about their competence to parent, and about their ex-wives. These myths potentially hinder parents and children living in these custody arrangements from having realistic expectations. They may even frighten potential fathers away from considering sole custody.

About This Book

If you have custody or are contemplating it, this book is meant to help you understand what other fathers with custody are going through. If you have a knowledge of what their lives are like, it is hoped you will be able to appreciate your own experiences and to put them in a proper perspective. As you read about the various aspects of single parenting, you will see that some things are more difficult than others but that rewards can be found in most tasks. Suggestions, provided at the end of most chapters, are designed to help you deal with the issues discussed in that chapter.

Chapter 2 describes the lives of two very different fathers. Dave gained custody without a court contest and is raising his young son, Jerry, with little assistance from Jerry's mother. For Dave, trying to balance work and child care and deciphering where to draw the line between the two, has been an important growth experience. Mark, on the other hand, has been battling his ex-wife ever since she deserted the family. Over the years she has gained custody of some of the children and is on the threshold of leaving Mark with none of them. Mark is philosophical about it, and hangs on to the hope that as the children get older they will appreciate what he has done for them.

Some of the myths about the childhoods, marriages, divorces, and custody arrangements of fathers with custody are debunked in chapter 3. We see that many of the commonly held beliefs, particularly about how the father gains custody, are not true.

Chapters 4 through 8 look at the everyday demands and joys of single parenting: running the household, getting along with the children, working, trying to establish a social life, and maintaining a relationship with the ex-wife. These demands are not easy but they can be managed successfully.

What happens in court concerning custody and child support payments is covered in chapter 9. It is clear that fathers now have a greater chance of getting custody than before, but it is a different story when it comes to child support.

Chapters 10 and 11 focus on the joint custodian and the widower. Even though the bulk of the book focuses on the divorced or separated father with custody, chapters on these two groups have been included because they are coping with many of the same issues in raising their children alone. Based on questionnaire returns and interviews with these fathers, portraits are painted that help to round out our overall understanding of fathering alone.

Chapter 12 is the story of one family twenty-five years after the children first began living with their father. Now adults, the children look back on life with their dad and consider what having been raised by him means in their attempts to establish relationships of their own.

The focus of chapter 13 is on the children. We discuss what children of divorce are going through when they move in with their father and offer specific suggestions for how to make that transition an easier one. The topic of children in therapy is also covered. In addition, twenty-six adult children offer their views on having been raised by their father. Most are optimistic about their future.

The last chapter offers a look at the changes experienced by the fathers and noncustodial mothers over time. What they have gone through, whether there has been a remarriage or a new custody arrangement, is all considered. A look to the future of single parenting is included.

A brief comment is needed about the noncustodial mother.

Her specter appears throughout this book. As is discussed in chapter 8, how she copes living away from the children can have a profound impact on the single father and his children. It is not easy for her. These mothers are greatly misunderstood. People are uncomfortable when a mother does not have custody and react negatively to her because motherhood has been deified for so long. When the mother is comfortable with the situation, life can be much smoother for everyone.

I hope reading this book will make it easier for you to accept yourself as a single father and your ex-wife as a noncustodial mother. Such acceptance will benefit not only you and your ex-wife, but the people you are most concerned about—your children. The message here is that you can raise your children on your own and you can do it competently, with nurturing, and with love.

2

Two Families

THE two families described in this chapter provide profiles of the single-father experience following a marital breakup. They are presented in depth so that you can see the types of experiences that fathers have had raising children alone. As will be seen, both families encountered some difficulty, with the first family ultimately having more resolution than the second. Dave's story is one of success, while Mark's is one of a continually unfolding struggle.

Dave

Dave, now forty-three, has been raising his seven-year-old son alone for three years. He has lived in Arizona his whole life, the son of a two-parent family. In his neighborhood, in the 1950s, divorce was virtually unheard of. His image of a family was of two parents, two children, and a dog. If there were space for a house in that image, it would be a two-story dwelling with a yard and a white picket fence. As a child, his image of himself as an adult was also naturally straight out of the 1950s. He would be the breadwinning, baseball-playing, disciplining dad that was so typical of those fathers he knew and watched on television every evening after dinner.

His father was a presence in the family, sort of like the rudder on a ship, but it was his mother who left an indelible impression on him. It is an impression he has thought about many times since he became a single parent. "My mother was always there. But things changed with the times when she went off to work as a part-time librarian. Like many working mothers today, my mother entered the work force to provide additional income for the family and to give herself a new challenge. It was during that time that she must have felt the way that I sometimes do now—torn between my family responsibilities and my career. This is undoubtedly also experienced by working mothers now, too."

Dave was well aware of the change in the time his mother could devote to the family, but it did not appear to hurt his teen years. Dave's high school years were also typical. "In high school I had the usual amount of boyfriends, girlfriends, good and bad years." When he went to college, he decided to be a business major, a field he would pursue upon graduation. College was not all work, he laughs. "I experienced much that was out there," he says, in terms of sexual experimentation. By the time he graduated and started his first job, he was ready to settle down. After his first week with the company, he met Rose, whom he would later marry. He was a middle-level manager and she was an executive secretary. "I was first drawn to her by her physical attractiveness. I guess that always comes first. She was very peppy, too." After a two-year courtship, they were married. Both were in their mid-twenties. His career path seemed set. Dave was constructing the image of family life he had held as a boy. He was going to climb up the corporate ladder. She would work for a few more years and then would stay home with the children they hoped to have. Life seemed stable.

Sooner than they had wanted, though, Rose became pregnant. Within a year after being married, Jerry, their only child, was born. Dave was not in the delivery room when Jerry was born, but became immediately involved in his care and upbringing despite his early images of fathers' operating outside that realm of parenting. "I was much more interested in being with my son than most fathers. I did the potty training, helped change diapers, sterilized the bottles and all of that. Things around the house were fifty-fifty."

Even though responsibilities were shared around child care, Dave did not feel they were shared in the marriage. "I felt like I was putting much more into the marriage than Rose. We were just drifting apart. I wanted to work things out but she just lost interest. She was having emotional problems then, too. There was not a lot of fighting; rather, she would get in these moods and shut me out. Then she began working part-time in the evenings and doing less and less around the home. I picked up the slack." The dream of the 1950s-style family was fading. Five years after being married, they decided to break up, with the understanding that Jerry would live with Dave. "Marrying her was just a mistake from the beginning. My having custody was the obvious arrangement. I was more into him than she was and I was better able financially to take care of him. My sense of family had always been quite strong. There was no court battle. If she had contested it, I would have done everything I could have to make it turn out the same way." No child support payment arrangements were offered or requested. Dave believes the judge would never have agreed to it given their disparate economic situations. Jerry was only four at the time, so, as is often the case with parents of young children, he was not given a choice about where he wanted to live.

Raising Jerry Alone

Dave continued on a success track at work with the help of his parents. But the facility with which he was able to balance work and home was short-lived. "Like most men, success is important to me. I watched my father succeed, have everything taken away from him by a cheating business partner, and then build himself back up again. I learned many lessons from that. When I was married, I had become very successful with the company. I pushed and strived, largely because of my upbringing. I began to troubleshoot and travel to other companies to help them out. When I first became a single parent, I was still able to do a lot of that because my parents helped out when I went on trips. But when they died (within two years of Dave's gaining custody) it became impossible for me to take on the extra responsibilities."

When his parents died, Dave suddenly felt restricted. It was the first time that the demands of single parenting came crushing down on him. "I could no longer do whatever I had to do to get ahead. I lost the edge. My role as a parent was placing serious limitations on my potential for career advancement. Because of my involvement with Jerry when he was younger, I felt physically prepared to take care of him alone, but it was still difficult at first psychologically." The death of his parents had left a hole in his life that no one could fill. Not only were they his role models of how people coped with adversity, they were providing the needed time off from Jerry.

No assistance was forthcoming from Rose. For the first two years after the divorce, she almost never visited. Visitation has slowly increased but father and son have had to build their life without her. Relying on her became too problematic. She would come one week, then skip the next two scheduled visitations, then reappear. By 1989, they had agreed on a visitation schedule of four hours a week. "She has all kinds of personal problems so this has worked out the best for us. She sticks with this schedule. Her behavior still baffles me, though," Dave said.

Just as Dave began having difficulties, so did Jerry. "He seemed to hold back from me and then get angry all of a sudden and blow up." Dave took him to a child psychologist. "I was concerned he might have negative feelings toward women because of his mother. Also he had experienced a lot of losses in his life then. His grandparents and his dog died about the same time that the divorce became finalized. He saw the psychologist for three months and it helped. I learned from this that Jerry is a survivor." Dave still has some minor concerns about Jerry, but these seem to be typical of the kind most parents worry about. "I don't know about his getting along with his friends sometimes. People comment that he seems a lot older than his age, more mature. Most of his contacts have been with adults. Luckily, some children are moving into the neighborhood, so he can make some friends his age."

The home has been maintained primarily by Dave. Jerry helps out with the cooking and with cleaning his own room. Dave is used to running the household, because he did it in the waning months of the marriage, when Rose had turned her interests elsewhere. "I do send my shirts out," he laughs. "I have to look good for work."

Time has given Dave the chance to cope with his parents' death and to get his priorities in order. While he wants career advancement to take a back seat to his life with Jerry, he finds it is not often easy to put work on hold. Perhaps remembering the successes and failures of his father at work, while providing him strength in certain areas, has also made him wary of letting that area of his life slide. He is acutely aware of the conflicts. "The demands of family life are strong. My best friend, who has no children of her own, calls children a major project. Having kids today is complicated. The balancing act a parent must perform to juggle everything is tough. Our normal schedule of school, sports practice, games, reading tutor, dentist, doctor, PTA, homework, summer camp, and the need for us to have quality time is often more than one can accomplish. And what do you do at work when the school nurse calls with an emergency? How many school trips can you turn down because of work? And how often do I get calls at home at night that I am needed at the office that minute? The demands of work and family are not ones that can be met by making a one-time commitment to act in a certain way. Both are constantly changing."

Dave has found time in his busy schedule for a new relationship. Initially after his divorce he shied away from dating. Then he jumped back in with both feet, playing the field as he had done during his college days. Recently a relationship turned serious and, as this book was going to press, plans were being made for a wedding. His fiancée is one more person he has to fit into the family equation.

"The line between family and job responsibilities is not always drawn in black and white. I have strived to fulfill both of these jobs to the best of my abilities. In my day-to-day life, I am a manager. At other times, I am Jerry's dad. However, in the final analysis, it is my son and family life that mean the most to me. I feel very fortunate that things have worked out well for us. Knock on wood. Having him precluded me from doing a lot of things. But you do what you have to do."

Mark

Mark is a 37-year-old divorced father of four who lives in Arlington, Virginia, a suburb of Washington, D.C., where he works for the post office. I have known Mark since 1984 and have interviewed him and his family on seven occasions. Four of the interviews have been in his home and have included a changing cast of his children. In fact, since 1985, his children have begun to slowly migrate from his house to the home of his ex-wife. Currently, only his youngest sons are living with him. He is a tall, thin man, initially reserved when talking. With time, he warms to the subject at hand and becomes expansive, particularly when the children are out of earshot. It is important to him to make a good impression during the interviews by showing that both his home and children are well taken care of. He willingly gives me permission to ask them any questions I think are relevant. He says he wants other fathers to learn from his experiences.

Mark was born in Georgia, the third of three sons. He was raised by both his parents but his father died soon after Mark went to college. He describes his parents' relationship as loving, though he feels his father never showed much affection for him or his two older brothers. It was a similar upbringing to Dave's— Mark never thought about parenthood, much less the possibility of raising children on his own.

At the University of Georgia Mark met a young woman and after a brief courtship, they married. Mark was only twenty. It was quickly obvious to them both that it was a mistake and the marriage was annulled. That experience, Mark says, made him gun-shy of any involvement with women for a while. His next few semesters were spent in the library. Two years later, when he was close to graduating, he met Ellen, the future mother of his four children. She worked near the university in a bank and had just completed high school. Despite the mistake of the first marriage, Mark again married after a very short courtship and agreed to move with her and her family to northern Virginia, where her father was relocating. Mark was physically attracted to her but wonders now if he was trying to escape Georgia and the burden of responsibility for his widowed mother. Mark, a liberal arts major, found a job working for the postal service. They set up a house near their in-laws.

One year later, their first child, Sally, was born. A second daughter, Polly, followed in quick succession. Three and four years later, two sons were born, Tommy and Lee. The marriage was shaky from the beginning. The newlyweds had little in common. Each was perhaps running from something when they married. Mark did not find the escape he hoped for in marriage and Ellen remained too tied to her family. Mark was working hard but having trouble advancing. Ellen longed for the south and felt constantly barraged by her parents' intrusions.

When Lee was eight weeks old, Ellen left town with a man who was a close friend of Mark's. For her there was once again the attempt at escape. Mark found himself alone with an infant, another boy in diapers, and two girls, five and six. His mother, who had remarried, stepped in and offered to take all four children. Mark considered it and refused. Even though he had never been very involved with the children, he thought he could manage. He also was furious at Ellen and wanted to prove to her that she was no longer needed. He slowly learned how to cook and do the laundry. A neighbor was hired to babysit for the younger boys and help get the girls to school on the days Mark left early for work.

Six months later, Ellen returned. Her new relationship had fallen apart and she wanted custody. Mark refused. He had become quite attached to the children and they were doing okay with him. The first of many court fights followed. The judge saw no reasons to change custody given the children's satisfactory progress. Ellen was granted visitation. During the next five years a series of court battles raged around custody, child support, and visitation. Mark wanted to hang on to the children while Ellen continued to try to chip away at his stronghold.

LIFE AS A SINGLE FATHER

Mark's fury at Ellen for leaving was unrelenting. They essentially did not speak for six years. The children's birthdays were celebrated at two houses each year. The children took vacations with each parent and celebrated holidays twice. Cooperation was a word that did not exist in their parenting vocabularies. Even visitation posed a problem for Mark. "When the children went to her house every other weekend, they were spoiled rotten. She would undo in a few days what I was trying to build up in-between. It was like she would dress them up to look pretty, play with them, and then put them back on the shelf when she was finished."

Children are usually aware when they are in the middle of

their parents' tug-of-war and Sally was no exception. The older the child, the more likely the judge is to ask the child to choose where he or she wants to live. As Sally approached her adolescence she began acutely feeling the pressure of having to make such a decision. She told me, "I have to decide (where I want to live) because I can't keep on thinking about it. If I go with my mom, my dad will be angry and my grandmother won't like it. I don't know what I am going to do. They are always fighting over me." Sally believed she would lose her father's love if she went with her mother. She also did not want to be separated from her siblings. Yet she began questioning how comfortable she would feel living with her father as she got older: "I am starting to develop. I wear a bra sometimes (her mother bought it) and I don't know what else will happen. I need my privacy sometimes and Mom would be better about that."

A few months later Sally decided she wanted to move out. Arguments were escalating between her and her father as well as between her and the other children. But Mark was still adamant about not letting Sally live with her mother. As he told me, Ellen's "attitude" was not right yet. Six months later, as the fighting with Sally escalated further, Mark relented and she moved out. She began visiting on occasional weekends which, over time, became less frequent.

During his years as a single parent, Mark had become psychologically withdrawn, which affected the family. It meant, for example, that the two oldest girls were occasionally put in charge of the younger boys, a situation the girls complained about from time to time. It also meant that they cooked for the whole family and often felt overburdened by the responsibilities. Chaos often seemed to reign. Polly described their mornings together as "rush hour. First you get up really early, have to get to the bathroom, feed the rabbit, and then get over to (a neighbor's house) for breakfast before going to school." Recognizing some of the problems he was having, Mark occasionally sought counseling for himself and the children, which had a Band-aid effect. Despite this atmosphere, the children were able to organize themselves to have a good time together. They once wrote a variety show they performed for their father and me.

Mark continued to work outside the home at the level he always had. His social life was nonexistent. When I asked Mark if he ever considered remarriage, all four children chimed in, naming women they knew and offering an opinion on whether Mark should or should not marry. Finally, everyone agreed that the most important criterion was that she be nice. "Yeah, someone nice like Mommy," Polly said. A long silence followed.

As the years passed, and perhaps hastened by Sally's departure, Mark's depression began to slowly lift. Polly, who had lived in Sally's shadow for years, began to assert herself more and moved into the role of family caretaker. Mark loosened his grip on his other children, no longer needing them as a defense against his own anger. He decided they should be allowed to live with their mother if that was their wish. A year later, Polly left.

Polly's stay with her mother lasted only nine months, though. Living with her sister, mother, and her mother's child from a second marriage, she felt left out, as if there were no place for her. She was having school problems, too. She had been held back a grade and was the oldest student in her class. Moving out of her mother's house would place her in a new school where she could make a fresh start. Polly also complained of constant battles with Sally about her involvement with boys. "Sometimes she would come home with two or three boys and they'd stay up late and make a lot of noise," Polly told me. When Polly returned to Mark's home, there was a great deal of discussion about who would be in charge. She wanted to forge a place for herself and immediately began talking as if she would assume a caretaking position. "They need me here. I want to get a job, earn some money, and fix this place up so that it is more cheerful." "Do your father and brothers need taking care of?" I asked. "Yes, they need a woman's touch," she replied with a big smile. Tommy and Lee were present but were hesitant to respond overtly to Polly's charge. They assured her, though, that they could take care of themselves. Mark predicted that trouble lay around the bend if Polly was returning with the idea of taking over.

He was correct. Polly did try to take charge. The three males resisted and conflict began. A battle also began on another front. The rules Mark set up for Polly, and Sally when she visited, were seen by them as Victorian. Mark defends one of his positions by saying that Sally should not have been allowed to hang out on the corner at night when she was only fifteen years old. Yet Sally had that freedom at her mother's house. Polly felt equally constricted. Serious school problems, which existed earlier, came into full bloom for all four children as the school year wore on. Counselors intervened and the whole family was seen in treatment. It was the first time in years they had been in the same room together. The counselors attempted to establish similar rules in both homes, a common therapeutic intervention when tensions following a divorce are high and expectations are unclear. It was to little avail and Polly moved out before the start of the next school year.

As Mark tells it, "Polly was missing her mother and her mother was working on her to come back after school was out. She moved out four months ago and I have not seen her or Sally since then. Polly told me that I was trying to run her life and that I did not know how to love. It is interesting. Those are the same words that her mother said about her own father (the girls' grandfather) when she tried to break away from him. My ex has also remarried and the girls get along pretty well with her new husband. Now Tommy is talking about going to live with them, too. That is his decision. In some ways having them go is kind of a relief because of all the fighting. But I miss them, too. And, yes, I would take them back if they wanted to come back. But it is not fair to have them bouncing back and forth all the time. It is not fair to them or to me."

Mark is now no longer depressed. His standing aside so his children could go live with their mother, while resulting in a sad outcome for him, is a sign of his willingness to move ahead with his life. This was a necessary rite of passage for him, yet one that he reached with great ambivalence. As long as he clung to the children as a way to get back at Ellen, he was potentially hurting himself and them. At the same time, Mark viewed their living with him as being in their best interests, as he believed for years that their mother was a bad influence. He was caught between respecting their wishes to leave, yet feeling they were making the wrong choice.

"What is most remarkable," Mark says, "is that I have a friend who is a few years ahead of me with this. His wife left him with three kids and he raised them alone for a while before they left to go with her. Now that they are all teenagers and older they are coming around again and seeing him. I think this period that I am going through will pass. I raised them alone for almost eight years and I am hopeful that, as my daughters think about it and get a little older, they'll come around, too. I guess we'll see."

Conclusions

Dave had no difficulty getting and maintaining custody, but Mark has had to struggle from the beginning and at some point may be without any of his children. Dave's experiences show how, when there is little interest on the part of the mother, a father is left completely on his own. Coming in to single parenting with experience in child care, Dave has other demons to battle—the most significant being balancing the conflicting demands of work and child care responsibilities. He draws his strength from the model set by his mother, who entered the work force while still raising children, and his father, who persevered through business difficulties. He is comfortable with most aspects of his life and even has commented that the problems of being a single parent are overrated. He is doing well.

Mark's experiences reflect the tortuous process that many other single fathers have had to undergo to gain custody and retain it. His demon is the terrible burden of giving children the chance to choose where they want to live when the other choice is not believed to be a good environment. Standing aside and allowing that choice to unfold has been excrutiatingly painful, especially given the anger that he felt toward Ellen.

Almost every father who reads this book should be able to see himself in some part of these men's stories. These two fathers are at different points on the parenting continuum. Yet what they have in common is a desire to do what is best for their children. Sometimes that desire works out for everyone. Other times it results in misguided attempts. Ultimately, as with all the child-related issues discussed in this book, the answer as to what has worked out for the best may lie some years in the future. In the meantime, fathers are handling their day-to-day concerns the best way they can with the knowledge they have at hand.

3

Ten Myths about the Fathers' Childhoods, Marriages, and Custody Arrangements

FAMILY life can be like a roller coaster ride. There are ups and downs, stops and starts, twists and turns, and periods of great momentum, all of which one can try to predict by studying the track or looking around the next curve. But the vagaries of the course nonetheless surprise, thrill, and sometimes scare the rider. When two people first consider each other seriously as spouses, they begin the climb up the steps to get on the roller coaster. If they are wise, they first study the structure, look at the person operating the ride, and wonder whether it is a safe one. When they get married, the ride starts. Traveling with them are all their dreams and expectations about the future, their experiences, and their present day-to-day lives. Their friends are there, along with their families and their workworlds. The curves of the ride are sometimes easy and sometimes treacherous. Many couples stop the ride before they make it once around the track.

When children enter the family, the roller coaster ride takes on more momentum. The turns become more treacherous, the thrills more exhilarating, the stops and starts more frightening. Many families can hang together and make the ride fun. Other families cannot and decide to jump off.

Usually, when families jump off the roller coaster, the children live with their mother and the father becomes the visiting parent. For the fathers with custody, however, something different happens somewhere along the route. The mother and father take on unconventional roles. Most fathers gain custody as the culmination of a number of events that slowly evolve. The ways fathers gain custody and the events leading to that point are as unique as the individual fathers, their ex-wives, and their children.

Because the phenomenon of the single father is still fairly new, people do not understand how these custody arrangements come about. When information is lacking, myths develop. Throughout almost a decade of involvement in the topic of single fathers, I have heard a number of myths about these men that need to be substantiated or eliminated. These will be presented here with discussion about their viability. A few turn out not to be myths but relatively accurate representations. Most, though, reflect a lack of understanding of these fathers.

Life before the Marriage

Myth #1. Fathers who gain custody were themselves products of single-parent families and were most likely raised by their fathers.

Among the fathers interviewed in the 1982 and 1988 studies, no clear connection was found between the types of families the fathers were raised in and their becoming single custodial parents. For example, about 80 percent of the fathers were raised in a two-parent family. The rest were raised primarily by their mother and only occasionally by their father. If the father was the primary custodian it was often because of the death of the mother, rather than because of a marital breakup. In research on mothers without custody, a similar exploration also evinced no clear trends in those mothers having been raised either in single-parent families or by one particular parent. Thus the parental structure of the home for the custodial father or noncustodial mother was not found to be clearly related to the father's later custody arrangement. At the same time, other research has found that being raised in a divorced family is linked to being more likely divorced as an adult.[1] This, though, is not tied to becoming a custodial father.

Myth #2. Fathers who gain custody were unusually interested or involved in taking care of children when they were young.

The fathers were asked whether they had thought about children when they were growing up. The majority, over 60 percent, said they had not given much consideration to fatherhood before they got married. Many added that they did not think about fatherhood even after they had married and were attempting to start a family. While no comparison data are available to tell us how fathers who did not gain custody would answer this question, this does show that for most fathers the desire for custody developed later in life, and not as a childhood quest. In fact, even among the fathers who did report a strong fathering urge, no one spoke of single parenting. Rather, as one father put it, "When you are brought up with a mom and dad, you just assume you'll have kids."

In addition, only a few fathers reported having spent an unusually large amount of time taking care of younger siblings or babysitting as a pastime. The fathers, by and large, did not describe childhoods or childhood interests that would help predict later assumption of custody.

Into the Marriage

Myth #3. As young adults and at the time of the marriage, the seeds of single fatherhood were being sown.

Is there a natural selection process that occurred? Did fathers choose their wives knowing subconsciously or consciously that they would end up with custody? Were the courtship patterns different among this population of fathers? The answer to all of these questions is no. When the fathers began dating their future wives, they were attracted to them by a number of qualities, but almost no father mentioned parenting ability or potential as being an attractive feature. Nor was mention made of concern about the mother's inability to parent. The rare exceptions were fathers who were marrying for the second time. They chose their wives in large part because they believed they would be good caretakers. In many instances those women were good caretakers even though they did not end up with custody. Much more common were fathers who said they married their wives for their physical attractiveness (the most common reason) and their personality (the second most common reason). Fathers occasionally listed intelligence or similarities between themselves and their wives as reasons. A few had married childhood sweethearts and said they could not remember, nearly twenty years later, what the initial attraction had been.

An unplanned pregnancy was rarely the precipitating event that led fathers into marriage. Almost 90 percent were married for at least nine months before the first child was born. Thus nothing outstanding was found in the courtship patterns that could have predicted later events.

Myth #4. Fathers with custody were present at the birth of their children and as a result established a unique bond with them.

Some support was found for this. Many were involved in the whole birthing process, taking special classes with their wives and attending the birth of the child as either a helper or an observer. About half the fathers were actually in the room at the time of the birth and a number of others said they would have attended the birth had they not been sent out of the room while a cesarean section operation was performed. (Hospital practices about allowing fathers in the room during this procedure have varied over the years.) Their presence during the birth resulted in many of them establishing a particularly close bond with their children, a common occurrence for men who do attend the birth. One father who reported not being especially interested in parenting before having children felt immediately bonded to his children because of being in the room: "It was fantastic. I really enjoyed it and I cried when both children were born. It changed everything I felt about kids."

A father with a similar orientation before the birth of his son said, "I was afraid I would not make a good father. I just didn't know. My wife and I had decided that we wouldn't have kids. Robert was an accident. But that day when he was born was the happiest day of my life. I was in the delivery room and I held him. I knew then that I would be a good father and I never changed my mind. I was always involved with him. Just like when he woke up for three o'clock feedings, I did it. His mother would sleep right through. You know how they say there is a mother-child bond and the mother hears the child even if she's asleep? Not in this case. It was Robert and me; we tuned in to each other. I knew that as soon as he was delivered. He cried and the doctor gave him to me."

Another father who was present at the birth said, "I think my older son and I have a closer bond because of my being there. I have a theory that it has to do with the fact that when he was born the doctor gave him to me first, right after he was born. When the younger son was born, my wife said she did not want that to happen again and so she ordered the doctor, 'Give him to me' right after he was born. That's the way it continues—the older one favors me and the younger one favors her."

Despite the impact that being in the room had on some of these fathers' feelings, it must be added that these fathers as a group were *not* more likely to have attended the birth of their child than other fathers in the last decade, according to comparisons with other research.[2] Some fathers who later gained custody felt they had no business being in the room. One self-described male chauvinist said in an interview that he was in a bar when his child was born and asked, "Isn't that where all men are?"

While attending the birth may have a significant influence on the later desire to have custody, this group of fathers was not more likely than fathers in general to be present at the birth of their children. Yet it was found that fathers who were present were more likely to describe themselves as being the parent most involved in childrearing in the year before the breakup. The connection can be made thus for this group that being at the birth was related to being more involved in childrearing. At the same time, other fathers who were present at the birth did not end up with custody, while fathers who were not present did.

Myth #5. Fathers with custody were very involved with their children during the early stages of the marriage.

Were the fathers very involved with their children from the beginning of their parenting? In most cases, not in the early stages. Once married, the couples tended to fall into traditional roles, with the male providing most of the income and the female running the household and taking care of the children. Although the fathers, *by their own description,* seem to have participated in childrearing and housekeeping during most of the marriage, many did not perceive themselves as being any different from the father next door. The fathers usually characterized their involvement as "average" when asked to compare themselves with other fathers they knew. Jeff, a mechanic, was one such father: "We started off like everybody else. I worked and she did the home. When the kids came, she took care of them. I was doing as much at home as the next guy. (It was not until) later, when she changed, I started doing more."

A few fathers did see themselves as being very involved from the beginning. One father said, "I was more involved than most during the marriage. So it was easy for me when I got custody. I had done a lot of the cooking, so it was not a big change when I had to do it all the time." Another father, whose involvement began with the birth of his child, shared most of the child care with his wife: "We took the birthing classes together, and I was there when our son was born. I stayed involved. It was part of who I was. I used to give him baths, feed him, and change him."

In some cases a father may in fact perceive himself as having a high level of participation with the children, only to find his children have a different impression. A father of three from Minnesota had a rude awakening about what he perceived as a high level of participation: "I was president of an athletic association that my kids and my wife were involved in. I was president of the recreation program. That took a lot of time. We spent a lot of hours and money planning improving the parks in the city. After the divorce, my daughter came to me and said, 'I know you did this and I know you did that, but when we had a problem you did not have time.' But they never really came to me and said, 'I have a problem.' They saw I was busy and went to their mother instead." The level of involvement of this group of fathers as a whole during the children's early years was not extraordinary.

Myth #6. The relationship between the custodial father and his wife was different than in typical marriages.

No support was found for this. The fathers describe a range

of relationships with their ex-wives that appear no different than others that end in divorce with the mother getting custody. Some fathers had very good, storybook relationships in which both partners shared interests while maintaining their own identity. When the divorce came, it was handled amicably. Manny, from Arizona, gives one example. He and his ex-wife split up when she fell in love with another man. He is not bitter or angry at her now (four years later) and said they had had an amicable marriage with an amicable divorce. She moved out, he kept the home and their two teenage sons.

Other fathers reported that their relationship was in trouble from the start but that they continued in the marriage, hoping things would improve or because they were afraid of a change. Following an initial attraction to each other, the couple may have slowly grown apart, sometimes resulting in hostility and sometimes in apathy. Some fathers stayed in the marriage because they felt trapped. Jan was one such father. He sensed something was wrong from the beginning. For religious reasons, after the children were born, he stayed married. When the youngest child was three, Jan learned that his wife was a lesbian. They stayed together for three more years, again for religious reasons. But after Jan slept with a prostitute and "learned what life was really all about," he asked for a divorce. Jan was an exception though. More often than not, it is the wife who ends the marriage.

TTe interactions during most of the marriages tend to be typical of other marriages that end in divorce. No unique patterns of interaction were found though some level of alcohol and/or drug abuse was found in at least one partner in a number of the cases. This conclusion is also based on extensive interviews I conducted with mothers without custody.[3] As will be shown with the next myth, though differences do appear in the ending stage of the marriage.

When the Marriage Floundered

Myth #7. The fathers were very involved with their children near the end of the marriage, which is why they gained custody.

Support was found for this to some extent. Approximately two out of every five fathers said they were the most-involved parent in the final year of the marriage. Only one in four said the mother was more involved. The remainder said the responsibility was shared. If the fathers rate their participation with the children as high, is it true? According to a sample of mothers without custody, no. When they were asked about the fathers' level of involvement with child care and housekeeping during the marriage, as compared with theirs, only a handful said the fathers were doing more.[4]

Further explanation is needed about this final period of the marriage. In many marriages there comes a time when one or both partners realize things are not going as well as they wished. It is at this point that the biggest shifts in behavior often occur. Sometimes these shifts result in the father's getting more involved in childrearing, which can set the stage for his getting custody later. The increased involvement usually occurs for two reasons: 1) to take care of the children, if the father senses a reduction in nurturing on the part of the mother, and 2) to preserve a sense of family for himself.

The fathers who became increasingly involved with their children because of a change in the mother's nurturing were more apt to be fathers who were disturbed by their wives' behavior. For example, one salesman with two sons said: "She started to go out on her own and spend more time away from the family. She would go out with friends. I took over some of the things she had been doing that weren't getting done with the kids and with the house. Then she said she wanted a divorce." Another father said: "She had a number of mental breakdowns and would be away from the family in the hospital. Her mother moved in for a while and helped out. But I ended up eventually doing most of it."

These fathers felt compelled to become more involved with their children due to their impression that the children's basic needs were not being met. It was the mother's withdrawal from the parenting role that resulted in their getting more involved.

This is in contrast to a second group of fathers who became more involved with their children in an attempt to preserve something for themselves. They saw their wives' parenting changing and felt a great closeness with their children that they wanted to maintain. One father of two boys, a psychologist, was asked at what point he took over responsibility for the children. He replied: "Two years before she left, we talked about the need for a separation. I felt she was off in her own world. I thought the kids should be with their mother. I was away from them for two days and I couldn't take being without them. So I came back and said if anyone has to leave it will have to be you. I don't know how I would have survived being a weekend parent. I knew this (having custody) was what I wanted and she made it easier by being the one to leave." There were also fathers in this group who assumed greater responsibility for their children because they wanted to hold on to a sense of family and not be alone. A few fathers did not like the idea of their wife's remarrying and having another man raise their children.

Not all fathers became more involved with their children when they sensed their wives changing their behavior. Some fathers, witnessing an abdication of the mothering role, responded by withdrawing, often leaving the children to drift. Fathers in this group candidly described turning to work for solace and not picking up the childrearing responsibilities. The reason? As one father said: "At the time I was not into kids."

It was not always the case that the mothers withdrew when the marriage floundered. In some of these marriages, the mothers became *more* involved with the children. Perhaps not getting what they needed from the marriage, the children became a source of solace and support for them. Fathers in this situation would withdraw or would increase their own involvement, competing with the mother for the children. This competition often provided the basis for custody battles that would follow.

Finally, some fathers sensed a shift in the marital relationship that bore no connection to the mother's participation in parenting. They perceived the mother as still fulfilling her parenting role at the previous level even though the husband-wife relationship was souring. Fathers in these failing marriages either turned away from their children and wives, maintained their prior level of participation, or increased their participation.

In the see-saw relationships described here, where a shift in the marriage often, but not always, results in a changed father-child relationship, there were five different groups of fathers:

1. Those who sensed a lack of involvement in parenting by the mother and responded by becoming more involved to fulfill their children's needs;

2. Those who sensed the mother's withdrawal and became more involved with the children to fulfill their own needs;

3. Those who turned away from the family as the mother turned away;

4. Those who turned toward or away from their children as the mother increased her involvement; and

5. Those whose involvement with their children was unrelated to the mother's parenting.

Thus, to some extent, fathers do become more involved with their children near the end of the marriage. This involvement lays the groundwork, in some cases, for their later acquisition of custody.

After the Marriage

Myth #8. These marriages end on more unusual notes than most marriages.

Mixed support is found for this. It is often believed that these marital relationships were characterized by extreme animosity and bizarre behavior or that some rare event caused the dissolution. Comparison with other research shows that these marriages ended in similar ways to other marriages. Some differences were found, though. For example, the fathers reported less infidelity on the part of their wives than men in other research. Yet they also reported more desertion (which may or may not have involved infidelity).[5] In general, with the exception of a higher frequency of desertion, the stories the fathers provide do not appear to be that different from stories of breakups in which the mother gained custody.

This is not to say that the divorce experience was qualitatively better or worse for these fathers. Divorce is difficult for everyone. Nothing else dissolves the family in quite the same way— pitting one spouse against another, changing the financial and living situation drastically, altering parent-child contact, and leaving festering wounds from interpersonal conflict. The psychological toll can be severe. These fathers were not exempt from the feelings of depression, loss, rage, bewilderment, and anxiety that accompany a divorce. In some cases there were also reactions of happiness and relief as an unhappy situation came to a resolution.

The divorce itself was not anticipated by many of the fathers studied: almost half said it came as a surprise and more than half said they did not want it. Only one in four initiated the breakup. A handful said it was arrived at mutually. These findings are consistent with other research that has shown women to be more likely than men to initiate a breakup. With many fathers unprepared for and not wanting a divorce, it is not surprising that almost three-quarters said it was very stressful for them.

REASONS FOR THE DIVORCE

Why did the fathers divorce? The fathers were most apt to blame incompatibility; that is, to give answers that indicated they were partially to blame for the failure of the marriage. Almost half the fathers in the 1988 survey gave reasons for incompatibility that included "communication problems," "sexual problems," "we grew apart," "we fell out of love," "we married too young," "money problems."

A quarter of the fathers reported it was the wife's infidelity that caused the breakup and only a handful reported their own fooling around as the cause. Is this an accurate account of the way these marriages ended? Not necessarily. It is interesting to note that in the study of mothers without custody about the same percentage of that group blamed the breakup on the father's infidelity.[6] While parents in both groups were not necessarily fudging the truth, certainly the impressions of such events tend to change depending upon which partner is asked.

About one father in five said the marriage ended because his wife deserted him. This figure is much higher than that cited by other divorce-related research. This is not surprising. Clearly those women who desert are more likely to leave their children behind.

A similar number (18 percent) said the wife had had emotional problems that caused the breakup. Examples of answers in this category were, "she was unfit," "she was on drugs/alcohol," "she could not cope," and "she abused the children."[7]

The overall impression is that while these fathers as a whole did experience a higher degree of desertion than most, the marriages ended for typical reasons.

Getting Custody

Myth #9. The mother was emotionally incompetent, which resulted in the father's getting custody.

This is not true for most cases. The reasons fathers gain custody are complex and involve a number of interlocking factors, ranging from the personalities and emotional and financial needs of the father, mother, and children to the legal climate in the state, the consultation of the lawyers and other professionals in the situation, and the judge. To understand what is involved in custody decisions we need to look briefly at each of these parties.

THE FATHER

With the laws having shifted to more sex-neutral decision making, the father is in a better position to gain custody than in recent memory. Yet much depends on the idiosyncracies of the situation. In a dispute, a father may be at a disadvantage. For example, the parent who is in the home with the children at the time of the custody dispute often holds the inside track, because judges are loathe to remove children from situations in which the children are adapting. Many fathers leave the home at the time of the breakup, perhaps assuming the children are better off with the mother. If they change their minds, they have this initial obstacle to overcome. The traditional view of the mother as the more competent parent also works against the father. This may be particularly true if the mother has been at home with the children and the father has been working outside the home.

But the father has a number of pluses on his side in a dispute. He usually has greater financial resources than the mother. His higher income can go a long way toward hiring a lawyer (some fathers, though, earn too much to qualify for legal aid but not enough to afford what they consider a decent lawyer), toward offering the children a nicer home, and toward buying the children material goods. The father with the stronger financial position can make life difficult for the mother by (illegally) threatening to withhold alimony or child support unless he gets custody.

The father has to weigh the benefits of fighting for custody against the costs such a battle may have on the children and himself. The more he believes himself to be the parent most capable of raising the children, the more likely he is to explore the possibilities of getting custody.

THE MOTHER

The mother is dealing with other issues. One of these is the societal pressure to maintain custody. She does not have to look very hard to realize there is not a great deal of support for women who are no longer raising their children. They are frequently believed to be selfish, emotionally incompetent, substance abusers, or sexually promiscuous. These beliefs make it more difficult for mothers to relinquish custody and to find a comfortable niche for themselves after they become noncustodial.

Most mothers, of course, gain custody without a battle from the father. Fathers and mothers generally believe that children are better off with their mother. Many fathers are convinced that even if they wanted custody they would have little chance of winning. If the mother desires custody, has a history of being a competent primary caretaker, and is on an equal footing financially with the father, she can be a formidable opponent. If the father shows a desire for custody and the mother does not have some of those criteria, she may have second thoughts. She has to make a decision about her chances of winning and about what is best for the children and for herself. Many mothers are deterred from fighting when they consider the financial and emotional costs.

Of course, custody does not have to be turned over after a court fight. Mothers may also be willing to have the father raise the children, seeing a shift in the child-care responsibility to the father as a fresh opportunity for everyone. They may perceive the father to be competent or even the more emotionally competent parent and welcome his desire for custody.

THE CHILDREN

Generally, the older the children, the more likely it is their wishes will be honored in a dispute. Sally in chapter 2 is one such example. The sex and age of the children can be a factor, too, depending upon the situation. Younger children have traditionally been placed with the mother. Increasingly, children are being placed with same-sex parents. Placement also is influenced by which home offers the most stability. Children often prefer staying in the home where they can maintain continuity with their neighborhood, friends, and school. In some cases, children who are not progressing well in their current situation opt to go with the other parent for a fresh start. Without a doubt, children are also influenced by what each parent has to offer. This can take the form of material goodies, emotional stability, nurturance, or the chance to get to know a parent from whom they feel distanced. Some children are attracted to the father because he has remarried and offers a two-parent situation. Others leave the mother because they do not like the mother's new boyfriend or husband, or a stepsister.

THE LEGAL CLIMATE, LAWYERS, OTHER COURT PERSONNEL, AND THE JUDGE

The legal system and those working in it also play a key role in how these custody arrangements come about. It is the legislation in a particular state and the way it is interpreted by lawyers, court personnel, and judges that ultimately affects how many custody decisions are made. Even in situations that do not go to court, impressions about how the legal process works seep into the parents' decision-making process. In states in which laws about equality of the sexes are less clear, in jurisdictions in which judges are known to favor mothers, or court-appointed mediators have recently decided against fathers, a father may be advised against contesting custody. The lawyer, in an attempt to offer a fair appraisal of the father's chances, may sound discouraging. At the same time, if it is known that fathers are winning a good percentage of cases, the father's lawyer may encourage him to contest, while a lawyer for the mother, reading the same tea leaves, may discourage her.

Reasons for Custody

Within this context, and with the additive of individual personalities, the custody decisions are made. Sometimes they are made quickly, when the mother leaves abruptly. Other times, they evolve quite slowly after months or years of painstaking discussion. Sometimes decisions are made for very healthy reasons and the feelings of everyone are carefully balanced. Other times they are made for less healthy reasons ranging from a need for revenge to an inability to handle responsibility.

The eight reasons the fathers gave most frequently (they could give up to three) as to why they have custody were:

1. "I was the more emotionally competent parent" (48 percent);
2. "The children chose me" (34 percent);
3. "I was better off financially" (32 percent);
4. "Ex-wife deserted us" (25 percent);
5. "Ex-wife wanted time away from the children" (16 percent);
6. "Ex-wife wanted a career" (13 percent);
7. "Children wanted to stay in the home" (10 percent);
8. "Children have spent more time with me" (10 percent).

Mentioned much less frequently were reasons having to do with the children's needing a stricter upbringing, with the father's abducting the children, with the ex-wife's remarrying, with the children's being of tender age, their needing a male role model, and the wife's being gay.

From the list we see that almost half the fathers viewed their being more emotionally competent (which does *not* necessarily mean the mother was incompetent) as a major reason for their

having custody. The wishes of the children, the different financial situations of the parents, and the mother's deserting were
also key reasons. Let us look at the other side of the coin. In the
study of mothers without custody the mothers listed money (34
percent), their own inability to parent (33 percent), the children's
choosing their father (24 percent), and the best interests of the
child (23 percent) as the main causes for their not having custody. In response to another question, 46 percent of the mothers
said they believed they did not have custody because their ex-
husbands had more money than they did.[8] These mothers had
another perspective on the situation than the fathers.

Using both studies, it can be concluded that custody is likely
to go to fathers for reasons having to do with the mother's incompetence in one-third to one-half of the cases, that money
plays a part in at least one-third of the cases, and that the children's wishes are key in up to a third of the situations.

Myth #10. The courts intervene in most cases in which the father gains custody.

This is not true. Only 11 percent said they won custody after
a protracted court battle and 9 percent said they won after a
brief battle. Most custody arrangements are arrived at without
the court's intervention. This is not to say that mothers willingly
give up custody. Many, surveying their options, see it as the only
way. If they had more money or better housing, for example,
they might have fought for it. Sometimes the threat of a court
decision will cause custody to be decided outside the judge's jurisdiction. Decisions that are about to be made in court may be
made literally in the hallway.

It should be mentioned that how a father gets custody is different from whether he wants it. Not all fathers seek it. Only 61
percent said they wanted sole custody very much when the marriage first ended. The rest said they either wanted it "somewhat,"
wanted joint custody, or did not want custody at all. Clearly,
many did not consider themselves as potential single father material at the time or believed that children should be with their
mother. As events unfolded, though, they changed their minds.
Maybe some wanted revenge or were hoping to save money by
not paying child support. Others may have realized how

much their children meant to them. For a variety of reasons, these fathers, along with those who initially expressed a desire for it, sought or agreed to accept custody. But the courts were rarely the final arbiter.

The Fathers' Stories about Custody

The individual stories that follow provide examples of how fathers have gained custody. The more negative stories included tales of abduction, split families, and children shuffled back and forth. On the positive side are custody decisions that involve caring and forethought and are handled optimally for everyone involved.

Jack, raising two sons, takes us from his courtship through the eventual custody decision: "We were junior year sweethearts. We parted, then got back together and married. She was a good woman when we married and the first few years were amiable between us without the horror stories of some marriages. We shared having babies and we knew that it wasn't the greatest between us. There is a fine line between love and hate sometimes. But the hatred becomes self-defeating after awhile.

"She slowly became agonized over whether she loved me or some other guy at work. Then one day I read something on her face and pursued her until she told me that she had fallen for this other guy. The guy was someone I used to work with. He was macho, a man's man. I thought he was using her but they went together after she left for five years. I first took it personally. But just because it was over did not make all the past bad. We came to a fork and parted, which doesn't mean either direction is wrong.

"After we decided to separate I didn't think she could handle all three kids alone. We were going to let them decide and we both wanted joint custody. But the court required that one of us have sole custody. So the two boys chose me and my daughter chose her. We wanted the kids to be happy. I had enough love and respect toward her that I didn't stay angry about her running off with the other guy."

Ken, raising an eleven-year-old daughter, related this story: "My daughter chose to stay with me. Her mother did not ask her to move in. She was up there living with her mother. She was only eight years old. My daughter was expecting me to go south to visit her for the winter. When I first arrived for the visit she wanted to stay with me. I said okay. I did not know if her mother would allow it. I asked her mother, and she said yes. I did not want my daughter's hopes to be built up, or mine, and I did not know until the last minute that it would be all right. Actually, I was down for the holidays and was going to leave five days later, but I was so afraid that her mother or someone in her family would talk her out of it, or not let her come, that I just rushed in and said we had to leave. I did not kidnap her, but I got her out fast. My ex-wife has remarried and sees my daughter every summer."

Slim, a policeman from Kentucky, said: "My son originally decided to stay with me, and my daughter went with her. Now both are with me. I felt I could supply a good home and they could stay in their home and go to school. If they had moved in with her, they would have had to have started over again with friends and everything."

Marcus gained physical custody of his two children when his wife moved out. His mother moved in for a short time and helped. Meanwhile, his wife got a job and an apartment. She wanted the children. Joint custody was arranged. All was working well until she remarried and moved two thousand miles away. To everyone's regret she had to give up sharing the children. The separation from her has been hard for the children but they prefer staying in their home town to moving. She writes and calls frequently and they visit her on holidays.

Leonard was in nearly the opposite situation: He admitted to having abducted his child three years ago. When a lawyer told Leonard he had no chance of winning custody, Leonard took his seven-year-old son, Paul, and moved to a different city in the same state. Leonard took Paul because he believed Paul was better off with him than he would have been with his wife. He explained to his son that he and his mother could not stay married, and that Paul would be better off living with him. Leonard said his wife hired a private investigator to track him down at first, and then fought him in court for many months. Finally she gave up fighting. The son and his mother see each other infrequently and have occasional contact on the phone. Leonard's desire to have custody, his belief that Paul would be better off with him, and the lawyer's pessimistic outlook on his chances all helped motivate the abduction. Leonard admits to feeling a little guilty but quickly adds that his son is better off with him. Incidentally, Leonard had to quit his job in the courthouse because he was afraid the judge who had tried his case would recognize him.

Sheldon, an engineer with three sons, has his children "because of an [paternal] instinct. I did not want the marriage to end and refused to leave the home. That forced the confrontation. She had to choose. She wanted out and so I got the children and the house. At first I got two of the children and one wanted to go with her. Then he came back with me and one of the ones I had went with her."

Gary, a mail carrier, describes his desire to live with his family: "In 1975 I did not have the chance to get custody as a man. My son wanted to stay with me, and she [his wife] allowed it. My daughter wanted her mother. My family was a very important part of my life, and that is why I pursued it. I did not want to give up the rest of those things that were important to me. I thought I was a good parent and did not feel her behavior was conducive to raising kids. I felt I was a better parent. At the time, the only way to get kids was to have them testify. If you really care about them, you don't want to do that. At the time, you just could not win otherwise. The lawyers say to men, 'You cannot get it,' so many men don't go after it. Many men do not want to assassinate their wives' characters, and many men do not want to involve the children in that either. I threatened, cajoled, and fought, and did everything I could to get them without going into court. It finally worked.

"Fathers are damn lucky if they have custody. It depends on the circumstances. You have to be lucky or the woman has to not care at all. I put pressure on her by threatening to fight, that there would be a war. More fathers would seek custody if they thought they could win it without hurting the child."

One father, Stephen, went through a long series of investigators and detectives before he could find sufficient grounds to get custody of his children through the courts. Nevertheless, he lost the court battle. The next day he heard from his wife that she was going to take the children and move out-of-state with another man. Stephen got a restraining order to keep her and the children in the state. She stayed for a year and a half, and then he got documentation that she had exhibited immoral behavior. He went back to court and won. Stephen wanted his children, but his desire for them was intensified because he believed she was not taking good care of them.

The quality of care the children receive from the mother is frequently mentioned as a reason for getting custody. Another father provided a similar story. He said: "The standards of my ex caused me to want to raise my daughter. [His ex-wife had run off a few times during the marriage.] She was not caring for her, so I wanted to do it. I never thought of raising her before the divorce, but when it happened, I wanted her. When I accepted the marriage was going to end, which I, at first, did not want to accept, I decided I wanted her. My ex had a daughter from her first marriage whom I adopted. When we got divorced, she went with her. Now she has remarried, and I do not know where she is." This was echoed by a father who said simply: "Five years ago I won the case. The children were not being properly cared for. I couldn't take it any more, so I got them."

Sometimes, following a divorce, fathers establish their own life without the children and then take the children in when they come knocking. Fred gained custody of his fifteen-year-old son two years after the son had left with Fred's ex-wife: "He showed up with his suitcase and jeans in arm and said, 'Dad, I want to live with you.' I did not have any experience, but it was okay with her. We never went to court."

Don was on his own for a year before his children came back: "I am raising them because she moved to another city, and they did not like it, and they did not like the stepfather. They came back because they wanted to stay where they were raised. And I am a little easier on them than she is."

There are also situations in which the wife wants to go off and find herself, and the husband becomes a willing partner in the arrangement. The children may be choosing the house, not the parent. John tells this story: "She wanted out. She wanted me to move first, and I told her no way . . . that I was staying. When she left, I don't know if she really wanted them at that time or thought it would be a hardship for her. We sat down to talk and she had nothing . . . no job or anything. I think it was planned for me to have them before she left. We sat down and talked with the children when I refused to leave because there was no reason for me to leave. I had been very active with the children and the community, and she even told me I was a very good father and husband. She knew they would be in good hands with me. I had done a lot for myself growing up. She was going to leave and had no place to go except where she was going to work in a motel. So she did not have any facilities for the children. We both had our say with the children, and they wanted to stay in the house, and whoever was going to stay in the house that's who they were going to stay with. It was kind of a mutual arrangement."

One final story from a father who worked as a salesman. He was left with a son and daughter by his wife, who thought she had missed something in life. What she wanted did not include her family: "My wife felt she had other, more meaningful things in life to do rather than be a mother or wife. She wanted to go out and have fun in life. She found someone to do that with after she left."

These stories paint a variety of pictures of how men end up with their children. In many cases, it is the wife's desire not to have custody that plays a major part in the father getting the children.

No More Myths

Perhaps, if the myths about these fathers' lives are put to rest, an understanding of them can develop that will make them more normal. They are not extraordinary men who have had extraordinary childhoods or marriages. They are fathers who, for a variety of reasons, end up with custody. As the following chapters will show, they do not bring any particular expertise to the many tasks of single parenting they face. As such, their successes are even more gratifying and encouraging, because they show that with little previous training men can adapt to raising their children alone.

4

Running the Household

WHEN a father starts raising his children alone, the issue requiring the most immediate attention is the home. Regardless of the emotional adjustments the father and the children have to make, everyone has to be fed and clothed. Secondarily, child-care arrangements have to be made and the home has to be cleaned.

Two common assumptions exist about the father who has to run the household: that he will not do it well and that, if possible, he will use outside help, either his relatives or a housekeeper.

There is good reason for these assumptions. Traditionally, men have left the bulk of the housekeeping—especially tasks such as cooking, cleaning, and laundry—to the wives, while they have tended to share the responsibility for the shopping. The child-care arrangements have also been left to the wife. It is in these areas that family responsibilities seem to divide the most often along gender-related lines. Although men now are more involved in these tasks than ever before, there is a great deal of research confirming that the wife is still the primary caretaker of the home and children. Even when both parents work full time, the wife does most of the housework and takes responsibility for the child-care arrangements.[1] Despite the media's view that men are sharing the housework and child care equally with their wives, in fact they do not do so. Blumstein and Schwartz, in their book, *American Couples*, write: "Working wives do less housework than homemakers, but they still do the vast bulk of what needs to be done. Husbands of women who work help out more than husbands of homemakers, but their contribution is not impressive. Even if a husband is not employed, he does much less housework than a wife who puts in a 40-hour week."[2] A 1987 *New York Times* poll found that between 85 percent and 90 percent of the family's cooking is done by the wife.[3] Perhaps to avoid the drudgery of housework, or perhaps to maintain some dominance, men have successfully held on to the image of themselves as being incompetent in the kitchen, a threat with a washing machine, and lethal with a vacuum cleaner. Women, at the same time, are partners in this dance. They maintain their hold over the housekeeping and child care—perhaps as a way of trying to prove, if they are working, that they can do it all, and perhaps as a way of dealing with guilt about not being home all the time.

Housekeepers are also believed to be the father's salvation. A look at some television images of single fathers that the baby boomers grew up with shows where this assumption comes from. Fred MacMurray in "My Three Sons," John Forsythe in "Bachelor Father," and Brian Keith in "Family Affair" always had a family member or a housekeeper to run the show while they worked. But it is more than television programs that feed this assumption. Because men are the primary wage earners in most families, it is believed they will be able to afford the luxury of outside help.

These assumptions of incompetence and the need for housekeepers do not hold up when applied to the custodial father. The fathers in this study were more like Dustin Hoffman's portrayal of Ted Kramer in the film *Kramer vs. Kramer*. The first morning after his wife has left him, Kramer burns the French toast. During the movie, the apartment loses some of its initial tidiness and luster. By the end of the movie, however, Kramer is shown to be a competent cook who gets help from his son. This is similar to what many fathers reported. After an initial period of mayhem, they established a routine and adapted comfortably to the demands of housekeeping. They did not use outside help to a great extent; when they did, it was usually at the beginning of solo parenting. In addition, most of the fathers feel comfortable with the child-care arrangements they have made for their children when they are not home.

This chapter will look at the father in his home. Attention will be paid to how the housework is divided up, the effect that the age and sex of the children in the home has on how much work they do, and the role that outside help plays. The ease the father feels with housework will also be examined, as will the arrangements the father makes for child care.

Who Did the Housework during the Marriage?

The fathers in this study left most of the housework to their wives during their marriage. Only about one father in eight reported that he was doing more of the cooking, cleaning, or laundry than his wife; only one in five said he was doing more of the shopping. Most often the wife was doing these chores; occasionally they were shared. It is important to consider these responses to understand single fathers. Even though these were fathers who ended up with children, the degree of sharing of household responsibilities during the marriage did not deviate greatly from the norm. The relationships in these marriages, many of which began in the 1970s, followed the traditional path for the completion of family chores: The wives did the housekeeping while the husbands did the breadwinning. Yet by the time of the second survey, fathers were reporting a greater level of involvement in those chores than fathers in the earlier survey. Thus a trend can be seen in fathers doing more around the home. This may, in part, be due to a higher percentage of women working outside of the home than previously.

Who Does the Housework Now?

Although fathers left much of the housework to their wives during their marriages, they had to decide how to handle the chores when they began raising their children alone. The fathers had four options. They could do the chores themselves, share them with the children, turn them over to the children or some other family member, or—if their income allowed it—hire outside help.

Fathers received the most outside help in the areas of cooking and laundry, but in no instance did the use of outside help apply to even as much as 10 percent of the sample. (The use of housekeepers may be infrequent because the average age of the children was over eleven years old, an age at which they were old enough to take care of themselves. Also, fathers may hire housekeepers only at first, when they are most uncomfortable in their new roles.) Fathers are most likely to do the shopping and the cooking by themselves and to share the cleaning and the laundry with the children. These latter two chores are left up to the children because they carry the least potential danger and need the least supervision. They also are the least important to the smooth running of the home.

As might be expected, when it came to the amount of money earned, definite differences appeared between the fathers in the amount of housework they and their children did. Fathers who earned more money were more likely to use outside help. Fathers who hired someone to do the cooking and cleaning had an average income that was substantially higher, over $36,000 than fathers who did the cooking and cleaning themselves.

Age and Sex of the Children and Housework

In most families, whether headed by one parent or two, as the children get older they take on more of the responsibility for housekeeping. Daughters may be groomed for certain roles and sons for others. For example, the girls may have to help out with the cooking, while the boys do the yard maintenance and trash removal.

As children get older, fathers tend to relinquish sole control over tasks and begin to share them with their children. An exception is shopping; in only a few cases do the children take over full responsibility for that task. Many fathers, however, end up doing more housework than they really have to, perhaps because of feelings of guilt. As one father said: "I feel the children have been through enough. I feel bad about asking them to do their chores around the house. I ask them to do it, but I feel bad about it." The father who believes he has burdened his children already with the dissolution of the family does not want to make further demands on them.

Another reason some fathers stay so involved in housekeeping is that they may think they have to prove to the world that they can take care of their children on their own. It is a sign of strength to do it alone and not ask for help. By being central in the home in this way they are maintaining control. Using relatives, friends, or hired help weakens the impression. This is part of a stiff-upper-lip mentality that many of the fathers interviewed demonstrated when it came to handling problems. The fathers also may feel it is important to let the world know they are not going to expect more from their children than may be perceived as normal. They may not want to give the impression of working them too hard or depending on them too much.

In some instances, a father may have won custody in court and may feel a need to show both the judge and his ex-wife that his children are being well taken care of. The father in this situation may believe that if he expects too much from his children he might not be upholding their best interests and might be brought back into court, which would threaten the custody arrangement.

Although some fathers absolve their children of doing much housework, it was found that fathers raising teenage daughters got more help than did those raising teenage sons. Daughters were, in fact, twice as likely to help out around the house than sons. No difference in the help received was found among younger children.

This finding is further proof of the traditional upbringing of many of these fathers. They turn to their daughters to take care of certain traditionally female tasks, just as they had left these tasks to their wives. In this way, some daughters become mother substitutes. They may receive support for this from various sectors. First, their family and friends may see it as a natural shift and place a spoken or unspoken pressure on both the father and the daughters to adopt this pattern. Second, the daughters themselves may voluntarily fall into this role. They may have been doing a lot of housekeeping during their parents' marriage and may continue or increase their work load when the mother leaves. This could be a natural progression that is comfortable for them and that also pleases the father. Finally, they may be aware of the need to get the housework done, unlike a son who was not previously involved in housekeeping. In any case, the result is greater participation by daughters in housework.

One father talks about what happened in his household: "When my wife and I decided to get a divorce, my daughters, who were then in their teens, stayed with me. I don't know how it happened, but they began doing the cooking and the laundry, I did the yard and the trash. We never discussed it. Sometimes they shop. I don't know, I guess I could cook if I had to but I like them doing it."

In summary, fathers do a good deal of the housework themselves when they have custody, and do not rely on outside help. As the children get older, and especially if there are daughters, fathers get more help.

Comfort in Housekeeping

Do fathers find it difficult to manage household chores without a woman around? Can they find happiness with a broom and a frying pan? Most reported they felt comfortable in these areas. Housekeeping did not pose problems. Shopping was perceived as the easiest chore by the fathers, cleaning as the hardest. (This is not to say that fathers enjoy it. Housework is little more than an endless progression of chores that are tedious and boring. No one looks forward to doing it. To paraphrase Joan Rivers, the problem with housework is "You make the beds, wash the dishes, then six months later you have to do it all over again.")

The fathers' generally high degree of comfort with housekeeping may be an indication of a number of different factors:

1. *The relative ease of the chores themselves:* Housekeeping, when one puts one's mind to it, is not difficult. Men have been scared away from it by tradition. When they have to do it, they do not find it that hard.

2. *The diminished expectations that fathers may have for the quality of how the chores are completed:* Many fathers cope with the demands of housekeeping by lowering their expectations about the way the house looks or the quality of the meals. Many women find a measure of their worth as a mother in how neat the house looks and how well-kept their children look. Fathers, however,

have not grown up with that message; when they gain custody, they do not put as high a value on these things. With lower expectations, they are more likely to feel comfortable with how the house is run.

3. *The relative ease of these chores compared with some of the other demands of parenthood:* Housekeeping is simple compared with some of the other tasks the father faces that involve situations over which the fathers have less control.

4. *The role congruence of housekeeping:* Keeping the house clean, for example, is something that involves only the father and the clutter in the home. No one else's expectations have to be considered. There is no boss to please and no ex-wife wanting to visit the children. The cleaning exists, it is stable in its demands, it is controlled by how the father feels about it, and doing it produces tangible results. For these reasons, compared both with other aspects of parenthood and with other situations that present more complex role demands, housekeeping proves to be an area in which the fathers feel a good deal of comfort.

Who Finds Housekeeping Comfortable?

Certain fathers find housework to be a breeze. For instance, the fathers who had had the primary responsibility for the chores during the marriage were the most likely to find those chores easy now. These fathers found the transition to doing housekeeping alone easier than other fathers did, as they already possessed knowledge about the washing machine, the vacuum cleaner, and the stove. They had also figured out how to do these things while holding down a job, which is no easy feat.

Fred, a salesman from Virginia, is one example. While married, he had been doing the bulk of the housework and working full-time. He thought his experience with the housekeeping contributed to his obtaining custody. Fred said about his wife's leaving: "She knew they would be safe with me since I was from a broken family and knew how to cook, wash, and iron. Better, in fact, than she did. I taught her most of it. She was ten years younger than I was."

Henry provides a slightly different example of a man with

prior experience. He was a fifty-year-old security guard from a rural Kansas town and had spent a number of years in the army before getting married in his late twenties. He believes his army experience prepared him for taking care of the home when he ended his marriage. When he began raising his two sons alone, he read a lot of books on cooking and cleaning. Now, when he wants to, he can get his house "spanking clean." His sons help him with the cleaning and the laundry; he does the cooking alone.

At the other end of the spectrum is Charles, who lives in Chicago, where he works as an electrician. He had no prior experience, and he stumbled around the house for the first few weeks after his wife left. He concentrated mostly on getting his four daughters presentable for school, while letting the appearance of the house slide. Eventually, like most fathers, he became comfortable as a housekeeper. Now he laughs at the way female friends he once went to for help come to him for advice with recipes. His children are also now old enough to help him out more with the chores.

Not only does experience and having older children help when it comes to housekeeping, feeling comfortable financially is also related to comfort with housework. Money is able to buy fathers more options that can contribute to greater ease in handling these chores. If there are greater financial resources, laundry can be sent out and housekeepers hired. For example, wealthier fathers use more outside help, which definitely makes a single father's life easier.

Fathers who sought the role of sole custodian also tended to feel more comfortable with the housekeeping. These were the men who were more psychologically prepared for that role and found the transition easier to make than fathers who did not seek the role of sole custodian.

The one recurring theme heard from the fathers is that the first few months on their own were the most difficult as they and the children struggled with the new situation and the loss of the mother. After this period, however, housekeeping did not pose great difficulty for the fathers.

The story of Alonzo is one example of what can happen. Alonzo is a manager of a medium-sized business in Colorado.

Five years ago, his wife left him and his two children—a four-teen-year-old son and a seven-year-old daughter—on the eve of the son's birthday. Alonzo and his wife had been discussing the possibility of getting a divorce for months, but she gave him no warning that she was leaving when she did. First, he had to straighten out who was going to carry certain responsibilities around the house: "Initially, everyone had a piece of the action. The first night I thought, what the heck am I doing to do? Okay, guys, a little family meeting here. Most of the burden went to my son and me, as my daughter was too young to help out. He was great. He practically raised her. He missed things after school to be with her. The neighbors helped out a lot, too. My daughter is twelve years old now, and my son has gone into the army. She cleans and does some of the cooking but still has problems. I'll call her and tell her to start dinner and what to do. Like, 'Okay, boil up some water and take the ravioli out of the freezer and start it at five o'clock.' Other nights, if she is busy with her schoolwork, I'll bring in food. Otherwise there is always good old frozen food. We are surviving but not having what I would call good old family eating, roast beef and things. Laundry? I did that most of the time until recently. Now she does it."

Alonzo had problems at first but has worked out a system that adequately meets his family's needs, even though he regrets not having family-style meals. Like many men, he forges through the problems that come up. Most men do not seem to be overwhelmed by the housekeeping tasks facing them as single fathers. With few complaints, they do what they feel has to be done. This approach—part of their male upbringing—may actually help reduce the strains the fathers experience. Not acknowledging problems that arise may make the problems easier to get through.

Child-Care Arrangements

Keeping a household running smoothly involves more than just housekeeping. Appropriate child-care arrangements have to be made. This undertaking seldom can be assumed lightly. Placing a child in someone else's care or in an after-school program is something working parents often do with reluctance. Many of the fathers gave a good deal of time and thought to the arrangements they made for their children. If they found good child care, it paid off for them. The satisfaction they felt with child-care arrangements proved to be a key variable in their satisfaction in many other parenting areas. In other words, if the father thought his children were well taken care of, other things fell into place for him. The fathers in this study were basically pleased with their child-care arrangements; almost three-quarters of the men reported satisfaction.

The arrangements the fathers made for child care varied on the basis of a number of factors, including:

1. The age of the children, with teenagers being left alone the most.
2. The father's income and the choices that income gives him for hiring people.
3. The presence of support systems—families, friends, and neighbors.
4. The father's impressions of the individual needs of the children, as children with certain personalities may need more supervision than others.
5. The father's feelings about the type of home life his children should have. Fathers who are more upset by the dissolution of the intact family make a greater attempt to be home with the children.
6. The father's work schedule.

Child-care arrangements were examined in two time periods: during school hours and after school hours. Most of the fathers reported that during school hours their children were in school. Fathers raising children too young for school tended to use day care and sitters. A few fathers were home during school hours.

Arranging child care after school is more difficult for all working parents. School is usually over by midafternoon; yet many parents do not get home until early evening. This often leaves a two- to three-hour gap, during which time some other arrangement has to be made for the child.

More than half the fathers in the survey reported that at least one of their children is alone after school. With the average age of the children in the study being between eleven and twelve, this is not surprising. Children at this age are usually capable of taking care of themselves.

After school, the youngest children—those in the one- to four-year-old group, tend to be either with their father, with a sitter, or with a relative or friend. One-fifth of the children in the five- to eleven-year-old age group are left on their own. The high percentage of latchkey children (children who let themselves into their own home and are alone after school) in this age group indicates the difficulties working parents confront in making child-care arrangements. Even someone who earns an income of thirty-five thousand dollars a year—well above the national average for single fathers—will have difficulty finding someone to watch the children. Other studies on latchkey children show similar findings. It has been estimated that 5 to 10 million children are left unsupervised after school, and that many of these children are younger than eleven.[4] This is more a commentary on day-care availability in the United States than on the child-care arrangements that single fathers make. It shows that fathers are not immune to the problems faced by single mothers or dual-career families.

Difficulties Arranging Child Care

It is most difficult to arrange child care for children in the five- to eleven-year-old range. Fathers raising children older than eleven and those raising children younger than five reported much less difficulty. This is most likely because of the lack of clarity on the father's part concerning how responsible these children can be for themselves. Should a child who is seven, eight, or nine be left on his or her own after school? Some fathers believe their children can take care of themselves at that age; others do not. At a younger age, the issue is clear-cut: The children must be taken care of. In the older age range, the issue is also clear-cut because the children are more capable of taking care of themselves. But concern about children between five and eleven makes arranging child care for them more difficult and requires greater care in making judgments.

Neither the father's income, the sex of the children being raised, the number of children he is raising, the number of years he has had custody, or whether he sought custody has a relationship to the difficulty the father experienced in making child-care arrangements. The father's concerns about child care rest more with the age of the children than with any other variables.

Conclusions

Housekeeping and arranging child care, when compared with other areas of adjustment for the father, proved relatively easy adjustments. The father's lack of experience in handling these matters during the marriage does not seem to have a great impact on the comfort and satisfaction he feels in handling them (although fathers who have had experience during the marriage do better). The reason for the ease in handling housekeeping is, most likely, that doing housekeeping and related home maintenance chores is not that difficult. The tasks themselves are not hard, and there is no question about who is in charge. The father does not feel uncomfortable doing the chores because of conflicting expectations placed on him. He knows they have to be done and proceeds with the tasks to completion, although he may have diminished expectations for the quality of the results.

These findings are different from the assumptions that exist about the father being incapable of running the household without the mother present and needing outside help. Even though men in intact families leave the bulk of the housework to their wives, it can be assumed that, after a short period of time alone, they would feel comfortable taking care of these chores. What this implies about married men who do not do much at home is that they are in an unspoken conspiracy with their wives to have the wives do the housework. There is much in society to reinforce this arrangement. Unfortunately, a sloppy house reflects negatively on the wife more than it does on the husband.

It was particularly interesting to learn that fathers get more help from daughters than sons. Despite the nontraditional nature of this parental arrangement, some things have not changed.

Suggestions for Dealing with Housework

1. Give your children time to adjust to new chores if those are required. Expecting them to follow a new routine immediately is unrealistic.

2. Be specific and clear about what the rules are: "Make your bed, dust your furniture and vacuum." These can be posted for everyone to see, with clear time frames in which they must be completed.

3. Have a few rules that are basic to your living together (rather than overwhelming your children).

4. Specify negotiable rules along with tasks you deem essential and non-negotiable. "You must do your homework before you talk on the phone" is a non-negotiable rule. "You can determine how often you need breaks while doing homework" is a negotiable rule.

5. Teach your children to do what they have to first; then they can do what they like after that.

6. Be positive with what they have done instead of being critical about how they have done it or what they left out. Use positive reinforcement, such as praise, for what the children have specifically done ("I really appreciate your remembering to do everything. Thanks for setting the table, folding the laundry and making your bed").

7. A schedule needs to be placed in a frequently visited place in the house (like the kitchen). Chores can be rotated depending upon their difficulty and the abilities of your children to complete them. For example, a young child should not cook, but he or she could set the table one week and throw out the trash the next.

8. Help your children remember their chores by making notes to help them follow through. For example, you can post notes on the refrigerator as reminders.

9. You and your children will need to check with each other frequently to evaluate progress and make modifications as needed.

10. Be flexible to allow for some change in the routine. You

may have a special meeting at work that precipitates a change in schedule. Your children may have special activities for certain periods of time that may necessitate a modification of schedules. Roll with the punches.

11. Parents are models in following through with chores and demonstrating responsible behaviors. For example, if you want your children to be on time you need to be on time.

12. Be careful not to overburden children with too many chores while at the same time not relieving them of an appropriate amount of responsibilities. Daughters, in particular, are likely to want to help out and to be encouraged by you to help out. This may not be the best situation if a daughter is helping out too much and is not spending time with her friends.

13. Be aware if housework is becoming a battleground on which other issues are being fought out. If so, talk about it with your children. At the same time, recognize that no one likes to do the cleaning. Expect a certain amount of unhappiness with these chores as normal.

SOME EXAMPLES OF TASKS CHILDREN CAN COMPLETE

eight-year-old:

- make own bed
- set table for dinner
- clear the table
- help in vacuuming
- keep room clean; put clothes, books away

eleven-year-old:

- watch a younger sibling one afternoon a week
- set table for dinner, make salad
- load dishwasher after dinner

fifteen-year-old:

- watch younger sibling one or two afternoons
- help make dinner with assistance from younger children
- help with housekeeping on all levels

Children can learn to consistently follow through with tasks when they are praised for what they do as well as when they have the opportunity to earn rewards. An eight-year-old youngster might appreciate an extra bedtime story or spending ten minutes of extra time playing a game with a parent. An eleven- or twelve-year-old might appreciate a financial bonus, playing a game with a parent, or having a friend sleep over. A fifteen- or sixteen-year-old might be happy with a special time out with a parent or extra time with friends.[5]

5

The Father's Relationship
with the Children
and How They Adjust

A BALTIMORE father said, "Having my kids with me is the best thing. I'd probably be alone otherwise. I don't date much so I spend most of my time with them. It's what keeps me going. My personal feeling is that whatever damage I've done with the split-up has been done." From a New Jersey father: "My relationship with my son is better than it ever was. We are very close. We touch a lot and say 'I love you.'" A father from Texas reported, "Things were okay at first with my son but not my daughter. Then my son started to withdraw and things improved with my daughter. He's still angry about his mother and it has gotten worse between us." A father from Boston told me, "Things were tough at first, and they still are tough for my son. He's having school problems. But they are better than they were before."

Regardless of the successes and failures of the fathers in their parenting endeavors, the most important area is the one in which the fathers have the most invested: their relationship with their children. It is the satisfaction the fathers derive from being with their children, their impressions of how the children are doing, and the way the fathers feel about themselves as parents that are the markers, from the fathers' point of view, of how this parental situation is working out. By the fathers' own accounts, it is going well. Over 80 percent of the fathers in both the 1982 and 1988 surveys give themselves a very positive rating as a parent. Between 1982 and 1988 the satisfaction the fathers report with their children's progress has increased: in 1982, 70 percent of the fathers were satisfied; in the most recent survey that figure grew to 82 percent, a marked improvement. Satisfaction with their relationship with their children has also been consistently high.[1]

This chapter will describe the father-child relationships that emerge, the possible reasons for the high degree of satisfaction with them, and the children's adjustment. Because the father's perceptions of the relationship and of his children's adjustment go hand-in-hand, both topics are being covered here. Suggestions for improving the father-child relationship are covered in depth in chapter 13.

FATHERS AND CHILDREN

Fathers have historically been depicted in a negative light (along with stepmothers). Examples of poor fathering and absent fathers abound in popular literature. The father of Mark Twain's fictional hero Huckleberry Finn, saddled with the dubious pleasure of raising his undomesticated son, spends his time either drunk, committing petty crimes, or beating up Huck. (Twain, in writing about Huck, was perhaps trying to deal with the loss of his own father, who died when Twain was twelve.) In Charles Dickens' *Oliver Twist* the father is unknown. (Dickens may also have been struggling to come to grips with his relationship with his own father, who spent years in debtor's prison when Dickens was young.) Fairy tales offer further examples of incompetent or absent fathers. Hansel and Gretel's pathetic father abides by the stepmother's demands to abandon his children in the forest so that the two adults can survive. Snow White's and Cinderella's fathers are barely visible, being mentioned only in passing at the beginning of the stories.

It is, of course, not only in literature and fairy tales that fathers appear to be marginal characters. Numerous research articles and books on American fathers have shown them to be peripheral, compared with mothers, in their involvement with their children.[2] Research has also found them to be viewed by their children as less affectionate, less accepting, and less emotionally responsive than mothers.[3]

It is clear that many fathers have been absent in childrearing while being more involved in breadwinning. To many men, this level of involvement is not only acceptable but correct, and is a true sign of a father's taking care of his family. To them, weighing caretaking purely on the basis of time spent bathing the children is using an unfair yardstick. In addition, the fathers' having responsibility for breadwinning does not mean that they are not *capable* of taking care of other aspects of the children's lives if need be. There are many indications and studies that attest to the fact that fathers can be excellent parents. One researcher, after observing fathers with their young children, concluded, "There is no research evidence that biological mothers are more effective than adoptive mothers or that women are more effective than men in caring for infants and promoting their psychological development."[4]

When the single father gains custody, he moves into a new world of childrearing, one for which few have been fully prepared. Unless the father had completely taken charge of his children before the marital breakup, he faces a list of new demands. In many cases the mother may have been carrying responsibility for all aspects of the children's emotional, physical, and social upbringing. Left to his own devices, he has to carry the full weight for the first time. A number of factors make building a good father-child relationship under these circumstances difficult. The father may be unaccustomed to handling his children's emotional ups and downs. He may not know what the normal developmental stages for children are. And he may be feeling angry and at a loss as a result of the marital separation.

It is not only the father who is struggling to establish a relationship. The children are facing many of the same issues. They are probably also reeling from the breakup of the family and, with custody going to their father, the loss of daily contact with their mother. There are financial changes and a possible new living situation, neighborhood, and school to be coped with. Perhaps unaccustomed to spending time with their father or having him supervise their activities, they have to slowly adjust to his style of single parenting. Both children and father enter this relationship feeling vulnerable. It can be particularly hard for them all to establish a satisfying relationship.

The Fathers' Preparation

Some fathers are emotionally prepared to begin single parenting. These are men who have thought about custody, want it, and plan out each step. They most likely have been fairly involved with their children before the breakup. At the other extreme are fathers who do not want custody at all, or who want it but are not prepared for it. They may have become parents without any warning, having had little previous experience in being alone with their children.

One example of a father who was prepared for single parenting is Henry, the security guard mentioned in chapter 4. Henry was married for thirty years before he initiated divorce proceedings three years ago against his wife, who was an alcoholic. Henry was prepared for single parenting both by the desire he brought to the custody arrangement and by the experience he had had in taking care of a home before he was married.

The relationship that developed between Henry and his sons is not atypical. His two teenaged sons wanted to live with him, and his daughter wanted to stay with her mother. The decision was worked out amicably.

Because Henry works the night shift, he does not spend much time with his sons. They see each other at breakfast before they go to school, and at night before Henry goes to work. When they were younger, they took bus trips together. As children grow up, however, their needs change, as does their relationship with their father. One of Henry's sons was trying out for the football team at the time Henry was being interviewed. That meant that even when Henry was not working, it was difficult to schedule time with his sons.

When discipline or school problems come along, Henry handles them the same way he handles his job—by laying down the law. Henry does not talk much, but when he does, his message is clearly understood. He has told his sons if they can find someone who treats them better than he does, they are welcome to leave. They have not left yet.

Henry describes his relationship with his children as "close" and, from talking with Henry, it seems to be close in a traditional male way. When they are together, there is an understanding and caring between the three men that they do not talk about a great deal. As with many men, actions speak louder than words; the fact that Henry indicated he wanted the children, and that they chose to live with him, says it all.

Henry wanted the marriage to end and initiated the proceedings. He had thought about the children and offered all of them the chance to come with him. His sons' choice of him as the parent they wanted to live with may have heightened the sense of belonging and improved the quality of their relationship. Henry has a fierce sense of belonging to his children and having them belong to him. The atmosphere in the house, had his daughter come to live with them, would not have been the same—would not be as "male," Henry says. Maybe, however, there would be more verbalization of feelings and more time together. Henry is not sure.

Charles, also mentioned in chapter 4, is living in almost the opposite situation. He was not at all prepared for the breakup. He has been raising four daughters since his ex-wife left him for another man a year ago. He was given only a few days notice that she was leaving, although he had had suspicions for awhile. The relationship he has with his daughters, in which he gets along better with some than with others, is also not atypical. He describes himself as a father who was not particularly involved with his children during the marriage. All four girls, whose ages range from six to fourteen, are doing well in school. Each has a different relationship with him. The two youngest enjoy being in his company, and he gets along well with them. The oldest is a handful. She grumbles about wanting to live with her mother, a matter still to be settled in the courts. Charles is reluctant to give her up, as he does not want to break up the children. The fourth daughter fluctuates between joining the two youngest in games with Charles and sulking in her room with her older sister.

Charles has tried to shield his children from the animosity he and their mother share for each other. He wonders whether he has been successful with his oldest. She had felt the closest to her mother during the marriage, and she misses her mother the most. There is the possibility that Charles tried to give her too many of his ex-wife's responsibilities when the marriage first ended. Issues surrounding housework remain a problem for them.

Charles spends a little time alone with each child every day, which has helped his relationship with them. He says that problems are discussed very openly in the house and that everyone gets lots of hugs and kisses. In this predominantly female household, one would think Charles would rule as king. Although he sets the tone, it is a tone that is greatly influenced by his daughters. He worries that he is deferring too much to his oldest daughter in an attempt to smooth things over with her. He tried that approach with his ex-wife, and it did not work.

Why Fathers Do So Well

The demands of rearing children alone are unusual ones for fathers. Yet the vast majority feel very positive about their children. Why? It may have to do with the type of the people who took part in the study (fathers wanting to crow about their success as a single parent or those who want to provide a good impression), but the nature of single fatherhood is also a contributing factor. For a father to have custody in the first place, he will, in most cases, have undergone a decision-making process that reflects a great deal of thought on his part. Most of the fathers had some choice in the matter and time to weigh the pros and cons. Only about one father in four was deserted and even among the fathers in that group there was the option to not retain custody. These fathers, essentially, went against the grain to get their children. When you fight for something or someone and get it, you are more likely to value it. In addition, these fathers may get along so well with their children because of factors that already existed in the relationship. Fathers are probably more likely to seek custody of children they have had a good relationship with than ones with which they do not.

Their strong desire to raise their children makes them work hard as parents. That desire may also blind them a little when it comes to objectively assessing that relationship and how the children are progressing. Such a task is difficult for any parent who wants to believe his child is doing well. For the father who has sought out this nontraditional role, the belief may be especially strong, as is his desire to make it come true.

The father may also believe things are going well with his children because they may have escaped a bad situation at home. Living with him, following a volatile marital relationship, desertion by the mother, or a court battle, might be seen as a relief from years of fighting. The father perceives himself as an oasis for the children and assumes they will do better with him than they had before. With noncustodial mothers being viewed negatively in society, he and the children may be hearing a great deal about the qualities of a mother who does not raise her children. This can reinforce the father's impression that his relationship with his children is a positive one.

The children may also have a desire to make things work. Children in these families often hear wonderful things about their fathers. A halo effect is created. The children, witnessing the praise heaped on their father, work a little harder on the relationship,[5] which in turn produces more praise and better feelings for the whole family. The children, having experienced a change in their relationship with their mother, will often seek out a closer one with their father to compensate. They are well aware that they are heading into a new situation following a painful period of time. As a result, they and the father may, at least initially, be on their best behavior.

When the father and children are first alone, a quasi-honeymoon period may occur. Simultaneously one can observe both the most difficult and the best of times. This period can be short-lived. It works as follows: the father is finding the initial few months the most difficult because of the need to arrange child care, work, and housekeeping. Yet everyone is attempting to be on their best behavior because they want the arrangement to work. As the pressures of the new situation mount up, they can tip the initial attempts at good behavior into a negative, albeit more realistic, balance. Family members begin acting themselves again. Just as the relationships assume a more realistic tenor, the other pressures (it is hoped) come under control. The result of these shifting family interactions is that usually, within a year, the family has begun to establish an interpersonal and household routine that becomes their identity. This does not mean that the children have adjusted fully to the divorce. That may take longer.

In a minority of cases, there is no honeymoon period. The children, understandably, are angry and unhappy about the new custody arrangement. They constantly test the father. They can be withdrawn or demanding. They may try to pit one parent against the other. In venting their feelings they are asking for structure. In doing so, they can make life hell for themselves and their father. The father, struggling to get the house and his new life in order, is going through a period when he is least able to cope with the emotional demands of the children. The reactions of others can also make this period more difficult for the father and his children. If acceptance from family members and friends is not forthcoming, the family can feel isolated and further stressed. Time and understanding can heal this as the father and children work to clarify their relationships both within the family and outside the family.

VARIATIONS IN HOW THE CHILDREN ADJUST

Children in the same family often adjust differently to a divorce and to a custody arrangement. Such attributes as their personalities, sex, age, needs, relationship with either parent, and sibling position can have a distinct effect on their own adjustment and the father's opinion of that adjustment. In addition, a child who seems to be well-adjusted at one point may experience difficulties when reaching puberty, for example, or when faced with new family demands. All this can affect the relationship that the father and children establish.

A negative cycle can be started. The father who believes his child is having trouble adjusting may start to examine his own role in the adjustment. He may blame himself and believe he is failing as a father. A man who thinks that action can take care of problems may feel over his head in the subtle complexities that develop around human emotions. When there is no clear or direct action he can take to make things better for his child or himself he may feel frustrated. This can turn to anger as the child gets blamed for having troubles. Naturally, in this situation, the relationship with the child is harmed.

A positive cycle can also be generated when things begin well. Early difficulties are faced and overcome. Adjustment problems are not viewed as personal attacks on the father's or the child's competence but rather as the result of growing pains. Having overcome adversity or having placed it in a positive context, the father and child move on to new challenges with confidence. The relationship is a positive one. Sometimes a better cycle can develop with one child than the next.

One father, a policeman, is pleased with his son's progress but not with his daughter's: "They have adjusted okay to living with me now. They were, at first, surprised by our breakup (two years ago), but after six months they adjusted to it. Grades have been up and down. My son's are up and my daughter's down. She is having a problem with one of the teachers in school and is starting to date. Adolescence is quite a thing to go through." The father later added that he felt he was losing a "certain closeness" with his daughter but hoped that by the time she became an adult, things would improve. Adolescence is frequently blamed for problems between father and child.

A factory worker from Indiana with four children has also had problems with one of his children. He blames his ex-wife. "The children are very upset by the divorce. My oldest daughter is having a big problem. She thought her mother would change her mind and come back. When problems came up between her and her mother, they became my problems, too. I got my daughter (age eighteen) a job. She got fired. She doesn't want to do anything. I helped her get a car and now I am making the payments. She has kind of dropped out. I tried to get her help; she refuses. She's a good girl around the house but she just dropped out. She said she will get herself straightened out, but I think I am going to get professional help. The other children are doing great."

A third father, a biologist from New York, is raising three children. He also describes great differences in their adjustment. He recounts how he pulled the wool over his own eyes in an attempt to give himself a better impression of his children: "Each child reacted differently. They are still paying the price. The oldest one pulled into herself and still is withdrawn. The middle one became unhappy and would cry. I would get in touch with his mother and that would help. The youngest had it the hardest. He was six and now has a hard time dealing with women. The more assertive his mother was, the more he fought her. They seem to have recovered now. I thought it was just me having problems, and I was wrong. They all were. I wanted to see them all doing well."

What these three fathers have in common they share with many of the other fathers: variation in how their children are doing. When questioned closely during interviews, however, many of the fathers who report problems see the situation either as an improvement over what the children had been going through or as an improvement over what they would be going through if they were still living with their mother.

They also feel they have grown a great deal in their own relationship with the children. Many fathers talked about how they had not known their children as well before they gained custody. They spoke of how the opportunity to raise their children, while not emerging from a situation they would have chosen, has worked out positively for their personal growth and for their growth as a parent. It is these good relationships the fathers turn to when they are searching for a silver lining on what many find to be a difficult parenting experience.

Not only did the fathers feel they had changed for the better, they often noted improvements in their children's relationships. The biggest positive change came in the children's relationship with the father, with 55 percent of the dads feeling that that had improved. The three other most positive changes were improvements in the children's attitude toward themselves (49 percent), their ability to talk about feelings (46 percent), and in their school performance (45 percent). Changes for the better were also noted in about one-third of the children in their attitude toward school and friends, and in their physical health. Only a handful thought things had gotten worse in those areas since the father gained custody, with the remainder believing there had been no change. The area that showed the greatest change for the *worse* was in the children's attitude toward the mother, with 36 percent believing that had declined.

For many fathers, then, three recurring themes emerged:

1. The children are doing well under the circumstances;
2. The father's having custody has resulted in positive changes for the children;
3. The father and children have become much closer since he gained custody.

Do Sex and Age of the Children Matter?

One frequently asked question is whether fathers should raise daughters or young children. The courts traditionally have been less willing to give fathers custody of either of these two groups in the belief that the mother was better suited to raising them. Daughters were thought to need a feminine touch and young children were seen, according to the tender years doctrine, as being more closely bonded with the mother. Let us first examine the question of sex.

Among all those surveyed, fathers are more likely to be raising sons than daughters. In addition, when fathers have one child living with them and another living elsewhere (a split custody situation) those children living elsewhere are more apt to be female. There is then a clear tendency for fathers to be raising sons rather than daughters. Based on tradition, this would be expected.

Some research on children of divorce tends to support this arrangement. It shows that children do best when being raised by the same-sex parent.[6] This is not to say that fathers should not raise daughters or that mothers should not raise sons. A daughter will be better off with her father if he is the parent best prepared to raise her. What was found from interviewing fathers, though, was that they often feel uncomfortable with certain aspects of raising daughters. For example, one father who had had custody of his three-year-old girl for six months said: "I keep wondering if there is some secret I don't know about raising girls." One father who felt uncomfortable discussing sexuality with his daughters believes his reticence led to their early experimentation. Perhaps if he had been able to talk to them they would not have felt the need to learn about sex at such a young age. A handful mentioned having to work to handle their own feelings about their daughter's sexuality. One or two fathers alluded to being sexually attracted to their daughters, a situation that parents must guard against and keep in check. Fathers also recognize that the needs of daughters are different than sons and worry more about their emotional development. Involving other women in their daughters' lives was one way of coping with this concern.

How might a father do this? One Philadelphia father talked about the help he received from the women in the neighborhood in getting his daughter ready for her first high school prom. Others spoke of asking teachers, nurses, sisters, and their own mothers to discuss sexuality and feminine hygiene with their daughters.

Despite the past research and the obvious discomfort some fathers feel with certain aspects of their rearing daughters, fathers in this research felt they had a *better relationship* with their daughters than their sons. The reasons for this are varied and have to do with the unique father-daughter relationship that develops. In the father-daughter relationship, the daughter may idolize the father. She may look up to him as the embodiment of what all men should be. When the mother is not in the home, she may be drawn into a caretaking role, and do the laundry, cooking, and cleaning in the belief that is how she can win her father's affection and attention. The mother's departure leaves a gap in the family's life that the daughter often believes she can fill.

As the daughter is moving toward a closer relationship with the father, he is seeking the same thing. Many men see their role as being to take care of females. With his wife absent, the daughter becomes the recipient of the male need to protect. Her position as "daddy's little girl" intensifies. This is quite different from how a son would be raised. The father might see his role with a son to be to raise him to fend for himself. In doing this, competition could be fostered between father and son, which is much less likely to happen with a daughter. The father and daughter then seek each other out and find themselves in a position in which each is trying to take care of the other. Establishing a good father-daughter relationship under these circumstances can be quite easy.

The age of the child can also have an effect on the father's relationship with the children. Because young children have traditionally been raised by women, both in the home and in schools, it is believed that fathers would have a hard time with this age. This was not the case. Fathers consistently express more satisfaction with younger children than older. Their relationships with them are more satisfying, they find them easier to engage with in activities and to discipline. Men raising younger children also give themselves higher ratings as a father.

Anyone who has spent time around a teenager should not be surprised by this. The issues teens present to parents are much more critical than those presented by younger children. Worrying about a fifteen-year-old's sexual and drug experimentation has helped sprout many more gray hairs than worrying about how well Junior is learning to make his own lunch for first grade. There is also more control over younger children, as they are more dependent. A father can send a disobedient six-year-old to bed. A sixteen-year-old cannot be handled that way. In addition, school performance as it relates to college and career goals becomes one more area of concern. With a younger child there is more time spent physically with child care, but there is probably less time spent worrying.

Other factors also may account for greater satisfaction raising younger children. With the loss of daily contact with the mother, an older child may turn to peer groups for support; a younger child, lacking that option, may turn to the father. For some men, this can provide a feeling of being needed that helps the parent-child relationship. The father, perhaps feeling unloved following the marital breakup, appreciates the attention. Many teens are also better able than younger children to make independent contact with the noncustodial mother. Such contact may stir up turmoil in the father and negatively affect his relationship with that child.

Conclusions

It can be concluded that while fathers may have more difficulties raising daughters, worrying about them more, being unsure what to do, and needing outside assistance, they also experience more contentment in their relationships with them. This is especially true for preadolescent daughters, the group with which fathers feel they have the best relationship.[7]

This discussion is meant to help you better understand the relationships that develop between you and your child. You should not be discouraged from seeking custody of children who are a certain sex or age. For many reasons, the children may be better off living with you than in some other arrangement. You must decide, or seek help in deciding, with whom the children will most benefit.

As mentioned, suggestions for raising children are discussed in depth in chapter 13. It can be emphasized here, though, that a positive attitude by the father and having wanted custody are linked to better father-child relationships and to the perception of a better adjustment by the children. Taking steps to feel better about yourself as a parent can benefit your relationship with your children and their adjustment.

6

Balancing Work on the
Daddy Track

How does a single father balance the competing demands of childrearing and work? Are these fathers shunted off a career path and forced onto a daddy track? Most of the fathers, when they were married, went to work each day knowing their children's needs were being taken care of by their wives. The father and mother were partners. He brought home the bulk of the income while she maintained the home and raised the children. If the child was sick, the wife usually was at home to shuttle him or her to the doctor. If the wife worked, she was more likely than the father to take time off. If school conferences or other special events happened during the day, the mother would attend; the father would show up only if his schedule permitted. Having the mother available freed the father to work as needed to support the family. Having her there enabled him to work overtime, to attend after-work meetings, to adapt to a different shift if needed, and to pursue work-related travel.

When a father gains sole custody, all that changes. Working overtime may not be as easy to arrange if it interferes with a child-care schedule. Traveling may be greatly reduced and the father may even miss work or have to cut short his workday. Perhaps most significantly, he may have to change his priorities. Instead of defining himself through success at work—that is, as a worker who happens to be a parent—he has to consider a new identity: that of a parent who works. Many fathers find this a difficult identity to assume. Some even feel that because of their children they are being pushed aside by their employer.

The adjustment fathers make to working while childrearing alone turns out to be one of their toughest, with five out of six fathers reporting difficulties. This should not be surprising. Even though these fathers had many years experience as the primary breadwinner, coupling the demands of the workplace with the demands of running a home, often a new experience for the father, is stressful. Work, of course, can be stressful in and of itself. As Studs Terkel has written, work can be violent to the body and to the spirit. It produces ulcers, accidents, daily humiliations, and nervous breakdowns. Many adults agree with Terkel's sentiments that the workplace can be a place of great tension, uncertainty, and inflexibility. During an economic turndown, these problems can be exacerbated. In times of high unemployment mental health problems and child abuse increase. Despite adversities at the job, our work is our emblem. It defines who we are and how we live.

The importance of work is deeply ingrained as part of the American work ethic. From the time these single fathers were young, they lived in a society that emphasized that being a man meant being a breadwinner. They were supposed to go off to work where, it was hoped, they would excel. Within the last decade, the importance placed on work has changed, but only slightly. Now it is more acceptable than before for men to modify their careers (if they are in white-collar positions) to share in housekeeping and child care. The assumption, though, is that this is a short-term detour. After the children are older the father is expected to return to the full-fledged pursuit of the golden ring. We should not be fooled into believing that society has shifted its still basically conservative expectations of men's and women's behavior. Polls of college student's attitudes about sex-role behavior, for example, continue to show that little has changed over the last twenty years despite the women's movement. Overall, work remains vitally important to a man's self-image.

When the father begins raising children alone, the stresses of the workplace do not go away. Instead, childrearing presents the father with another job to cope with. And this new job is often in open conflict with the work the father does outside the home, as epitomized by Dave in chapter 2. Confusion abounds.

The father is pulled in two directions. In fact, work can take on greater importance. His family has to be kept financially afloat as the mother's income and time commitment to the home is often lost. In addition, he needs his work because his own self-esteem has been battered by the marital breakup. The workplace may provide stability and an opportunity to build himself up. Yet he is tugged toward home, too. He is needed to handle the daily emergencies and to deal with the emotions of the children, which have been rubbed raw by the breakup. Thus it is not surprising that working while childrearing was difficult for so many of these men.

When the Father Gets Custody

What does the father do about the daily pressures at work? About three-quarters of the fathers underwent at least one change relative to work, with the average father experiencing at least three. The most common adjustment is arriving late at work or leaving early (39 percent of the fathers). Reasons fathers cut short their workday are usually related to teachers' conferences, after-school activities, child-care emergencies, or child-related illnesses. Having to miss work altogether, often for the same reasons, is the second most commonly mentioned job-related change (35 percent). Other frequently cited changes are reducing work-related travel (32 percent), going on flextime (25 percent), bringing work home (15 percent), and taking on additional work (14 percent).

The fathers that had to take on extra work needed to do so to make ends meet. They often had older children in the house who did not need them home as much or they had their parents who could help out with the child care. The lack of the wife's income left a hole in the family budget that the father had to fill.

Some men were subject to even more drastic changes. Seven percent said they had to quit their jobs because of being unable to balance work and childrearing. Another 5 percent admitted to having been fired. Harry, a Minnesotan, was one of the fathers who had to quit. When he began raising his two small children the day he and his wife separated, he ran into problems as a store clerk. He found he could not take his three-year-old to his job, nor could he afford to hire someone to care for her. Describing himself as "old-fashioned" in not wanting to leave his child at a day-care center (a common feeling among fathers), he found a job as a resident manager of an apartment complex. That position enabled him to work out of his home and take his youngest child along on his maintenance calls.

Pierre, a Canadian father, was fired from his job as a trucker because he could no longer work overtime. "They have this bullshit rule that single parents are not allowed to work overtime. Well, I couldn't and I was fired because I couldn't put in the hours they needed." Pierre found a different truck-driving position in his province where a union protected him from having to drive overtime.

Bob, a Virginian, lost his job because he couldn't cope. He makes a cogent point about the way single parents are treated. "Due to my health problems and stress from the divorce and raising the kids, I lost my job of twenty-two years. I think companies should have programs for people going through divorce. They have programs for alcoholics. Why not for us fathers?"

On the Daddy Track

It is hard for fathers, whether married or single, to take time off from work. Research on fathers in the workplace shows that they are loathe to make use of paternity leave and that it has a negative connotation to employers. When fathers do take time off from work for parenting responsibilities such as the birth of a child, they tend to attribute it to other categories of leave taking such as sick days or vacation time.[1] Clearly this atmosphere presents problems for working fathers, even those whose leave taking is only temporary and whose children will be the ultimate responsibility of the mother. Imagine what it can be like for fathers who are faced with more long-term responsibilities.

Harry, Pierre, and Bob, whose situations were just described, provide some examples of fathers whose jobs were imperiled because of their custody arrangement. Less visible are those men who, with or without their knowledge, are placed on hold at work. An observant boss sees that the single father is distracted by telephone calls, is leaving early, or is missing work. As a result, she decides to pass him over for a promotion or a new assignment. In the film *Kramer vs. Kramer,* Ted Kramer loses his job because of his responsibilities to his son. He begins to miss important meetings, to turn in his work late, and to accept urgent phone calls from his son during conferences. The outcome? A lower-paying job.

Having less income because of solo parenting means a number of adjustments for the father and his family.

One father, a policeman, worked the day shift on the force for a number of years. He also worked part-time in the evenings to supplement the family income. When he left his wife, he had to give up his part-time job and the extras that work had brought him. He was philosophical about the changes: "If you don't have it to spend, then you don't spend it."

Mark, a salesman who worked on commission, was not as amused by his changed circumstances. When he was married and had someone at home to take care of the children, he could attend sales meetings, take clients out to dinner, and travel. He was the typical salesman—always on the go. Like many people in sales, he knew that the more time he put into his job, the higher his income would be. At one time he earned well over thirty-five thousand dollars a year. Mark never had to worry about his children during the day because his wife, who did not work, was always there. When he ended up with custody, the family's life-style changed dramatically. Mark's income dropped by a third because he could no longer attend sales meetings or be as free about taking clients out to dinner. He had to sell the house, split the proceeds with his ex-wife, and move to an apartment. "I guess when the children are older, I'll be able to earn more again. But I sure hated to lose my house."

In addition to the financial adjustments, fathers must make psychological adjustments when they can no longer pour themselves into their careers. An accountant in Virginia was very articulate about having to shift the way he viewed himself: "When I got out of school, I worked very hard trying to become the best. But then, when I got my kids, I was no longer the guy who was going to earn forty thousand dollars a year by the time I was thirty-five. I was raising a seven- and a nine-year-old, and I had to completely revise my self-image. It has been damned hard." Another father, an engineer, said simply: "I'm stuck where I am. I can't move elsewhere. I can't go up. I'm stuck."

Another aspect of childrearing causes discomfort to single fathers—the loss of the ex-wife as a child-care provider. Not having the children home with their mother has meant reevaluation of the importance they may have placed on the nuclear family's being able to take care of its own. Other child-care providers, such as day-care centers, become options that fathers grudgingly accept; but they feel their children are suffering, and this concern pulls them more and more away from work.

A few fathers who were interviewed welcomed this change in their priorities. They were unhappy with the pressures placed on them by their work and their upbringing. Being a parent first and a worker second has enabled them to enjoy their lives more and to learn more about themselves. When they were concentrating on work all the time, they were too busy to appreciate their children.

Difficulty Working

What makes working more difficult for some fathers than for others? As might have been anticipated, the more job-related changes a father undergoes, the greater the difficulty he experiences. As shifts in work schedules, reduced overtime, and missing work add up, work becomes harder and harder. Not surprising, the fathers who are fired or quit usually have the greatest difficulties.

Although one would think that lower occupational status, less education, and lower income would all be related to less job flexibility and hence more difficulty, this turned out not to be the case. There is no link between these characteristics and the difficulty of working while childrearing.

It *was* found, however, that although the actual income earned has no effect on the father's difficulties, a change in his income does. In other words, a father whose income falls from thirty thousand dollars a year to twenty-five thousand dollars a year will find things more difficult than will a father earning twenty thousand dollars a year who experiences no drop in income after the breakup. The fathers make ends meet with whatever they have; but when what they have is reduced, it is harder for them than if they did not have the extra money in the first place. Tom's story illustrates this: "Before the divorce, my wife and I had all the basics. She was working twenty hours a week. We could make ends meet. Not any more. Her income does not go to paying for the food like it used to. It goes for her own place. There just isn't as much." The problem is further exacerbated for this man because he cannot put in overtime at work. To do so, he would have to leave his children alone at night.

Fathers who did not seek custody but had it forced upon them tended to find working—and many other aspects of parenting—more difficult. When the father does not want sole custody but finds himself thrust into the role—either because his ex-wife does not want the children or because she is physically or emotionally unable to take care of them—he may feel a great deal of anger about the interruption in his work schedule that childrearing introduces. He may not be psychologically prepared to assume the role of full-time parent. He may find himself unwillingly upsetting his workday and his career goals to take on the responsibility of his children. He may also feel guilt because of his feelings of anger. This makes his reaction to parenting much different from that of the father who willingly accepts his children with some idea about what that might mean for his career goals.

Younger fathers are more likely to find working and childrearing difficult than are older ones. This could be expected for two reasons. The older the father, the more experience he will have had at work and the greater his freedom to come and go as he pleases. He also may have become more indispensable to his employer over time, so that his boss may be more accommodating. The second reason is that the older father is more likely to be raising older children, who need less supervision.

Just as certain characteristics of the father affect his difficulty working, so do some of the characteristics of the children.

Characteristics of the Children

The more children there are to raise, the more child-care demands there are. There are more parent-teacher conferences to attend, more doctor's appointments to make, and more phone calls to field from battling siblings. With one child at home, there is the potential for only one crisis at a time. For the father raising three or more children, the potential for crises is greatly increased.

The age of the children can be a factor, too. As discussed in the previous chapter, the father raising children in the five- to eleven-year-old range turned out to have the most difficulty working. It can be presumed that the reason for this is that this age group poses particularly tough questions for the father concerning children's ability to take care of themselves.

Even when elaborate and satisfactory child-care arrangements are worked out that allow the father to work as he would like, things tend to happen that throw everything out of kilter. Frederick, a manager raising a five-, a three-, and a two-year-old, was able to manage everything with his two oldest in day care and his youngest at a sitter's home. With the hours offered by the day-care center, he thought he had all bases covered. But when the two oldest became sick with chicken pox one day and were not able to go to day care for two weeks, he had to stay home with them. Because he missed so much work, he was fired. He now has a new job and a more understanding boss. Instead of being on salary, however, he is working on straight commission. He says he is not earning the kind of money he used to; as a result, his self-esteem has suffered.

Some of the fathers discuss their concerns about the children even when the children are past the age of needing constant adult supervision. James has been raising four children aged twelve through twenty for about two years. He told me that he worries about his children even though they are older and even though he works only four blocks from his house. His oldest son, who is sixteen, works; but the twelve- and fourteen-year-old are too young to work and too old to be watched by the twenty-year-old, who is looking for work. Summers are especially trouble-some because the children are home for long periods of time.

Satisfactory child-care arrangements can go a long way to-ward helping the single father to adjust to working. Some men are able to go to greater lengths than others to assure that their children are well taken care of in their absence.

One man who has had custody for five years provides such an example. Samuel lives in one city but works in another, one hundred miles away, where he has assumed responsibility for his father's business.

His son is eleven years old and attends school in their home town. Samuel commutes daily between the two cities by train. Because he runs the family business, Samuel has more flexibility than those fathers who have to answer to a boss. Yet he also has greater responsibility for management, which makes his job stressful. He has been able to arrange a system of beepers be-tween the two cities that permits him to be called at a moment's notice if there has been some change in his son's child-care ar-rangements or if his son needs him. With this arrangement, he feels comfortable that his son is always well taken care of.

Fathers adapt their work lives to the child-care needs of their children in a variety of ways. One father, who could not find a sitter for his children after school, remained in the army longer than he had planned to so that he and the children could benefit from the safer environment on the military base where they lived. Another father started a business at home, where he made seasonal gifts. Working out of his house, he was able to be at home when needed for his small children. In these diverse ways, fathers adjust their work lives and their home lives to find the best match between the two.

Involvement of the Ex-Wife

The involvement of the ex-wife also affects how the father feels about his work experience. Just as she was important to the fa-ther during the marriage, when she helped him pursue higher career goals by taking care of the children, so too can she be helpful after the breakup. The more contact she maintains with the children, the easier it is for the father. The nature of the relationship that develops between the custodial father and the ex-wife is described in depth in chapter 8, but a number of advantages of a good relationship can be touched on here. There is a greater likelihood of child-care assistance, of financial assistance, and of the children being less upset by the divorce and hence less dependent on the father.

One case illustrates this point. Herman's ex-wife, Sue, lives in the same city as he does and takes their son on the weekends. Sue has lived with her mother and father since the divorce. About once a year, Herman goes to a week-long convention that is important to his career. During that time, his ex-wife takes their son. She works during the day, so the child care is left to her parents. Without the help of Sue and her parents, Herman might have had to miss some of these conventions in the three years he has had custody. It is easier for him to travel knowing that backup support is there.

In a minority of cases, an ex-wife who is very involved with the children can make working *more* difficult for the father. Tom, who for a variety of reasons does not like his ex-wife, gets phone calls from her while he is at work. She may call to change visitation or to suggest a new way of approaching a problem with one of their children. If she were not so involved, Tom would have to try harder to schedule child care; but he also would not be bothered by his ex-wife's calls when he is at work.

The Need for Flextime

One message that keeps on coming through loud and clear from the fathers is the need for flextime; that is, the ability to come and go at their jobs as they wish without having to give up any hours over the course of the week. Fathers want to be able to take time off from work to be with sick children. They want to be able to bring work home if they did not finish it because they have been on the phone with their children for half an hour. Emergencies do not always happen when the father is at home. The ability to leave work without having to relinquish an arm and a leg to do it is what the fathers constantly say they need.

One father wrote that the lack of flextime was the hardest

thing for him about single parenting: "I've raised my son from the bottle and diaper stage. My life wouldn't be complete without him. But it is hard when he gets sick and I can't leave work." Bringing work home is, unfortunately, something that is less possible to do at a blue-collar position.

The father's need for flextime increases as the adequacy of his child care declines. Fathers who have good child-care arrangements do not feel as great a need for flextime. Of course, the need for flextime is not unique to fathers. In any situation in which both parents work, or there is a working single mother, it can be useful. A fictional example of the problems facing a working parent was seen a few years ago in the movie *E.T.* In this case, it is a single mother who is raising her three children after her husband has run off to Mexico. With some trepidation and many instructions, because she cannot afford to miss work, she leaves her son Eliot home alone after he has faked a high fever by placing the thermometer against a hot light bulb. Luckily, Eliot has the extraterrestrial to take care of him. The situation, though amusing, does raise the issue of the problems facing parents when no one is home to take care of a sick child.

Some fathers feel hesitant asking for time off to be with their child, especially if they have asked for it before or if the climate at work is not favorable to such requests. The hesitancy stems not only from those factors, though. It may also stem from having to ask for a favor, something those who believe they should be self-sufficient have difficulty doing. It can stem from their believing they are an integral part of the work situation and that they are letting the "team" down if they have to leave. In addition, if the father was hired with the expectation that his wife would handle the child-related emergencies that arose, his having to ask for time off reminds him of the failure of his marriage and does so in a public way. The importance of single parents' having the ability to leave work when emergencies demand cannot be overestimated.

Fathers do not only need more flexibility at work; some, naturally, want more money. Others, harking back to Terkel's view of the workplace being stressful, want less responsibility. Specifically, they say they want less travel, fewer nights out with customers, and less overtime, or in the case of those needing extra money, more overtime. Some dream of being self-employed. Many want greater access to the telephone so they can be available when the children need them or so they can call home to check that everything is running smoothly in their absence.

Understanding from the boss and co-workers is also needed. A workplace that is aware of the father's conflicting demands, one dad suggested, would make many fathers more productive.

The experiences of the fathers are not universally dismal. Ray, in stark contrast to the men who reported being fired or having to quit, found support in the Baltimore steel mill where he worked: "I have a very good foreman who knows me. His boss knows my problem. I talk with my immediate supervisor if I have a problem. They are pretty lenient. They don't like me missing work, but thank God the kids have not been sick where I would have to have missed a lot of time. Knock on wood. When I was going through the divorce, I had to go to court and take time off. They were pretty nice about it."

Trying to be Superdad

The problems faced by the working single father are more than merely the logistical problems shared by all working parents. He has to change the way he feels about himself as a *man.* It is not simply that it is difficult to make work schedules and child-care schedules mesh. Many fathers believe that since they have become single parents, they have been sliding by at their job; they think they are not giving the boss his or her money's worth. Others think their bosses have not been understanding of their situation, and that too much is expected of them. Still others long to be self-employed, to be able to work less, and to be able to earn more money—desires they did not feel as acutely when they were married.

What many of the fathers cannot escape—and what does not feel good—is that they are not earning as much money as they used to, and that they are not able to focus on advancement. They had always believed they would be able to get ahead, to achieve status in the world through success at work and earning a decent income. Instead, they are achieving a different kind of status—that of being seen as a good father. Although that particular status goes a long way toward making many men feel wonderful, to others it is not enough.

Some fathers want it both ways. They want to be able to work at the same pace they did when they were married *and* be the father they think their children need. They want to be like the so-called supermoms—women who try to excel both at a career and at motherhood, and often burn out in the process. They want to continue the professional climb while handling the home front. These men, newer to the role conflicts of working and childrearing than many women, have not learned some of the survival skills that can prevent burnout. Their awareness of these conflicting demands is a few years behind that of women who have seen through the illusion of the superparent and have begun to come to grips with its impossibilities.

Other fathers accept more easily the fact that they cannot have things both ways. They have put their career aspirations on hold until their children are independent. These fathers, and there are many examples of them, feel that their life has taken on new meaning. With a greater emphasis on parenting, the fathers are finding joy in what they used to consider the mundane aspects of life.

Clearly, in various forms, the daddy track exists, though a more accurate name for it might be the parent track. A father (or mother) who signals to the higher-ups that his first responsibility is to his children or even that he considers time with his children as an inviolable part of his life may find himself shunted aside when assignments are given out that require extra hours. Until society places more importance on parenting and adapts the work environment accordingly, this is likely to continue.

For most men, the voice that has told them since they were young to get ahead, to excel, and to earn money can never be completely silenced. For some, however, it can be quieted for a few years.

Suggestions for the Working Father

1. Do not try to be a superdad. Accept your limitations and the fact that being a single parent means that something at work may have to give.

2. Decide if you should talk to your boss about your new responsibilities. The wisdom of this varies by worksite. In some work situations, letting your employer know you have new responsibilities at home can make things easier. If the employer tells you that single parents make bad employees (a rare occurrence, thank God!), convince her or him of your commitment.

3. Try not to make any major work changes (if you can avoid it) immediately after getting custody. Give yourself a few months to adjust to your new lifestyle.

4. Explain to your children about the demands of working in a way that will not make them feel guilty. They need to know the pressures you may be under but should not be made to feel responsible for them.

5. Find out if nonemergency calls are allowed at work. If not, explain to your children what would be defined as an emergency for which they could call—brother has hurt himself, sister is sick, and so on. Give children possible times when it is okay for them to call you if it is not an emergency.

6. Find out if you can call home at a certain time. This would enable you to check on the children.

7. Find out whether the children can come to your place of work in an emergency.

8. Find out how your co-workers are handling their child-care demands.

9. If you are looking for day care, call the local day-care centers and go for a visit. Make sure they are licensed as required by the state. Call the licensing board to see if there have been any complaints about the day-care center. Go for a visit and see if you can picture your child being happy there. If you take your child for a visit, his or her reaction is important but should not be the deciding factor in your using that center. Ask to talk to other parents whose children are at that center.

10. If you are looking for someone to do child care in your home, call the local centers to see if they have the names of people who are interested in that type of work. Place an ad in the newspaper. When people call you, have a list of questions for them so you can screen them on the phone before meeting them. Ask them, for instance, how they would discipline your child. Under what circumstances would they call you at work? Try to

get someone with experience. Get references and make sure they are from former employers or professionals who know them. A relative or friend is not a reference.

11. Let the children know your work schedule and whereabouts if you are not based at one location at work. For example, if you are a salesman, consider giving them the numbers of your clients for that day so that they can reach you in an emergency. You will feel more comfortable at your job if you know you have a system in place for reaching you. Try and stay on your schedule. This will reassure them.

12. Make sure the children and any caretakers who are with your children have backup numbers of other people they can call in case you cannot be reached. For example, if you cannot be reached in an emergency, the children's pediatrician may be authorized to treat them. Friends and relatives can also be given such authorization. Find out if your city has a number for latch-key children that your children can call if they need to talk to someone.

13. Teach your children how to handle phone calls when you are not home. The child should not, for example, say you are not home. Instead the message should be conveyed that you cannot come to the phone at the moment. That would discourage anyone from coming to the house in your absence. In addition, the children should be taught to handle unexpected visitors in the same way.

14. Set up clear rules to be enforced in your home in your absence. For example, will you allow friends to visit your children? Can your children leave the house once they are supposed to be home from school? What food can they eat? Can they turn on the stove without you there?

15. Some experts believe older children should not be placed in charge of younger ones. Rather, you should give rules that you enforce when you are not there. Even with this approach, be prepared for telephone calls from big sister saying that little brother is not following your rules.

16. Be willing to renegotiate your rules as your children get older.

7

Social Lives of
Single Fathers

THOMAS, a forty-year-old salesman raising three sons in California, is a veteran of the social scene: "I usually date frequently, but I have been involved with one woman now for a few
months. I only bring home dates after I have been dating them
for a while and only if they are decent, nice people so the kids
make a nice friend. They are battle-scarred veterans because
they have seen women come and go all the time. They make
comments as to my taste. The person I am dating now gets high
marks. They sometimes spot problems before I do. They kept
telling me a woman I dated for a while did not like them and
that she was competing with them for me. I ignored them for
the longest time. I don't let them decide who I date but when we
broke up, that was one of the reasons."

Socializing! Dating! Getting close to someone again! Having
sexual relations! These are all activities that raise anxiety in single fathers. Yet as difficult as it may be for many, these are activities that help a father get back into the swing of things and can
signal a return to normalcy. Much more is involved in single parenting than the adjustments necessary to running a household,
arranging school and work schedules, and raising the children.
The father must adjust to being single again. That means coming to grips with the divorce and learning how to deal with being
alone. Ultimately it means emerging from the protective shell
that the newly divorced usually build around themselves.

Few fathers find this process easy, but some have a smoother time with it than others. There are fathers who date frequently and find their social and sexual life completely satisfactory. But there are also those who date rarely and are unhappy when they do venture into the social scene. What makes socializing so difficult for these fathers? The reasons are multifaceted and have to do with some of the common perceptions that exist about men.

Generally, in American society, men are thought to be in the driver's seat when it comes to dating. Long-lived is the image of the carefree bachelor, able, like a honeybee, to flit from flower to flower. The perceptions held about men are that: 1) they should be the initiators of dating; 2) they are able to have sexual relations without commitment; 3) they can be sexually assertive and aggressive; and 4) they can have sexual relations without guilt. In addition, it is believed men can be content staying single.

These views about male behavior are shared by some men but certainly not by many single fathers. Acutely aware of the expectations placed on men for assertive behavior, fathers often feel restricted rather than liberated by them. They feel pressured to act in a certain way. Fathers (and men in general) react by thinking they are not supposed to get too involved, that they are supposed to treat women as sex objects while turning to other men for intellectual stimulation and friendship. Ultimately, these expectations upset those who are not fulfilling them. Fathers may wonder what is wrong with them if they do not feel like being assertive or if they cannot perform sexually. These messages about male behavior have become increasingly complex during the last decade as women's roles have changed. It is now more acceptable for a woman to be an initiator and to be sexually active. This adds to the confusion that already existed in the social scene as the definition of correct dating behavior becomes more murky. As a result, dating is often undertaken in an atmosphere filled with tension and ambivalence.

Fathers, as they consider dating, are also buffeted by feelings that remain from the divorce. The reactions to being single vary from relief and elation to withdrawal and depression, depending upon the circumstances. Marital breakups can give rise to emotional and physical ailments, feelings of disorientation, guilt, and anxiety. Self-esteem suffers as the father wonders if he will ever be able to establish a meaningful relationship again. Adjusting to a divorce means accepting the end of the dream of a happily married life and reassessing one's values and goals. For many men, the loss of the marriage and the companionship of a once-loved woman can be extremely painful and can take years to overcome. These feelings inhibit many fathers' capacities for dating and initiating new relationships.

Loneliness is natural during this period. The presence of children does not mitigate it for many fathers. One father, an engineer, reported, "I don't mind having my wife gone. It was my idea. But I was not prepared for the loneliness. After being married for twelve years, it is rough."

Also affecting the fathers' feelings about socializing are the children. As will be discussed later in this chapter, not only are the fathers often reluctant to bring new women into their children's lives, the children may actively resist it. Such hindrances can add to a father's sense of frustration and anxiety.

How Socially Satisfied are the Fathers?

With all these constraints on fathers, it is not surprising that most who were surveyed said they were not satisfied with their social lives. The lack of satisfaction does not come from staying home every night to do the laundry. Almost half reported dating at least once a week and another quarter dated once or twice a month. Only one father in sixteen said he never dated.

As fathers date for a while, they are likely to get involved in intimate, long-term relationships. They are also likely to have sexual relationships. It usually takes the father about six months to a year before he begins dating. It is not until he has been single for more than three years that the typical father has what he considers to be his first meaningful relationship (not to be confused with having a sexual relationship). Sexual relationships begin soon after the father starts to date. They are a fairly typical part of dating for these fathers. As might be expected, those that date more are most likely to have sexual relations, with slightly less than half the fathers having relations at least every other week. Despite this level of activity, only about a third of the fathers reported being satisfied with their social lives. Sex does play an important part in the fathers' social satisfaction. Without it, there is little chance of finding social satisfaction. Of two hundred fathers who reported they were *never* having sex, fewer than one in ten said they were socially satisfied. At the same time, satisfaction with sexual relations does have a limit. It is helpful only up to a point. Fathers who are having fairly regular sexual relations are likely to see their social satisfaction increase socially over the years and peak at the four-year mark. After that social satisfaction declines slightly.

A clear point needs to be made here in discussing sexual relations. A father should not feel that he is not adjusting, or that he is any less of a man, if he is not having sex. For some men, feeling comfortable having sex may take much longer than for others. Sexual relations are best when the father feels comfortable and has the consent of a willing partner.

Barriers to Social Satisfaction

Some general hindrances to having a satisfying social life were mentioned previously: myths about male performance; residual feelings from the divorce; the presence of the children. Other reasons also serve as barriers. On a fundamental level, the advent of AIDS and other sexually transmitted diseases scare men off from casual relations. The way the father became divorced is also a factor. Most fathers did not want the marriage to end in the first place and experienced a great deal of stress when it did. Almost half indicated the request for the divorce came as a surprise to them (see chapter 3). Thus, a significant number of fathers were pulled into a divorce they may not have wanted. Not wanting to be single, and feeling caught off guard, many naturally have trouble adjusting. Reentering the social scene with little preparation and feeling hurt and vulnerable, the fathers are gun-shy of new relationships.

As mentioned, they have their children to think of, too. Many feel guilty about the failure of their marriage and about subjecting their children to a single-parent experience. As long as their children seem emotionally vulnerable, they may take great pains to not further aggravate the wound. If they believe some postdivorce stability has been established in the home, they are unlikely to want to upset that by introducing the often inflammatory issues that come with dating. Fathers also may be hesitant to date because it means less time with the children.

The result is that the more sensitive fathers end up putting their children's needs first. Sometimes this comes at their own expense. One father epitomizes this: "I used to feel guilty if I went out. My ex-wife had been taking off and leaving the kids with a sitter. I wasn't willing to do that when I first got custody." As a result, he stayed home, putting his own needs on the back burner.

The pain of the marital breakup and worries about the children are not the only concerns these men face. If they finally do date, they may experience culture shock. The average father in the surveys had been single about four years and had been married before that for about twelve years. That means that most men were last single in the mid-1960s to early 1970s, when expectations for men's and women's behavior were much different than they are now. At that time, it was more acceptable for a man to be the initiator. By the time these men divorced and became single again, things had changed. Many women do not assume the passive role they once did when it comes to dating.

These changes place incredible demands on fathers, even though the thrust of many role changes was intended to be liberating to both men and women. One fifty-five-year-old father, a lawyer from a rural Ohio town, described being single after thirty years of marriage: "Men and women are not the same as they were when I was first married. Women who believe in old-fashioned values are hard to find." The woman with old-fashioned values is the kind of woman he married in the 1950s and the kind of woman he is looking for now. Another father said, "The dating was awkward for me at first. I mean I forgot what you were supposed to do on a date and what to say. I guess I go through cycles. I'll date or get into something for a while and then break up and hit a dry spell. It's been that way for a while."

Some fathers feel in a double bind when it comes to dating. They believe they should date only single mothers, because only another custodial parent would understand the need to place their children first. Yet that also means that both parents will have little free time to work on developing a relationship. The result for those fathers can be an increasing feeling of isolation or a series of relationships that never develop a deeper intimacy.

When Fathers Start to Date

When a father decides to date the concerns just mentioned are quickly replaced by realities. One of the first hurdles is discussing dating with the children. Some fathers handle it by avoiding it, dating secretly until they are sure they want their children to meet the person. Others cope with it more effectively. Some face it head on, by telling the children they are starting to date and, when it is convenient, they might enjoy meeting the new friend.

Another major concern is money. A number of fathers do not have discretionary money they can spend on a social life. Dating is seen as a luxury, not a necessity. Having trouble making ends meet, they avoid situations that cost money or that they perceive require them to make a good appearance. One father wrote me and complained that his financial situation was such that he could not afford to buy clothes to attend a Parents Without Partners meeting. Because of the costs of parenting, fathers could not spend as much on dates as they had when they were single. The expense of nice restaurants, shows, sporting events, or day trips, when added to the possible cost of hiring a babysitter, puts many plans out of reach. As a result, the father who dates finds himself cutting corners.

The father's financial situation is a marker of how he feels about himself. Men in our society often place a high value on income and measure their self-esteem by the weight of their wallet. As would be expected, the more comfortable he is financially, the more the father socializes. For example, in the 1988 sample, fathers who earned more than thirty thousand dollars were more likely to date and have sexual relations than those who earned less than thirty thousand dollars. Money clearly buys the opportunity for dating and thus the opportunity for sexual intercourse. If the father associates being able to afford to date with his self-esteem, he is likely to suffer a blow to his masculinity when funds are short.

Some fathers, regardless of their income, may use their financial situation as an excuse to avoid socializing. Feeling uncomfortable with their personal situation, money becomes an acceptable scapegoat. Rather than attempt to date and risk being emotionally hurt, they avoid the arena altogether.

For fathers who wish to bring dates home, additional hurdles exist. Harking back to their single days when they were child-free, they quickly find their style cramped. It is difficult to have a romantic dinner in one room while the children are making popcorn and watching Cosby show reruns in another. Having sexual relations while the children are awake is clearly prohibited. If the father wants a woman to spend the night without the children knowing, he has the problem of sneaking her out in the wee hours of the morning or of risking being interrupted by a child's request for a midnight glass of water.

Many fathers, for good reasons, do not have their dates sleep over when the children are in the house. As one North Carolina father put it: "The kids have been confused enough by the divorce. I don't want to confuse them any more." This protection of the children's feelings is essential to their well-being and to the father's own sense of himself as a parent. Foregoing certain experiences for the benefit of the children can be appropriate and can help the father in forging a stronger sense of his role as a parent. But if the father goes too far in depriving himself, he becomes a martyr and the children will be perceived by him as persecutors. Thus, like in most parenting issues whether one is single or married, the needs of the children have to be balanced against the needs of the parent.

Not having a woman sleep over can be wise for another reason. One Michigan father told this story: "I was able to get custody from my wife because she violated the court order by being immoral and having guys sleep over. I know she is waiting to catch me do the same thing." In ongoing court battles, charges of immoral behavior can be grist for an opposing lawyer's mill. Legion are the cases in the court system that include charges of immoral behavior by one of the parents. Some cases include charges (whether true or not) that the child witnessed sexual behavior between the custodial parent and another adult.

It is not just sleepovers that need to be carefully monitored.

Examples also exist of fathers who adopt one standard of dating behavior for themselves and a different one for their children. Curfews can appear to be applied in unfair ways. One Baltimore father found his seventeen-year-old daughter emulating his late-night patterns. When he confronted her with her behavior, she replied, "If you can do it (stay out late), why can't I?" As a result of these issues, many custodial fathers are circumspect about their sexual habits.

Despite the natural concerns of not wanting to upset the children by dating or "confusing" them by having dates sleep over, most fathers do allow the children to meet women they have serious feelings about. This usually happens when the father believes his relationship has reached a point at which a long-term commitment is being considered. The woman may begin to spend more time with the family, including taking trips with them and spending nights at the home. Regular sleepovers do not usually begin until after plans for a marriage have been announced. Some fathers talk to the children first to get their impressions of the girlfriend. Many fathers have a good impression already, as the children have been offering unsolicited commentary for months.

It is not uncommon for fathers to gain custody after being without their children for a few years. These men have to go through a different kind of adjustment period. While they were first free to date without the constraints of having children in the home, they later had to restrict themselves. Some of these fathers, when they became single, threw themselves into the dating scene like a man who had been lost in the desert for days would approach a well. They sowed their oats in a way that a father with children in the home could not. Later they slowed down. George, who is raising an eleven-year-old daughter while his two sons live with his ex-wife, is one example. "When we first broke up, I went out a lot. I was like a kid again. I go out still. But it used to be better. I can't run the street every night because of her (his daughter). I wouldn't anyway since I am forty-six years old and I can't play that hard. I have to rest. You know you get off from work, you have to go home and be with the kid."

Many fathers who were single when they participated in the studies have remarried in subsequent years. Remaining single is not for everyone. About one-third of those fathers who were re-contacted had remarried within six years of being single. They tended to marry divorced working women who were raising children alone. Many fathers had met their wives through contacts made in self-help groups.[1]

The Children's Reactions

Having discussed some of the issues fathers face with dating, we can now turn to what the children experience. The father's dating is often the beginning of a difficult time for the children. Some children welcome the chance for their father to have a new relationship, but others are greatly troubled by it. To understand why, it may be helpful to briefly review some of the experiences of children who go through a divorce. They are often beset by feelings of anxiety and depression, unsure of where they will live and the status of their relationship with one or both parents. The permanence of their family life, which they may have taken for granted, is profoundly shaken. Children are often oblivious to what is going on in their parents' marriage and never consider what life would be like in a single-parent family. The noncustodial parent often becomes a visitor in the child's life, rather than a daily stabilizing influence. This may result in a great deal of reliance on the father as well as a new investment in his well-being. It may also result in an idealization of the mother or, conversely, in her being pictured as the bad parent. With the wrenching experience of the breakup and the frequently hostile remarks and actions that accompany it, a child may have a particularly difficult time developing a new picture of her parents that is at all comforting. These experiences leave a child feeling at risk and needing both parents. The father's move to replace the mother by dating shakes this foundation.

One of the fantasies commonly held among children is that their parents are going to get back together again. The Walt Disney movie *The Parent Trap* even plays out this fantasy. In this 1950s movie, two twins who were separated from each other at a young age when their parents were divorced engineer a happy remarriage. Certain obstacles have to be overcome along the way. For example, they torpedo the plans of a woman who wants to marry their father. Then they arrange for their parents to be alone together in a quiet setting. Certainly this film fired up the hopes of many children experiencing a divorce at the time. But in real life things usually do not happen so nicely. For the child who has clung to the hope of seeing his or her parents reunited, meeting a permanent replacement or even a casual date can be devastating. It destroys the fantasy of the family getting back to the way it was.

Dating does not often begin immediately after the breakup. This time lag provides an opportunity for the children and father to discuss issues around socialization. With intimate relationships starting an average of three to four years later, the notion of a more permanent relationship also has time to germinate. Yet even with ample preparation the children may be upset.

Their reactions may vary a great deal, depending on their age, their experiences, and relationships with their parents, siblings, and friends. Children may verbally comment on the choice of dating partner, as was pointed out by the father whose quote begins the chapter. They may withdraw, display clinging behavior, be hostile, or act out sexually. The more sexually indiscreet the father is the more indiscreet the children are likely to be.

While the focus has been on the pitfalls of dating, it is important to note that many children revel in their father's socializing. They may be the driving force behind his starting to go out and may suggest people for him to call. They may be eager to have a new woman in their life, to see their father happy, or to have permission to socialize themselves. The father's dating has the potential to send an important message to the children. Some men circle the wagons around themselves after a divorce to protect their own feelings as well as the children's; when they start to go out they send a message that life goes on after a divorce. As the father comes out of his cocoon, the children may feel more free to come out of theirs. Conversely, if the father refuses to open up and go out, he is sending a message to the children that they should not socialize with their peers either. Family members are most likely to be happy in families where both the father and the children are interested in his establishing a social life.

It is not only the father's and children's feelings that affect the father's social life. The feelings and reactions of the women they are dating also need consideration. The woman who begins dating or becomes seriously involved with the single father is confronted by a number of obstacles and questions. She may be unsure whether the father is interested in dating her because she would make a good wife for the father, a good mother for the children, or simply a companion for himself. Attempts to clarify this with the father may prove futile, as he may be unsure about his own needs at the moment. Problems can naturally arise.

A dance begins between the father and the woman that is bound to lead to disappointment. For example, when he hesitantly reenters the dating scene he may appear vulnerable and in need of care. With the children in the home, the family may seem to be in need of a "woman's touch." This appearance can trigger caretaking responses in a woman who is interested in getting involved with a family. The father's confusion about his own needs and those of the children may draw the woman further in. The father may express great appreciation for the woman, and encourage her further. The dance continues, with the woman playing an increasingly important part in the family's life, until the father realizes that what he is looking for and needs is quite different from what the woman has to offer or is willing to give. He may have seen her involvement as the helping hand of a friend. She, on the other hand, may have interpreted his initial shy behavior as his needing time to find himself and that the progression to a romantic relationship was inevitable.

Most women realize that they are naturally competing with the children for the father's attention and respect that quality in him. But as they become more involved, they hope there will also be a place for them in his life. Some women have stayed involved with fathers for years in the hope that as the children age, his commitment to them will change and room will be made. Sometimes this happens and, as noted, marriage is a possibility. In other situations, women give up hope and leave the relationship. A number of women, spotting potential quicksand, avoid the custodial father from the beginning, believing there may never be an appropriate place for her.

A few fathers complained that women were not interested in

dating them because of their having children. To them, the children's presence is perceived by the women to be a clear liability. The women may have children of their own or be afraid of the extra responsibility. Thomas, quoted at the beginning of this chapter, said, "Some of my relationships have ended because of this. It raises the question about how single parents are willing to deal with another single parent's children." The woman's uncertainty about her part in the father's life is fodder for continuing discussion between the adults and the children and is one more source of stress in what is already a difficult dating situation.

Finally, the role of the ex-wife must be considered. Her involvement with the children and the father may affect the way the children view the father's dating. If the mother maintains contact with the children and the father, the children may be encouraged to believe their parents are going to reconcile. The children would then discourage the father from dating. In ideal situations, the mother and father maintain contact but they have communicated clearly to the children that a reconciliation is out of the question. The children in these cases feel secure enough to believe that regardless of what happens with their father, they will always have a stable relationship with their mother. Here, dating poses few problems.

If the mother is not involved with the children, the father's dating holds open the possibility for a new mother, and may be encouraged. On the other hand, without much maternal contact, the children sometimes become overly invested in their father. In that case, his dating poses the threat of diverting his attention from them to someone new.

Who Is Most Satisfied Socially?

Fathers who earn more money and are raising older children tend to be the most socially satisfied. The reasons are fairly obvious. Money gives the father more opportunity to date the way he wants to. Older children make fewer demands on the father because they require less physical attention and are more likely to have their own social life. In addition, fathers with older children are likely to have been single longer, giving them more time to adjust. In summary, the following points can be made: 1. Most fathers did not initiate the breakup, nor did they wish to be single. 2. Fathers do tend to lead active social lives that include sexual intercourse. 3. However, they are not particularly satisfied with their social lives. 4. Satisfaction with the father's social life is likely to improve with time until the three- to five-year mark and then may decline slightly.

From the fathers' descriptions, a portrait emerges of struggle when it comes to dating. For the father who has not remarried a few years after being single, no guarantee exists that life will improve. While the frequency of dating is likely to increase, the satisfaction the father feels may not improve. At the same time, there are upbeat stories. Some fathers do feel more at ease with their social life over time. Given a number of months or even a few years, they have begun to emerge from their self-imposed isolation and are enjoying life again. Having worked through some of their own doubts about reentering the dating world, they may also have worked through some of their children's hesitations. With their self-esteem repaired and with support from their children, they are able to approach intimate relations with fewer encumbrances than fathers who are still struggling with these issues.

Mark, a thirty-three-year-old technician from Washington, articulately describes the course he took and how things have worked out for him. He is raising two teenaged sons and has been single for about two years: "I held back. I kept away from the singles bars. I wanted to be careful in the beginning not to just jump right back into a situation just because of need, physical or otherwise. I'm glad I was able to hold back. I needed to wait until I was ready. I never thought that I'd ever feel independent or confident or not lonely again. But somehow or other I have reached that point and I'm not afraid to be alone anymore or to get married. You have to be able to get past the loneliness. Now I can be more confident in myself before getting involved and looking for those qualities in someone else. I'm not bitter. I'm okay."

Even though the focus here has been on dating, the fathers

socializing also included their children. Going out with the children is an important family event in many of these families and in some ways serves as a bridge to the father's eventually going out alone. Three out of four fathers enjoy some activity outside the home with their children at least once a month, with many families going out as often as once a week. Common activities include going to a restaurant, a sporting event, school function, or an activity sponsored by a singles' organization. If the family goes out with others, those people are most likely to be relatives and other one- and two-parent families. Activities with relatives are especially important in these families, as they provide familial connections and continuity, which are threatened by divorce.

Jim, from Alabama, said, "Every Sunday we have dinner at my parents. That's how we did it when I was married and that's how we still do it now." What Jim receives from those visits is a sense that certain things in life are maintained, even after a divorce. Al, a neighbor of Jim's, values his family outings a great deal and uses them to discuss family issues. "I found sitting around the house and talking about problems to be too heavy. But if we go bowling or drive someplace, it's easier to talk."

How are the fathers doing socially? Not great. The various demands of single parenting make dating a trouble spot. But going out can be satisfying, particularly when a father has worked to clarify his own expectations and has talked with his children in advance.

Suggestions for Dating

1. Be aware that the expectations for men and women in dating situations have changed greatly since you were last single. Talking to people to learn what to expect is helpful. Being honest with your date about your confusion is critical.

2. Join a self-help group in which you can meet other single parents in an environment that is comfortable for you.

3. Do not feel you have to rush into dating. Give your wounds time to heal. At the same time, staying out of the social scene for too long is not a good idea for you nor does it send a good message to your children about their own socializing.

4. Before you start dating, talk to your children about it. You

might say, "I have no plans to date in the immediate future but I know at some point I am going to start. Children usually have feelings about their parents' dating and I would love to hear yours." The children may ask at this point if you and their mother are going to get back together again. They may want to know who you are going to date and when they can meet them. Answer their questions as honestly as you can. Preparing your children in advance is much better than springing a new relationship on them.

5. Gently convey the message that your social life is your own because you are an adult. When they are adults and are socializing you will respect their privacy. This leaves open the option for you, when appropriate, to be able to supervise their socializing without their supervising yours.

6. If money is short, think of less expensive activities: walks in the park, museum-hopping, and sporting events all cost less than a play or expensive dinner. Take a date out for lunch or a brunch. These also cost less than dinner and are more informal. You also will not feel under as much sexual pressure if you are seeing someone during the day.

7. Let your children know where they can reach you when you are out on a date.

8. Find a balance between your needs to socialize and the needs you and your children have to be with each other. In some situations, you will need to spend a lot of time with your children reassuring them about your relationship with them. But you cannot be a martyr for your children. Their seeing you happy and being socially active can be an important part of their own happiness.

9. If you are feeling insecure socially, be careful about putting that insecurity on your children and restricting their social activities. One father who was not dating did not want his sixteen-year-old to date either.

10. If you are still angry at your ex-wife for the breakup of the marriage, be aware of it and try and work through it. Do not take that anger out on other women. At the same time, work to see what your own part has been in the marital breakup. Accept responsibility if that is appropriate and do not continue to blame others.

11. Be circumspect about romantic interludes in your house when the children are there. You should teach your children responsible interpersonal and sexual behavior. The father who brings a different date home for dinner every Friday night can anticipate his own children's playing the field.

12. Be clear what the rules are for teenagers who are dating. You do not have to stick to the exact same rules yourself but if your behavior is wildly different you can anticipate complaints.

13. Learn to live with loneliness and being alone. It is a natural part of life and cannot be wiped away through constant dating.

14. Do not be self-destructive in your dating behavior. Take good care of yourself.

15. If you are interested in remarriage (a lot of fathers are not), make sure you do not rush into it. Getting remarried just to help the children will often backfire. Accept that you may be single for a number of years and adjust your life accordingly.

16. Do not feel you have to have sexual intercourse to prove your masculinity. Do not feel concerned if you go through a lengthy time where you do not want to have sexual relations.

17. If you are having sexual relations, practice safe sex.

8

Getting Along with the Noncustodial Mother

O F all the demands of single parenting with which a father must contend when raising the children alone, the one that is potentially the most troubling is his own and his children's relationship with his ex-wife—the mother of his children. It is she who has played the most vital role in the father's gaining custody of his children. And it is she who has the potential for continuing to play a vital role in how the children and the father adapt. If the children have a smooth, ongoing relationship with their mother, their adaptation to the father-headed family can be simplified. If the father feels comfortable relating to her, his daily life can also be made immensely more easy. Their mutual support of each other's parenting efforts, as well as her own consistent involvement with the children, are cornerstones upon which a family foundation can be built for the benefit of everyone.

Yet in many cases the continuing relationships between the mother, the father, and the children have not been good ones. They have been marked by distrust, anger, and hurt. High levels of conflict are not unusual. Visitation is sometimes sporadic, occasionally nonexistent. Arguments over child support payments, alimony, custody, discipline, and the way each is influencing the child are common. In such an atmosphere it is more difficult for children to flourish. They are already buffeted by the breakup and emotionally "at risk," and ongoing acrimony between the couple can upset their attempts at establishing a semblance of order. Most single parents are attuned to their children's needs but may find it difficult to act rationally toward the other spouse when feelings left over from the marriage get in the way. Single fathers are no exception. Their ex-wives can "push their buttons" in a way that no one else can. Concerning their children, their buttons may be especially easy to push.

Part of dealing with the noncustodial mother involves understanding her. Parents, even after they divorce, remain locked in a system in which the behavior of one often has an influence on the other. Like being on a see-saw, the father and mother are affected by each other's ups and downs. For example, a custodial father who perceives that his ex-wife is adapting well to her noncustodial status may have no concerns about visitation, whether she will parent well when with them, or whether he will receive child support on time. To at least some extent, her well-being affects his and the children's well-being. Without a grasp of some of the issues facing noncustodial mothers in our society, the father may be at a loss for integrating her behavior into a framework that he and his children can live with.

Understanding the Noncustodial Mother

Easily one of the most misunderstood populations of single parents, the mother without custody is subject to a constant barrage of negative feedback. People often perceive mothers who do not have custody as immoral, mentally ill, uncaring, cold, sexually promiscuous, or drug and alcohol abusers. The belief is that these mothers are unable to take care of their children or are unwilling to. So strong is society's need to believe that children must be raised by their mother that when the father becomes the primary parent the assumption is something is wrong with her. Another side of that message is that children do not belong with their fathers.

It is not only outsiders who pressure the mother to raise the children following a breakup—the mother herself often holds that view, too. This is the result of the way most of us have been raised. The same voice that makes it difficult for fathers to become primary custodians because it interferes with their career or is not masculine (i.e., places them on a daddy track), tells mothers that their role is to be with the children. Thus mothers have a very hard time giving up custody. As a result, many keep custody when such an arrangement is not in the family's best interests. Or, if they become noncustodial, they have difficulty adjusting and feel guilty, uncomfortable, and long for more visitation with their children.[1]

These mothers feel misunderstood. Many, by their own admission, give up custody because they are unable to handle the children, at times because of their own emotional problems. But many become noncustodial for other reasons. Money plays a key role, as mentioned in chapter 3. A child may be given a choice and select the father. Sometimes it is the father who gains custody because he is staying in the family house or will be the most available to the children by virtue of greater job flexibility. A mother also may not pursue custody because she believes it would not be in the best interests of the children. Putting her children's needs ahead of her own desire to be with them, she nonetheless is criticized for being a bad mother.

Given the criticism that awaits the mother, some hide their status. Others are unsure when to tell a new acquaintance that their children are with the father. Still others avoid situations that could bring up the topic. School conferences, children's sporting events, and school plays have become painful reminders that the children are living away from them.

Visitation holds the potential for being both the high point of the mother's calendar or the emotional lightning rod. Picture the common situation, where the children choose to live with the father. The mother calls the house to arrange visitation and notes a hesitation in the child's voice. A mother may see that as a lack of desire to see her; in other words, a replay of the custody decision, where she was rejected. For the child, it may very well be an attempt to avoid the mother or it could be a hesitancy because of having to make a choice between spending time with her or with friends. In a world that already sees these mothers negatively, it is easy for the mother to read into the situation the worst possible scenario.

If the mother does not have custody because of her own emotional problems, she may be especially prone to misinterpreting a reaction from a child. Because of low self-esteem she may skip a planned visitation or avoid contact altogether in the belief that the child is better off without her. If she deserted the family it may be hard for her to face the children's anger or their feelings of rejection and hurt. If the children are not progressing well, she may blame herself and be unsure whether she should visit the children or stay away from them. Conversely, if the children are doing well, she may not want to rock the boat and may maintain an infrequent level of involvement with them, again believing they may be better off without her. Her staying away may be seen by her as good mothering. To some extent she sees herself making a sacrifice for those she loves.

On a more positive note, other mothers may insist on a high level of involvement with the children because of their love for them and because they correctly assess that the children need their involvement. The thought of losing ongoing contact with their children may never have been their interpretation of giving custody to the father. They still see the children as belonging as much to them as to the father. They take every opportunity to call them, visit them, and learn about their lives. They want a say in the children's religious instruction, schooling, vacations, and upbringing.

At some point, these behaviors in the mother may bump up against the lives of the father and the children. Their impressions of what is needed from the mother may or may not jibe with the mother's impressions. If the mother initially withdrew from the family, they may have circled their wagons and begun building a life without her. When she returned to the neighborhood wanting more contact with the children, she was naturally treated with distrust. If the mother has remained highly involved and a custody battle has determined the living arrangements, animosity is likely to be high. Every move by the mother is likely to be interpreted by the father as a maneuver to regain custody. The result of these familial developments is that there can be much misunderstanding. Add to this the history of the marital breakup and its residual pain and it is clear to see how ongoing relationships between these family members can be fraught with tension. In fact, it can be seen as remarkable that so many of these relationships do work out, that parents do see each other in a favorable light, and that each is able to adapt to this nontraditional family arrangement.

To further understand the relationship between the noncustodial mother, the father, and the children, let us first look at her level of involvement in their lives.

How Involved Are Mothers?

Mothers tend to stay somewhat involved with the children after the father gains custody. One fifth of the fathers in our survey describe visitation by the mothers as taking place on at least a once-a-week basis and one fifth say it occurs on an every-other-week basis. One in seven of the fathers report the mother and child having face-to-face contact once a month, with it occurring in the other families either during holidays, summer vacations, or on a sporadic basis. Mothers never visited in one out of eight families. Overall, slightly less than half the fathers said the mother visited at least every other week, while only a small minority had dropped completely out of the picture.

Involvement also takes the form of spending overnights with the mother and having telephone contact. (If the father's children spent more than eight nights a month with the mother, an average of two nights a week, the father was considered to be involved in a joint rather than a sole custody arrangement.) Half the fathers said the children spent no overnights with the mother. Another 42 percent said their children spent four nights or less a month with the mother. For those children spending the night with their mother, a fairly typical arrangement is to schedule such visitation for every other weekend. When thinking about these visitation patterns, it is important to note that one-third of the mothers live more than one hundred miles away from the father and the children.

Telephone contact, particularly for the mother who lives a good distance away, can be most beneficial to both the child and the mother. Half the mothers called their children at least once every other week. Small percentages said there was telephone contact once a month, a few times a year, or once a year. Fifteen percent said the mother never telephoned, about the same number that never visited.

How reliable an estimate have fathers given about the visitation of the noncustodial mother? Are they underreporting contact? When mothers without custody were asked how often they visited their children, they reported only slightly more contact. About half said they visited at least every other week (versus the fathers' reporting 45 percent) and almost 10 percent said they never visited (versus the fathers' 12 percent). The average number of overnights spent with the mother as reported by her was slightly higher.[2] Given normal differences in recall, the figures for both groups are remarkably similar.

Visitation is usually handled amicably, according to the fathers. Only one in six fathers said there were recurring problems with arranging it to everyone's satisfaction. Despite a somewhat low level of problems around visitation, conflict does flare up between the mother and father. One out of four fathers said conflict was at a high level and another one out of four said there was "some" conflict. Conflict can, of course, come from issues that have little to do directly with visitation. Parents may not like each other's behavior. One father said the conflict was caused by his "ex's emotional problems because our daughter chose to live with me rather than her." Another blamed "her drinking and her boyfriends."

A few fathers see the root of their ongoing conflict as being difficulties that both parties share. One dad said, "We have problems agreeing on how our daughter should be raised." Another father, a serviceman earning very little disposable income, said their problems continued because of money.

Not all parents have a conflictual relationship. Half the fathers felt their experiences had been congenial. To a large extent, if there is little conflict in the relationship, visitation is going to be arranged more amicably.

The father's perception of the mother's parenting abilities also plays a part in the ease with which visitation can be arranged and in the level of conflict between the parents. Generally, the view is not a positive one. When asked how they rate their ex-wife as a mother, almost 70 percent give a rating of poor or fair, with the remainder falling into the adequate to excellent range. Trying to arrange visitation with mothers who fathers believe to be of fair or poor quality as a parent is, by its very definition, fraught with emotional land mines. Many fathers clearly are ambivalent about the mothers' involvement with the children. On the one hand, they may recognize that she is a valuable person in the child's life because she is the parent. On the other, the father may be harboring a great deal of unresolved anger from the marital breakup that affects the ongoing relationship with her. He may also have very real concerns about her parenting abilities. If between a third (by the mothers' own descriptions) and almost half the mothers (by the fathers' descriptions) have had emotional problems that have interfered with their ability to have custody, good reasons must exist for the fathers to doubt the mothers.

Naturally there are noncustodial mothers who behave inexplicably, just as there are noncustodial fathers whose behaviors also defy rational explanation. Working to build a relationship under such conditions is a teeth-gnashing, hair-pulling experience. It would be difficult for a father, potentially caught up in his own unresolved feelings about the mother, to clearly separate her weaknesses from her strengths. Yet that is what he must do if he is to open up the possibility of less conflictual contact between himself and the mother. He also must make that same leap when it comes to visitation. When societal views of mothers without custody are negative and reinforce the father's belief that the mother is incompetent, making that leap must seem like jumping across the Grand Canyon. Yet these parents are able to manage visitation relatively smoothly as witnessed by the small percentage of visitation-related problems that exist. In many cases they are able to overcome the ghosts of their relationship and work together.

Jerry is one example of a father who has made that leap. Even though he left his wife because she was unfaithful to him, he recognizes the positive influence she has on his daughter. He understands the differences between his feelings for her as his ex-wife from his feelings about her as a mother.

Making that separation is more difficult for fathers who do not believe the mother is making much effort to help them out. Only one father in eight felt their ex-wives were very supportive of their having custody, with half the fathers replying the mother was not at all supportive. In-laws were seen as being more helpful. Three out of every five were described as being supportive. It is not uncommon to hear stories from the fathers of grandparents who remain interested in the well-being of their grandchildren and their ex-son-in-law. Some in-laws help out with child care on a regular basis. Others take sides with the father in condemning the actions of the mother if her behavior resulted in the father's getting custody. In extreme cases, the noncustodial mother becomes the black sheep of the extended family, having little contact with her parents or her children.

In sum, we see a wide range of ambivalent feelings on the part of these fathers. Conflictual relationships and a negative rating of the mother are common characteristics, but visitation, when it occurs, is handled fairly amicably. A good number of these couples are able to put aside their unresolved feelings for each other so that the children can maintain contact with both of them.

When the Mother Visits

Two patterns of visitation were found that warrant mentioning. First, mothers were slightly more likely to visit when the father was raising only daughters than when he was raising only sons. From interviews with mothers and fathers, a number of reasons have emerged that explain this. Daughters may reach out to mothers more than sons do. Interviews conducted with adult children who lived away from their mother (see chapter 13) reveal a longing on the part of the daughters to have a woman to talk to. Many of these daughters felt their fathers did not understand them in the same way a woman does. As the daughter needs her mother, the mother in turn feels more needed and makes a greater effort to stay involved. Because of the division of the sexes that occurs as children grow older, with boys spending more time with fathers and girls with mothers, the mother is likely to feel a greater pull toward a daughter than toward a son and feel that her involvement is more critical to the daughter's development. In addition, the father may reach out to the mother more often for assistance with a daughter than with sons. This reaching out would further encourage the mother's visitation. The greater involvement by the mother with daughters makes sense from a number of different perspectives.

As the children get older, visitation patterns of the mothers change. The older the children, the less the mother visits. The children become increasingly involved in activities with friends and have less time for either of their parents. Teenagers do not like to miss a school dance or the chance to see a James Bond movie for the fourteenth time just because they are scheduled to have dinner with their mother. This is a normal stage of adolescent development, the stage in which children begin asserting themselves and experimenting with independence. In addition, there is the likelihood that part of the family will have relocated, putting greater physical distance between them.

Particularly interesting is that visitation between the mother increases again when the children reach young adulthood. At that stage, they are no longer minors under the influence of the father. They have also achieved a more adult perspective, which often includes a need to reconnect with the mother.[3]

Does visitation help the father? It depends on the situation. Some fathers long for more contact from the mother, while others do not like the high level of contact they have. This results in two patterns:

The Mother as Occasional Visitor. If the father has a negative impression of the mother, he rarely wishes she would visit more. If he thinks the children need her, and he is not threatened by her visitation, he is likely to want her to increase the time they spend with her. A sporadic visitation pattern is usually the most troublesome to the father. Here, the mother may come and go unpredictably. She may visit only a few times a year. She may come every week, establish a pattern, and then not show up for a few months. This unpredictability wreaks havoc with the children and the father. Neither can rely on her. If the children adjust to not having her play a major role in their lives and then find her forced on them, they are unsure how to react. If the children begin to form a bond with her that is then broken, it is also problematic. The father in these cases is left to pick up the emotional pieces and help the children understand what has happened. The father's perception of how involved she should be may also be at issue. He may believe that mothers in general should be very involved with the children, a common societal view. When her level of involvement approximates that of other noncustodial parents (usually males), the father may perceive that as inadequate. This may taint future contact between the father and the mother, and thus discourage visitation. The more regular the contact the easier it is for all concerned.

The Mother as Frequent Visitor. When a high level of visitation has been mandated by the courts or by some other mutual agreement, the father may perceive the mother as being an integral part of the children's lives or as interfering. Fathers do rely on mothers in some cases, consulting them about the children and involving them in every major decision. In these situations, the visitation arrangement has worked to everyone's best advantage. But when the father sees the mother as interfering, other issues come into play. Of course, his impression of her as interfering or being a negative influence can be an incorrect one, engendered more by his own discomfort than by an objective appraisal of her value to the children. But in other cases, it may be that the mother is interfering by stirring up the children emotionally. She may be promising them things she cannot deliver, upsetting the children by badmouthing the father, or countermanding previous discipline established by the father.

Overall, fathers and children usually benefit from a high level of contact between the mother and the children. Such a level of involvement is often born of a great deal of work and some initial favorable circumstances. When the mothers are very involved there often has been a relatively friendly divorce. Both parents feel they had a share in the demise of the marriage, rather than one partner blaming the other. The reasons custody went to the father were mutually agreed upon by both parties and indicated that the father's home was seen as the best place for the children to be raised. For example, a mother who believes the children are better off with the father, for either financial or emotional reasons, is more likely to stay involved with the children than mothers whose children chose the father over them. In cases where there has been a court decision, some mothers remain involved as mandated by the courts, while others drop off the face of the earth, upset by the public defeat. The relatively good feelings emanating from a less conflictual divorce and custody decision can help divorced parents remain involved throughout their years together as single parents.

Three Families

The experiences of three families help illustrate what evolves when the father has custody and the ex-wife is very involved with the children. Within these high-contact relationships, feelings between the parents range from the warm and supportive to the angry and distrustful. But in all three cases described here the fathers acknowledge (to varying degrees) the importance of the mother.

Joe, a Marylander, gained custody of fifteen-year-old Mark after Susan had been raising him for three years. Their marriage, which had been surviving tenuously for years, fell apart completely following the accidental death of one of their children. Susan first had custody because that was the norm in situations of divorce. She also had been the more involved parent and was staying in the family home. Over time, as Mark entered adolescence, difficulties grew. Susan found disciplining to be a problem. This period for her was especially frustrating because as a schoolteacher she believed she should know how to handle this developmental stage. Shortages of money also became a problem, with the house occasionally going unheated.

During the years Susan had custody, Joe had remained very involved as the visiting parent. He saw Mark frequently and maintained an excellent relationship with Susan. They even were able to discuss their social lives with each other. When Mark announced to Susan one day that he wanted a "divorce" from her because of the mother-son problems they were having, Susan agreed to move out of the home and have Joe move back in. Previously Joe had not been prepared to assume that full-time responsibility, but now he was. His career was going well and he was in a better position financially and emotionally to give his son what he needed. Father and son adjusted quite well.

Susan maintains a very active role in Mark's life. Even after she remarried they continued to spend a good deal of time together, with Susan making every effort to integrate Mark into her new family. Major decisions like college choices, tuition, and driving are discussed at great length between Susan and Joe. They remain close friends, interested in each other's lives and aware that whatever problems they have between them need not affect their parenting of Mark. As Joe said, "When our other child died, we learned that fighting over household possessions and other issues were trivial. Dealing with the death has given me the faith to deal with things."[4]

Bill lives in Illinois with his four-year-old daughter, Peggy. Bill describes a stormy marital relationship that grew worse after Peggy was born. When Peggy was two, Bill believed things had reached an unbearable level between his wife and himself. His wife had physically attacked him on a number of occasions; although she had never harmed their daughter, he feared she would. He took Peggy and moved out. After many months of costly and lengthy legal battles, the custody situation was legalized.

Currently, and with court approval, Bill's ex-wife sees Peggy every day. She is very involved with the child, and Bill no longer worries that Peggy will be harmed when she is with her. Bill pays his wife alimony and child support for the period of time each day that she is with Peggy. His ex-wife constantly threatens to take Bill to court to reverse the custody situation. Bill sees this as a ploy to get more money from him. Bill finds his ex-wife to be a great source of stress to him; yet he knows the value of her spending time with Peggy.

Jim, a father living with two children in Virginia, has had a totally different relationship with his ex-wife, Alice. He and Alice started growing apart after seven years of marriage and thought they could no longer communicate with each other. The problems were probably made worse by Alice's job, which required her to work nights. This meant a shift in each of their roles. Alice had taken care of the children when they were babies; later that responsibility became Jim's. A trial separation, with Jim moving out and Alice balancing work and childrearing, ended in reconciliation. Jim resumed the responsibility for the childrearing. A few months later their marital problems began again, and this time Alice moved out of the house, leaving Jim with the children.

Alice moved out for a number of reasons. Primarily, she thought Jim had a better relationship with the children at this point than she did, and she believed his relationship with them would be damaged if he moved out. Secondarily, she was finding the forty-mile commute to her job in a large metropolitan area difficult. She and Jim also agreed that moving the children to the city with her would not be as beneficial to their development as letting them remain in a small community. Jim was happy to get the children.

Despite the forty miles separating them, Alice stays very involved with the children. She takes them to her home every other weekend. She attends school conferences, and Jim consults her about any major decisions that have to be made about the children. For Jim, Alice's continued participation in the children's lives makes parenting much easier.

Jim also feels sympathy toward her because he believes she was caught up in the changing role expectations: "I feel sorry for her. She grew up hearing one thing about how women are supposed to act, and now she hears something else." Jim thinks people give her a hard time because she is not raising the children and, because he still cares about her, that hurts. Bonds of caring and trust still exist between them even though the loving relationship they once had has changed.

The feelings expressed by Joe, Bill, and Jim are held by a minority of the fathers. Yet they can serve as a guide for how other fathers can begin to move past a cycle of behavior and feelings that may be preventing appropriate interactions between the mother, the father, and the children. Working out such arrangements is not easy, and in some cases, may be impossible. If the mother's behavior is so inappropriate, attempting to reconstruct a relationship with her visiting may be ill-advised. Even in that situation, though, there may be room for the children and the father to work to understand her situation better. In that way, the possibility is left open for a future relationship.

Suggestions

1. Do not allow your unresolved feelings toward your ex-wife from the divorce interfere with your ability to work together as parents.

2. Find ways to resolve any negative feelings that you have toward her. Harboring them will not help you as an individual or as a parent.

3. If you feel yourself getting emotionally upset or angry when talking with her, take a time out. Learn how to let off steam.

4. Do not let the children get caught in the middle of your battles with your ex-wife. This is the most important thing to remember as a single parent.[5]

5. Respect your ex-wife's privacy and help her to respect yours.

6. Treat her with respect. This does not mean that you have to like her or agree with what she is doing. Treating her with respect, though, will help the children see her in a better light and thus they will be able to see themselves in a better light.

7. Work together to make rules the same in both homes. This will reduce disagreements with the children who may say, "Mommy lets us do it at her house—why can't we do it here?"

8. The noncustodial mother must respect what has been established in your home and not try to hurt your relationship with your children by badmouthing you. In turn, you should not badmouth her. You do need to be realistic with your children, though. If they have negative feelings about their mother, listen to them and support them for having feelings. Their feelings may need to be validated by you so they know that what they are feeling makes sense. When they say, for instance, "Mommy is bad because she did not keep her visitation today," you can answer by saying, "I can understand that your feelings are hurt. Here you were expecting her to come and she did not."

9. If the noncustodial mother lavishes gifts on the children, talk with her about it and try to get her to channel her energies and her finances in a way that you and she can agree on.

10. Support your children's sending Mother's Day cards and birthday cards, and calling her when they want to (as long as the telephone bills are not too great). Even if she does not respond to these cards, it may help the children feel that they are making some concrete attempts to establish a relationship with her.

11. Try and maintain contact with her parents. Your children can benefit from visitation with all their grandparents.

12. Move on with your life. Do not become fixated on your relationship with your ex-wife. As you move on with your life, it will help the children to place their relationship with their mother in a healthier perspective.

9

Dealing with the Courts and Child Support

A FACTORY worker with a six-year-old son said: "I don't get any child support. Is it 15 percent of whatever she makes? What is 15 percent of nothing? She's going along for a free ride. She lives with a guy who's twenty-five years older than her. I suspect she's married but she denies it. If she is married I could go after his money. I got full custody as part of the deal that said that as long as she wasn't working she wouldn't have to pay child support. So why should she ever work?"

A mechanic wrote: "I did not lose anything by going to court, because my ex-wife did not fight very hard. I am convinced if she had fought for the children [two boys, who were six and eight at the time of the breakup] I would not have been successful."

A management consultant, who was interviewed, told this story: "She left without the children. We decided I would have custody and she would visit. Then she decided she wanted to go to California, and she wanted the kids. She threatened, but never went for it. Then she attempted to snatch the youngest. I had had the foresight to get custody so I was able to prevent her from getting the kids, and the school was helping. She decided it wasn't worth it.

"We had some situations afterward, which meant going back to court, but by that time I had established I could do a good job. But it required spending a lot of money, hiring a court psychiatrist. I had enough money, so I was fortunate. If you have enough, it can be easier. A lot of men I have spoken to have had problems. Basically, if you get your children at the beginning, you stand a good chance of getting them. Otherwise, all things being equal around here [suburban county of major eastern city], it goes to the woman. In situations where one person has a measurable problem, that makes it simpler. My ex had mental problems, which made it easier for her to not seek custody, and when she later sought it, it was too late. I had everyone behind me—the schools, family, even some of her relatives. I wanted the kids and was providing a healthy environment, so I got them.

"A lot of guys I have met seem to want their kids to get back at their ex-wives. That disturbs me. It isn't good for anyone. They want revenge. They are going for the vendetta. Some men sincerely do want to have their children and suffer because their children are not with them. . . . The men who want their kids to get back at their wife eventually probably do not end up with the kids. They decide it isn't worth it."

A fourth father said, "I feel that based on what I hear from other men, a man has to do more to prove himself than a woman does."

The custodial fathers' complaints are the most vehement, their tales of financial woe the worst, and their fears the greatest when they discuss their experiences with the legal system. They complain that they have to spend thousands to protect what is theirs; that mothers are given the upper hand; and that there is no guarantee that, once they have custody, a new judge will not reverse it. Their worries about losing custody are ongoing. Nothing seems to upset their lives and frustrate them more than their court appearances. It is in this area that they believe they have the least control over their own destiny and are at the whim of an archaic set of values that, though no longer legally existing in most states, is still exercised by judges. As negative as are these fathers' feelings about their experiences, it must be remembered that these are fathers who won in court. Fathers who fight for and lose custody have even more complaints.

Fathers are seeking custody in greater numbers now than ever before. More equitable criteria are being used to determine if they are capable of single fatherhood. In the past, a father could get custody only if he proved his ex-wife unfit. Even then he might have to do battle with grandparents or foster-care agencies that might step in to insure the best interests of the child. No longer is the mother given preference in most cases solely because she is the mother. Other criteria are used. The parenting abilities and financial strengths of both parents are weighed, as are who the children feel closer to, who will allow the most visitation, who will provide the most consistent home environment, and who is in a stable relationship. Some women's rights activists believe money is too often the deciding criteria.[1] In such a contest, the father usually wins. Others claim that legislation that is supposed to be sex-neutral is not being followed and that fathers are still at a disadvantage.

In fact, there is enormous variation from state to state, county to county, and judge to judge. A case that may be decided in favor of the father in one jurisdiction may be decided against him in another. Even when fathers do win custody, they may feel the system has been unfair, yet another sign of daddy tracking. One father said, "The courts are heavily biased. They made me feel ashamed to ask for custody. Laws seem equitable but are not practiced by older judges as they should be. They stereotype a lot. To get custody you have to be head and shoulders above your wife. Fathers don't seem to get custody when the wife is seen as competent."

Fathers and Courts

Most fathers (80 percent) gained custody with the court playing a minor role—that is, rubber-stamping a prearranged agreement—or no role at all. The fathers whose custody was decided by court intervention were equally divided between those who characterized their battle as a brief one and those who said it was long.

In most cases the fathers had legal representation when they went to court. Most of those who sought the advice of lawyers found it helpful, but a significant minority, 40 percent, said that seeing a lawyer at some point during the custody process was not helpful to them.

The lawyer is obviously a key player in the father's experiences when there is a court battle. He or she not only provides the father with legal and emotional support but helps set the tone for the case. With the input of the father, the lawyer has to decide which issues to raise in court and how to include the children, being aware that the children's inclusion may be stressful to them. The lawyer also provides some impressions about the judge, if that information is available, and how other cases have been decided. Child support, visitation, custody agreements, and property settlements have to be negotiated. Finally, the lawyer has to pay special attention to the impact of any bias that may be held against the father or against the mother. Such bias can easily influence the case for or against the father. Two fathers' stories illustrate the kinds of experiences one can have working with a lawyer on a custody case.

John works in a refinery and is raising two children. His wife walked out on him and wanted to get custody. He earned about twenty-seven thousand dollars at the time and felt financially strapped by his legal fees. When asked about his court experiences, he answered: "Lousy! The lawyers, too. I finally did find a lawyer after the first one did nothing. He was not for anyone but he knew I was getting the shaft. My wife, believe it or not, was getting thirty dollars a week and I had the kids. My first lawyer had said to me there was no way I would have to pay alimony. But he was wrong. I did, and then I lucked out. My ex was living with her boyfriend and she let the children know about it. What she was doing with the alimony was going partners with him. She was working and they were splitting all the bills. I notified my new lawyer. 'Don't send more alimony,' he said. Her lawyer found out about it and we went to court. In fact, I went to court four times. I saw the judge, though, only once. Everything was always settled outside the courtroom.

"One time we got there and when my lawyer saw who the judge was, he told me I was going to get screwed. He said we were going to have to work out a deal before we got in there. We talked her lawyer into something real fast."

Jack, a chef, had a more positive experience. "My lawyer was good. He was friends with the judge. The judge seemed to lean over backward to me when I came before him. He chewed out my ex and gave her visitation but me custody. She did not have to pay anything. For me, the system worked fine."

What leads a father to a court battle? The profile of those

fathers who went to court is different from those who gained custody without a battle. Some of the differences are to be expected. First, the fathers who went to court tended to come from marriages in which there was more conflict. If the marriage ends on an acrimonious note the parents are more likely to carry their angry feelings into the custody realm than they are when a marriage ends more smoothly. Second, the fathers who battled for custody were more likely to be raising daughters than sons. One reason is that a mother may be less willing to give up daughters than sons without a fight. Third, fathers who fought for custody reported better relationships with their children once they had custody than those who did not fight. This can be explained by a number of factors: fathers are more likely to seek custody of those children with whom they get along well; once a father has battled for custody he is more likely to see the prize (the child) in a positive light; and the battle may have drawn the father and child closer.[2]

One approach to having spouses resolve their own divorce-related problems is mediation. Now found in most states and usually court-sponsored, divorce mediation is geared toward helping the often bewildered and angry parents work out their custody, visitation, and child support issues before or without seeing the judge. While approaches vary, the usual course is to have the mediator meet with the couple (often without their lawyers) to help them work out as amicable an arrangement as possible. The parents might first be seen individually. At that stage work may center on trying to define what each parent wants and what the mediator may see as issues confronting them. The mediator may attempt to heighten the parent's awareness of the children's needs by asking each one what he or she thinks the children are experiencing because of the divorce. Slowly, specific agreements are negotiated that realistically meet the needs of the parents and children. Sometimes, psychological testing of the children and therapy are recommended to help in the evaluation process. As the final issues are worked out and written down, each party reviews them with a lawyer.[3] The agreement may then be filed by the lawyers, or a judge may intervene as a final step.

Mediation programs have been successful in reducing parental conflict, as well as lawyer fees and court costs. But, like every other part of a potentially adversarial system, they are not always seen as fair. Michael experienced clear bias. "There was initial arbitration for custody. My wife had deserted us and was not really sure if she wanted the children. I took advantage of her psychological disorders and won custody. But the arbitrator kept asking my wife to reconsider giving up custody."

A mediator may also be hired privately by the parents. This is usually someone who is not connected to the courts but has experience with both counseling and legal matters. Couples often find it is less acrimonious and less expensive to hire a mediator to help them work out their issues than for each to employ a lawyer. A lawyer, though, may be needed by each party to review the final agreement arrived at through mediation.

The agreements vary greatly by couple. Sometimes the mediation agreement will spell out the exact pickup and dropoff time for visitation, who will give the children breakfast in the morning, and who will supervise their homework. Other times the agreement is left more open. A joint custody agreement will involve more details than a sole custody agreement. Regardless of the form the agreement takes it must be one with which both parents can live. For an agreement to be fair usually means that each parent had to compromise on an important point. For example, the father who goes into mediation with a certain conception of what the agreement should look like may have to leave mediation with half of what he wanted. But in the process he may have learned a great deal more about the feelings of his children and the needs of his ex-wife.

Returning to Court

In most cases, after the custody decision has been made the partners do not return to court. The original decision, then, either has been found satisfactory *or* the court experience was so unsatisfactory that neither party wants to go through it again. Disputes are then left unsettled or are worked out in some other fashion. Only one in four fathers had gone back to court.

Dick, a father raising two children, is one of those who did return to court. One year after gaining custody, and while he was planning a second marriage, his ex-wife sued for custody. "She was driven by the idea of another woman raising our kids.

We went through a five-month ordeal and evaluations by the court psychiatrists. As I was making wedding plans I was going to court. During the hearing, she withdrew because the children said loud and clear they wanted to stay with me."

Returning to court because of a custody dispute is not uncommon among those who do re-litigate. Other reasons for re-litigation are disputes over visitation and the father's seeking more child support.

Occasionally, charges of physical or sexual abuse bring both parents back to court. This can be a ploy to change a custody arrangement or to prevent the noncustodial parent from visiting. It can also be a serious charge brought for the protection of the children. In 5 percent of the cases, fathers reported that child abuse charges had been brought against them in court. One father of three daughters described being investigated for sexual abuse of the oldest child. This occurred after he had had custody for two years. The charges were unfounded. The experience, though, had a great impact on him and made him feel vulnerable toward future charges. As a result, he stopped showing affection to any of his daughters in public.

In about 10 percent of the situations fathers brought charges against the mother and, very occasionally, brought charges against the stepfather or boyfriend of the mother.

Fathers may also return to court to have a split custody agreement formalized. Split custody refers to having one child live with the father and the other with the mother. In these situations the father originally may have had custody of all children. Over time, though, as the needs of the children and the parents change, it might be decided to have a child live with the mother. If both parents and the children agree, this shift in custody can be made with relative ease. This occurs most often when the child initiates a move to live with the mother rather than at the provocation of either parent.

Issues around Child Support

Historically, any discussion of child support has focused on the ability of the noncustodial father to pay. The popular image of this father is that he rarely makes his payments and is late when he does pay. This image is not an unfair one. About half the fathers required to pay the full amount do so, with the other half either paying less than they are supposed to or nothing.[4] No popular image exists of the noncustodial mother paying support. Yet with recent federal legislation, the Child Support Enforcement Amendments of 1984 (P.L. 98-378), women are being held increasingly to the same standard as men. Legislation, written in gender-free language, is supposed to be in effect in each state for the collection of child support.

If so, it would be a marked change. Traditionally what has happened is that the noncustodial mother often has not been asked to pay support when the custody decision is made. In a 1983 sample of noncustodial mothers, only one in seven paid some child support.[5] The custodial fathers provide similar information. Slightly less than one in four (23 percent) said the mother was ordered to pay child support. The amounts they were ordered to pay range from one dollar to four hundred dollars a week. Less than half (43 percent) who were supposed to pay always paid child support. The rest contributed occasionally (22 percent) or never (35 percent). Two-thirds of the fathers think the amount their ex-wife was ordered to pay is too low. The other third believes it is a fair amount. Besides specific child support payments, many noncustodial parents contribute in other ways. About one-third of the fathers said the mothers helped out sometimes with doctors, clothing, and gifts for the children.

The picture that emerges, then, is that most fathers are unlikely to get any child support payments. In some cases, child support is not wanted by the fathers; in others it is needed and sought. At the same time, some mothers refuse to pay, while others want to financially support their children. While these situations may change as women's income increases and new legislation goes into effect, it is important to consider the reasons for the present situation.

Overshadowing all child support arrangements is the obvious inequity between the earnings of men and women. It is rare that wives earn more than their husbands. When divorced, the man would be expected to continue to out-earn his wife. Her potential ability to pay child support must be seen in this light. It is she who is likely to be strapped for money. At the same time, the father is acquiring new expenses. If he cannot provide the child care, for example, that she was once providing he will have to pay for it. More than half the mothers in the United States work outside the home at least part-time. A large number of women do provide a second income. Without her assistance the family could suffer financially. Thus it would be fair to expect her to make some payment toward the rearing of her children. Nearly half of the fathers reported a decline in the family's income when the mother left. Both sides of this issue must be considered when the payment of child support is calculated. To understand this further, let us examine fathers' and mothers' reasons for paying and not paying child support.

Fathers Who Do Not Want Support

Some men do not encourage the mother to pay support. Because of societal norms, they think it is an insult to their masculinity, or feel threatened, if the mother pays support. This is the case particularly if the father has been providing the sole support of the family. The circumstances around the breakup may affect this, though. The more anger the father feels at the ex-wife, the more he may want her to pay.

Some fathers do not want support because they worry about the access that may give the mother into the children's life. They are better able to control custody if they are the children's sole support. If the mother pays child support, she may have an influence over the children that may affect the father-child relationship. The father may also believe that her paying child support may improve her position in the eyes of the court in the event that she petitions for a change of custody. In addition, a father may not ask for support at the time of the original custody decree for fear of losing his bid for the children.

Some fathers do not want child support because they fear they will come to rely upon it. Being self-sufficient is easier than having to rely on the mother's largess. Others are ambivalent about it because they are sympathetic to the mother. One father said, "I feel discriminated against because of not getting child support. But a man is reluctant to force his wife to pay when he feels she is just getting by."

FATHERS WHO WANT SUPPORT

Many fathers want support. They believe the mother should have to pay because she is not carrying the financial burden of single parenting. For them, it is an issue of fairness. If the mother has remarried and is working, the father is especially likely to feel the mother should contribute. In other cases, it is more than just an issue of fairness—the father needs the money.

Some fathers are motivated by the notion that it is important to the children to have their mother paying at least a token amount. Payment keeps the mother involved with the children and gives the children the feeling that their mother still cares about them. Even if it is a minimal amount, the children learn that they remain in the mother's thoughts through the support. Money becomes one more symbol of her continuing concern for their well-being.

MOTHERS WHO DO NOT PAY SUPPORT

It is not merely the desires of the father that affect whether support gets paid. He is not in total control. The mother has to be a willing participant. If she is ordered to pay and does not, she runs the risk of being held in contempt of court. Most mothers do not pay because they have not been ordered to. Seeing her unhappiness at not having custody, the judge may be loathe to pour salt in her wounds by having her give up a portion of her income. The judge may also have assessed her financial situation relative to the father's and absolved her of responsibility. The father, as mentioned before, may not seek payment for a variety of reasons. If she has been ordered to, she may not pay because she simply cannot afford it or because she sees no logical reason to pay. If she refuses to pay, the father has to weigh the relative costs of taking her back to court. If the sum is small, often he will forget it.

Mothers also may not pay because they did not receive support when they had custody. This is likely to be true when the mother had initial custody after the marriage ended. If the father did not make payments on time to her, she might refuse to pay him when the tables are turned. Anger is another reason why a mother does not pay. If she was abused or treated harshly during the marriage, she might feel no obligation to pay someone who treated her so poorly.[6]

MOTHERS WHO DO PAY SUPPORT

Some mothers pay because they are required by the courts to do so. They fear legal retribution. They may resent it deeply and believe it to be unfair, but they pay it. Mothers also pay because they consider it the fair thing to do. They believe it is their responsibility to the children and to the ex-husband. They may have received payments if they had custody initially. Finally, some mothers pay as a way of staying involved with their children. They believe it entitles them to that involvement. They also may see it as a way of protecting themselves in a future court decision.

The Fathers' Experiences

The fathers have a range of experiences concerning child support that have been worked out informally or through the court system. These can best be reported in their own words.

"Their mother is on welfare and cannot handle her own life too well so I never filed for support."

"At the time of our breakup, I filed for bankruptcy. I was out of work for five or six months and needed support from her. I asked my lawyer about it but he never went after her because she was a woman. When I applied for welfare I also expected they would go after her, since they do this if it's a man who has abandoned the family. But I was told that in this state (in the South) they don't do that."

"The courts say I am supposed to receive seventy dollars a month (for two girls) but I never have."

"I receive support. We reached a mutual agreement before the attorney got involved. It was all very friendly and she pays me forty-four dollars a week for the two children. I think it is fair and she always pays on time."

"I did not originally ask for support because I was afraid it would hurt my getting custody. The judge, however, insisted I get something. It was arranged that she should pay contingent on her getting support from her first husband. She never gets paid so I never got paid until last month when I got a hundred dollars for the first time. It has all happened out of court. It's too expensive to take her back."

"The court originally ordered her to pay one hundred and twenty-five dollars a week (for two children) which she paid regularly, though sometimes she was late. Then a year ago, I got engaged to a woman with three kids and bought a big van to accommodate all seven of us. That made my ex real angry and she asked the court to have her payments cut in half. I didn't think that was fair because she was not reporting all her income. She could have paid me more. I did some research and took her back to court to get a better settlement. She now pays in-between what I want and what she wants—eighty-two dollars a week. At least she is never late with it, which I appreciate."

The Father's Status

The status of the father in court has improved dramatically over the last two decades. Despite this great improvement, many fathers still feel discriminated against because they are male. This perception has been shown to discourage some men from even seeking custody, and makes those fathers who do seek it more wary. Some shy away from seeking child support for fear it will hurt their chances of getting custody. As men increasingly enter the legal system seeking custody, the system is bound to become more sensitive to them. As long as this does not set off an unfair backlash against mothers, this increased sensitivity is a step in the right direction.

Suggestions for Dealing with the Court and Child Support

1. Get a lawyer with whom you feel comfortable. Discuss the expected fees in advance.

2. Study the custody and child support laws in your state so you know what your rights are.

3. Join a self-help group that is knowledgeable of legal is-

sues. Get from them the names of lawyers who are sympathetic to fathers having custody.

4. Keep all records of child support payments, visitation, etc. This will be needed in case there are future court appearances.

5. Consider seeing a mediator for help in resolving custody and child support issues.

6. Keep to the visitation schedule you and your ex-wife agreed to. Have the children ready when it is time for visitation.

7. Do not confuse the payment of child support with visitation. Try and make it easy for the mother to visit even if she has not been paying support.

8. Be aware of your ex-wife's financial situation and work history to understand her if she is having difficulties paying.

9. If child support becomes an issue with your children, talk to them constructively about it. Do not put them in the middle. They may feel she does not love them if she has not been paying. Love and financial support must not be confused.

10. Remember that the position of fathers in the courts is improving. Be optimistic.

10

Fathers with Joint Custody

J OINT custody of the children is an option that parents are increasingly considering when they divorce. This custody arrangement usually refers to a physical sharing of the children, a legal sharing of the children, or both. In the first instance, children actually spend half, or close to half, their time with each parent. This usually involves the children's moving between the parents' residences. In the second instance, that of legal custody, the children may spend a clear majority of their time with one parent but important decisions about the children (which school to attend, what type of religious upbringing to foster, how to handle critical health-related matters, and so on) are shared. As a custody arrangement, it has gained great popularity since its inception in the 1970s. By the end of that decade, six states had legal statutes that permitted joint custody provisions.[1] By the 1990s, well over half the states have joint custody statutes.

Despite its prevalence, the definition of joint custody is not universally agreed upon and the statutes that dictate it vary by state. Because of the variations, its viability is hard to document. What a father with joint custody is experiencing in one state may be quite different from what a father in another state is going through. In addition, joint custody is hard to evaluate. We cannot, for instance, systematically study a family's experiences in joint custody and then have them switch to sole custody to see which worked out best for them.

The rise in joint custody's popularity has been remarkable. Now, in some states, couples have to indicate why they are not agreeing to joint custody. The reasons for this rise are: 1) joint custody is often easier to arrive at legally because both parents stay involved; 2) neither parent is giving up anything; 3) it reduces the need to assign child support; and 4) it is often thought to be less painful to the children who maintain more contact with both parents than in cases of sole custody. Fathers particularly seem to benefit from joint custody because their involvement becomes greater than with the more usual arrangement of maternal custody. Common patterns of joint physical custody include having the children spend half the week with each parent or having the child spend most of the week with one parent and the weekend and one mid-week night with the other. If parents live far from each other, spending large portions of the summer and holidays with the distant parent is likely. Legal custody arrangements may follow the same visitation pattern or involve much less visitation, with both parents still maintaining an equal say in child-related matters.

Research generally shows that most parents involved in joint custody arrangements are pleased, but it is not for everyone. Parents in a high-conflict marriage and divorce are going to have a harder time working out joint custody and being satisfied with it than those in low-conflict situations. Joint custody compels them to work together in a way they would not have to if one had sole custody. If parents are amicable at the time of the breakup, they are most likely to have a positive joint custody experience.

While joint custody would seem to have obvious advantages for the children, who can maintain regular contact with both parents, the outcome on the children is not clear. Moving back and forth from one home to the other has disadvantages that may not necessarily be mitigated by having a great deal of contact with both parents. The children may never feel at home in any one place if they are there only half time. Traveling to and from school and friends' houses can be a problem if the parents do not live close to each other. Books desperately required for homework may be left at the other parent's home on the night before an assignment is due. A favorite teddy bear that is needed for bedtime may suffer the same fate. Friends may not know where to call the child on any one night. Particularly in high-conflict situations, children may be continually drawn into unresolved issues between the parents. While this can also happen in sole custody arrangements, the likelihood of it occurring increases when there is greater parental contact.

When it works well, joint custody allows the child free and normal contact with both parents. It shows the child that parents can work things out and continue to cooperate in the child's best interests. It allows the child time alone with each parent, which may foster a deeper relationship between the two. In addition, the child, if he or she is old enough to make a decision, does not have to choose between parents. The opportunity for siblings to stay together may also be maximized. The key to joint custody's success is the parents' ability to constantly monitor the child's progress and to relate to each other in a consistent and sane manner.[2]

The Voices of Forty-four Joint Custody Fathers

To learn more about the experiences of joint custodial fathers, a sample of forty-four was gathered that will provide the basis for the discussion that follows.[3] Learning from them can help other joint custodians understand the demands and joys of this parenting arrangement.

The profile of the typical joint custodian was similar in a few ways to the sole fathers discussed in this book. He is in his late thirties, was married for about twelve years, and has had joint custody of between one and two children, usually male, for about four years. Major differences between the groups are that: 1) the joint custodian is better educated and earns at thirty-nine thousand dollars, a substantially higher income; and 2) the children involved in joint custody are, with an average age of nine, younger than the other children.

DURING THE MARRIAGE

Why does a father become a joint custodian? Is there some special bond he observed in his own parents? Was he more interested in parenting than his peers? While no early childhood experiences were found in these fathers' lives that would later predict joint custody, most of the men did enter marriage with a great deal of preparation for doing housekeeping. Yet once the children were born, almost every one said their wives took over the child care and housekeeping responsibilities. Rick, thirty, speaks for many when he says, "During the marriage, my wife generally did all the cooking, laundry, grocery shopping, clothes shopping, and cleaning. Once or twice a week I may have helped with cooking." In fact, many of these fathers did not see themselves as any more involved in home maintenance during the marriage than the typical father. This level of involvement extended to time spent with the children. Here again, the majority described their wives as more involved than they. Morris reported, "I was not very interested in the children but got interested during the last year when we were about to break up. Compared to other fathers I was weak and uninvolved, like Jell-O. I wish I could have gotten involved with my children sooner." Like many of the fathers who ended up with sole custody, they were taking a back seat in the upbringing of the children. This is not to say that they were not fulfilling the traditional role of breadwinner. Many joint custodians saw their role as being central to the family in that they were the financial force that permitted their wives to spend so much time with the children.

It was not until the final months of the marriage that many of the fathers began to shift to a more active role in the home. Slightly over one-third said that in the last year of the marriage they were more involved than the wife in child care. The same number said child care responsibilities were split evenly in that last year. Jason, a forty-year-old lawyer, took over completely. "She started going out with her girlfriends. Either I did it or it wouldn't get done." Morris, a thirty-eight-year-old engineer, had a similar story. "She did everything around the house until she started to go to L.A. to be with her lover." Some fathers blamed the mother's career for their assuming the household responsibilities. One dad said, "She began working crazy hours so a lot shifted to me. I was left to do it alone." This sense of abandonment not only led many fathers to take over but also set the stage for the impending marital breakup.

The mothers were not always to blame for turning their attention outside of the home. Eric, a forty-two-year-old sales representative, said, "I was inconsistent as a parent and probably as a husband, too. I was not very giving. I was very resistant to her needs. I missed birthdays, made other plans on anniversaries. I had no romance in our marriage, no candlelight dinners for her. I thought the only thing I needed to do was to be a good provider. I traveled for my job, which took me away a lot. It was not her fault, it was just suddenly too late. She had already withdrawn and stopped communicating. All I did for so long was bust my butt and it hurt my marriage."

Why They Divorced and Gained Joint Custody

More than half the fathers said their marriage broke up because of incompatibility. Another one-third charged their ex-wives with infidelity. Reasons commonly given by sole custodians, like desertion and the mother's mental incompetence, were rarely mentioned.

When the marriage began failing, many fathers decided they wanted custody. Each father insisted on remaining a part of his children's lives either because he wanted the closeness with them or because he believed it was best for the children. As will be seen from the stories that follow, many of these arrangements were not easily arrived at.

Dick, a forty-two-year-old systems analyst, worked very hard to get custody. "I pursued it. The kids and I wanted to salvage the marriage but it wasn't possible so I went for custody. I spent months trying to convince her to let me have them. I said it was not fair because she didn't really want them. The divorce is not final and she wants the children divided sixty-forty her way. But I want them and I'll fight for them."

Eric said, "I fought for them and believe me, it cost me a lot of money. She said she was willing to sign for joint custody but she wanted more money. I said unless I have them half the time I am not giving you seven hundred dollars a month. It was a real battle but we worked it through and had everything written in the divorce decree. We agreed that neither of us would move fifty miles away or we would lose joint custody."

As is typical from the stories of other fathers, a good deal of the fighting between Eric and his ex-wife went on outside the court. In fact, it was rare that joint custody was decided by a judge or through mediation. The courts were generally just used to rubber-stamp a decision. "We basically settled out of court because we both had lawyers who cost too much. Our emotions were so high at the time it caused more fights. I was really angry and wanted to kill her boyfriend. I went bananas. Our emotions caused the negotiations to be stalemated. Finally I invited her out to lunch and we went for a long drive. We could only agree that in the end the lawyers would win and it was costing us too much money. So we thrashed it out until we came up with joint custody."

Morris initially had sole custody before moving into joint custody. As sometimes happens, one spouse wants to end the marriage, almost at any cost, and is eager to leave regardless of the circumstances. With time, though, one or both parents may realize the importance of trying to maintain contact with the children and will seek a change. "At first she wanted to give up custody because she had a female lover. She told me she was a homosexual and we agreed on visitation. I thought it would have been unhealthy and detrimental. But we later decided to set it up as joint so we could both see the children. My ex is still dealing with her homosexual issue but the kids are pretty secure and don't find her sexuality a problem, though it is probably too soon to know and some problems in my son may be coming up."

For Rick, career conflicts were at the core of the eventual divorce and joint custody. "My wife and I had problems early on partly because of her career. We are both lawyers and when she joined a firm and started working full time, she said she wanted a divorce. Time was a real problem for her. We went through a long adversarial process and decided to go to divorce mediation. During mediation she said to me, 'Of course you'll have the kids half the time.' I actually wanted them all the time but I felt it was unlikely I would get that in our county."

Kurt, a forty-five-year-old teacher, also wanted sole custody. "I was not the one who wanted to dissolve the marriage and I wanted to stay in the family home with the children. She left so she was willing to give me joint custody and they are split fifty-fifty but I am tired of it. They get moved around too much and she doesn't want them some of the time and is inconsistent."

Some arrangements were worked out amicably despite significant problems. Arthur and his ex-wife continued living together for two years after they decided to break up so that they could pay off their debts. His infidelity and sexual incompatibility were the reasons for the divorce. "I knew after a while that she didn't trust me anymore to be faithful or even to make it as a businessman. But we didn't want the kids (four and six years old) to suffer. We wrote up our own agreement. I cut the pie and she got to pick her slice, so it was as fair as I could make it. We felt that if we were going to break something up, let's not have it be the children."

Child support payments in joint custody tend to fall into one of three patterns—neither parent pays; the mother pays the father, who has the children most of the time (a rare payment arrangement); or the father pays the mother, who has the children most of the time. When no payments are arranged, it is either because the incomes of the parents are similar or the father has custody slightly more often than the mother and is not in great need of the extra money. The most common arrangement, in slightly more than half of the cases, was for the father to pay the mother. In these situations the father was clearly earning more money. In only one in six cases was the mother court-ordered to pay.

Just as child support varies greatly based on the financial positions of the parents, it also varies because of the visitation schedule. For example, one father pays child support during the months his daughter is in her mother's care, but stops payments during the months he has custody.

Court Experiences

Court personnel were generally described as sympathetic to the fathers' attempts to gain joint custody, but Rick's experience was a notable exception. "I think they were apprehensive. I don't think in (midwest state) they take fathers seriously who say they want joint custody. They think we just say we want our kids as a ploy or as a bargaining chip to reduce the amount of child support or alimony we'll have to pay."

Only a handful of fathers had been back to court after custody was legally established. In fact, a fewer percentage of joint custodial fathers returned to courts than sole custodian fathers. Reasons for going back had to do with attempts to change custody, visitation, or child support payments. Abduction of the children occurred in one situation and was threatened but never carried out in another. The abduction occurred shortly after the marital breakup and was resolved a few weeks later.

Jason is one of the fathers who has been back to court. A report of alleged child abuse was the reason. "Four months after the separation my daughter, who was then six, said to me, 'Don't hurt me like Mommy does.' We had joint custody at the time. I asked her what she meant and when she began to talk about threats and occasional beatings I went right back to court. Her mother has been behaving better since then but it was scary for a while. The judge gave her a strict warning." Jason wants to file for sole custody but is waiting until his children are old enough to testify on their own behalf. Jason's case was the only one in which child abuse was mentioned.

Rick also went back to court, but by prearrangement. "We agreed to go back every two years to reevaluate our arrangement. The only thing that got changed was to increase the amount of child support she got."

Joint custody may benefit the parents' relationship after the divorce or it may be born of better relations to begin with. For example, the amount of conflict at the time of the breakup was as great for the joint custodians in our survey as it was for the sole custodians. Yet at the time of the study, the joint custodians were reporting much less conflict with their ex-wives. The rating of the ex-wife as a mother was also much higher for the joint custodians, with nearly half saying she was an excellent or a good mother. By comparison, less than one in six of the sole custodians gave their ex-wives that high a rating. Thus, despite the problems described within these relationships, in many ways they are more satisfactory than what sole custodians are experiencing.

How well can joint custodians get along? Arthur, the father who continued living with his wife for two years after the breakup, continues his tale. "There has been little or no bitterness on my part, since I believe bitterness only consumes the one harboring such feelings. Hurt there is, but that heals with time. This arrangement has enabled all four of us to talk together, learn of each other's plans, share our hopes and dreams. I personally feel our son has learned a valuable lesson in how mature, sensible adults should act under such a stressful situation. Now that the house has been sold it is time for us to move on."

Other Aspects of the Fathers' Lives
HOUSE CHORES

Keeping the house shipshape is usually not an enjoyable task for these dads. When the children are younger, the fathers usually take care of everything, leaving only minor tasks to the kids. As the children age, they naturally assume more responsibility. If younger children are involved in chores, they tend to be required to clean their own rooms, help with light housekeeping, and fold the laundry after the father has washed it.

Eric, who is living with his thirteen-year-old son, shares everything with him. "We do the cooking, cleaning, laundry, and shopping together. Sometimes we both get lazy and things pile up for a few weeks. Then we spend a day and take care of it all."

Morris's situation is in flux. When he was initially raising his twelve-year-old daughter and ten-year-old son, he would do most of the chores himself, while leaving heavy cleaning to a college student who was hired every other weekend. Now he is engaged to be married and his fiancée has moved in with the family. She is picking up some of the chores, too.

Various systems of rewards have been worked out to get the chores completed. One father raising two daughters, eight and ten years old, has them choose which five chores they do during any one week. They get paid a two-dollar allowance if they complete all their assigned chores.

Do fathers assign more chores to daughters than to sons as the sole custodians did? Are fathers who are living in this somewhat nontraditional family arrangement more sensitive to the division of household labor? Most of the time, the distribution of the housework appears to be equitable. In only one situation was a daughter taking on more of a responsibility than her older brother. These fathers, perhaps because of their involvement in a custody arrangement where they are constantly evaluating what is fair, are highly sensitive to the demands placed on their children.

WORK

At work the joint custodial father is constantly in the position of having to juggle schedules to meet the needs of the children. Most parents find this difficult. School plays, sporting events, teacher's meetings, doctor's appointments, and childhood illnesses can all throw a monkey wrench into a single parent's work schedule. Having the mother involved does not always free the father from attending these functions. In fact, he may feel it is more important to attend if he has difficulty sharing parenting. He may feel he has to protect his turf with the children. As a result of these demands, fathers frequently report arriving late at work or leaving early (50 percent of the fathers), missing work altogether (36 percent), and working more flexible hours (30 percent).

These job changes might affect the relationships of some single parents and their bosses and co-workers, but this group felt a fair amount of support. When asked how supportive bosses and co-workers had been of his having custody, only one father, Jason, said he felt unsupported. His problems, though, stemmed more from having gone through a divorce than having custody. "My supervisor was from a religious order where they did not approve of divorce. He was not very sympathetic to me. He did not like me talking about divorce at work and he nailed me on my annual evaluation."

SOCIALIZING

Starting a social life is no easier for a father with joint custody than it is for the sole custodian. The same fears, ambivalence, and pain that come from a dissolved marriage remain regardless of the custody arrangement. These fathers are also not freed from expressions of concern from the children either. The children are likely to have the same objections and worries about their parents as children of sole custodians. Because the children are still an active part of their lives the social schedule tends to be built around them. As a result, a father will date when his children are visiting their mother. This allows him more time with the children, avoids any conflict he and the children may have over his dating, and places less pressure on the dating relationship itself. Eventually, the father will start to introduce women he is serious about into his children's life.

Over half the fathers date at least every other week. One quarter said they were having sexual relations once a week or more and another quarter said they were having sexual relations once every other week. Sexual relations are a common occurrence for those fathers who date. Despite this level of social activity, only one father in four was satisfied with his social life.

One father spoke of the evolution that takes place in the social scene. "My ex-wife joined PWP immediately and began having a good time. I joined a few years later and did not start getting involved with people until more recently. My extended family is now the church singles group I joined. There is competition there, though, among the men. They all try to sit next to certain women. None of us are in a friendly clique like women sometimes develop. My other social outlet is my antique car club. More and more divorced people are joining it and it makes it easier for me."

The Children

Some fascinating impressions were gained from the fathers about the children. First, the fathers tend to say that the children's attitude and progress is unchanged since joint custody was worked out. Attitudes toward friends, school, the mother, and their feelings about themselves are about the same. Thus, joint custody is not seen as having an especially positive or negative impact on them. One area that did show marked change was in the children's ability to talk about their feelings. And this change is in both directions. More fathers noted improvement and more fathers noted a change for the worse in this area, as compared with all the others. This would not be surprising, given the amount of negotiating that frequently goes on before a joint arrangement is worked out. It is clear that working out a joint arrangement can include a great amount of talking with all family members about their feelings, preferences, and how the arrangement is working out. Children are often under pressure to remain communicative with both parents. For many children, this situation opens them up more. But for some, it results in withdrawal.

Children who are less able to talk about their feelings are probably those whose parents are placing them in the middle of their conflicts. When a child gets put in the position of having to relay information back and forth or is asked to keep a secret, he or she may adopt the course of saying nothing for fear that whatever is said may inflame the parents. They are living in a situation where they may not trust one or both of their parents. If that is the case, their withholding is a wise defense against the pain of seeing conflict escalate between the parents.

Generally, the joint custodians in our study thought things were going well with their children. They rated their relationships with their children very highly (higher than the sole custodians rated theirs), they were satisfied with their children's progress, and they gave themselves high marks as parents.

Despite this high level of satisfaction with the children, some doubts were expressed about how well the joint custody arrangement was working out. One father said it was getting hard on his children because they were always forgetting something at one place or the next. Another complained that scheduling was becoming a problem and that his children were missing activities they were interested in because they had to be at the other parent's house.

Pitfalls for these children are many, as have been discussed. Each situation must be weighed not only for how it is working but for how a different arrangement might succeed. Forcing children into joint custody is not the answer. Yet, at times, it may be preferable to sole custody. If a child is having difficulties while living in joint custody, it does not mean that he or she would be better off with only one parent. Careful evaluation is needed to make that determination. Professional help in making the initial arrangements or in evaluating one that is in place can often help to clarify some of the issues the family is facing. This help can come in the form of legal assistance or mental health counseling.

In fact, every father we interviewed had had some counseling for himself and many were counseled with their children. The reactions to counseling varied. One father raising four children said, "I went off and on for probably two years once a week depending upon my work. When I was unemployed and depressed I went to my pastor. Even though my ex-wife refused to go, it definitely helped. I never would have made it without counseling. The children have not been. They first said they wanted to go, then changed their minds. I never forced it."

Rick also found it helpful. "We went when we were breaking up. We met with a counselor for about five months once a week. It was the only time we ever talked about the divorce and we haven't since. The children did not go."

Eric went for marital counseling before he and his wife broke up. "After we separated we went with our son for two months because we thought we were pawning him off on each other and we wanted to stop that. It helped."

Morris benefited from the process more than most fathers, but he may have had farther to go, too. "I went, then the children went, then we all went together. I realized I was very insecure, especially since my wife left for another woman. I had to find out who I was again and where I was going. We set goals and I now feel more sure of myself. But with children it's a slow process. My son is still going and has been for two years."

Not everyone found counseling helpful. Kurt and his children went for a few visits before he stopped. "I thought it could help us get along better but I did not like what he told me. He said I would have to let go of the kids and with them both being under ten at the time, that did not make sense."

In another situation, a father and daughter were ordered by the court to seek counseling. Again, the results were not favorable. "We went because we had to. It was expensive and I did not get much out of it. There were no real problems to begin with anyway."

Has It Worked Out?

Are they pleased with joint custody? Almost everyone we interviewed said yes. But it has rarely been a smooth road as they are dealing with many of the same issues that place the single fathers on a track.

Morris said, "Generally, joint custody is not easy at all. There are always things to do and you need to be extremely well-organized and the kids need to be well-organized. There is less time for yourself but you get to know the kids better."

Kurt said, "It is a very long row to hoe, but worth it. Get help from God."

Rick's view of the situation changed over time. "At the beginning I was convinced that all fathers should have joint custody. Now I realize that many couples have too many deep emotional scars and old wounds run too deep for it to be a good arrangement for everyone. I feel very happy and lucky that this has worked out so well for us. But I am no longer an advocate for fathers' custody. It is not for everyone.

"From the kids' viewpoint the pro is that it gives them more contact with their parents than they would have. I realize it may not stay this way when they are older. Our kids realize that we are divorced and when they compare with other children they really like what they see. Just sometimes my daughter says she needs more time with her mommy."

Eric has found that people are impressed when they learn he has joint custody. "I get many compliments. In most situations of divorce fathers split from the kids. But my son and I have gotten closer. Once his principal called my ex-wife and I in and said we were to be congratulated for being very supportive parents. We are probably both more involved with him now than we were before and that's an improvement."

Jason said, "My upbringing was kind of good. I was born with a silver spoon in my mouth compared to my wife. I had never been tested and I saw this as a chance to deal with something important to me. I refused to feel self-pity. I knew I could handle it. Now it varies from my not believing how hard it is to its being great. I've gotten a lot of support along the way, which I've needed."

One key factor in how the father feels about joint custody is his relationship with his ex-wife. Because of the amount of contact, this continuing parental relationship is much more important than when a single parent is in charge. The joint custody parents need to be in frequent communication to make the relationship work optimally for all. A child's positive or negative experience at school, for instance, should be communicated to the parent who did not have custody that night so that both parents are kept abreast of these sorts of developments. In this way the parents are truly working together. When things are going smoothly in this relationship, the father tends to feel much more optimistic about joint custody. While some of the fathers saw no improvement over time in their relationship with their children, and a few thought it had worsened, most thought things between them and their ex-wives had improved. Descriptions of the current relationship ranged from "bitter and distant" to "I'm tolerating it" to "We are good friends now. Before we were always fighting."

Complaints about the ex-wife revolve around her parenting abilities and her behavior since the breakup. For example, one father said, "We have a businesslike relationship. What happened between us in the end was real messy. Many of our friends, as well as I, lost respect for her. We are civil to one another but we do not even share coffee."

Jason has mixed feelings about his wife. "When I talk to her on the phone, I want to get back with her. But when I see her in person I want to wring her neck."

Rick is more upbeat. "It is very satisfying for us both now. Workable is the way I would describe it. We talk about the kids, not each other anymore. We are trying hard to make it work for us."

The joint custodians appear to be a little less bitter, a little less war weary, and a little less cautious in dealing with their ex-wives than do the sole custodians. These fathers have worked things out with their ex-wives and their children in a way that may not have been available to the sole custodian. Their children may benefit from the continued contact with their mother that the children of the sole custodians do not have. This closer involvement with the mother reduces some of the burden that a sole custodian would naturally feel. These joint custody fathers are not carrying the parenting load by themselves to a large degree. They do have more time to themselves. And, importantly, the financial burden is not as great. Few are paying anything to their ex-wives and many have ex-wives who are partially supporting the children.

Joint custody is not a magic solution for life after a marital breakup. Nor is it for everyone. From the descriptions of these fathers it is clear that it takes hard work and perseverance for joint custody to meet the needs of the parents and the children. If there is great acrimony between the parents, it may not work. It should be viewed as one option among many when parents decide who will raise the children.

Things to Remember If You Are a Joint Custodian

1. Remember that joint custody is not a solution to a divorce. It is one way of handling custody arrangements. As such, the children, you, and your ex-wife may still need professional assistance with the feelings that follow a breakup.

2. Do not let the feelings you have for your ex-wife affect how you and she co-parent. Treat her with courtesy and respect but do not expect her to meet your emotional needs. She does not have to praise you for the great job of parenting you are doing.

3. Do not pull the children in-between you or use them as pawns to get back at her.

4. If dealing with your ex-wife is difficult, find safe ways to blow off steam. Try exercising or taking a time out period if you find yourself getting especially angry.

5. The children may need help with organization. Traveling back and forth between two homes is a daunting task. Not much is known about the toll it takes or what a normal reaction to it should be. Thus, support and guidance are called for when the children become tired from the moving or forget schedules or

homework. Such lapses should not be interpreted as a rejection of a parent.

6. Remain flexible about the success of joint custody. Just because you both have worked it out to your satisfaction does not mean it will work for your children. At the same time, keep in mind that problems that arise during a joint custody arrangement may have been worse if sole custody had been in place. Evaluate carefully before suggesting a change.

7. Consider joining a self-help group for single parents. Learn how others are managing and how they deal with the little daily crises that always spring up when children are around.

8. Keep to the schedule that has been agreed upon unless you and your ex-wife agree to diverge from it. If you do not treat your agreement with respect, havoc may follow.

9. Remember that you and your ex-wife are a team. You can support each other as parents without having to love each other.

10. Try and keep the rules in both houses the same to reduce the natural discrepancies in parenting styles that are going to occur.

11. Post a schedule in each house as to where both parents are during the day. That way, the children can always reach the other parent if needed.

12. Try not to pump your children for personal information about their mother. She is no longer your wife. She needs her privacy just as you need yours.

13. Spend quality time with your children. Do not assume that your ex-wife is still doing many of the parenting duties that she did during the marriage. She may believe you are the one talking to the children about their feelings, school work, friends, and other matters.

14. Dating is important and should be handled carefully (see chapter 7). The children still spend a good deal of time in your home and their reactions to your dating must be considered.

15. If you have joint custody but your ex-wife is living far away from the children, encourage them to write and call her.

16. Having time to spend with one's children and being able to establish a new relationship with them is wonderful. Enjoy it.

11

Widowers: Raising Children Alone

A FEW years ago, John's wife committed suicide. While it is always a shock when someone kills herself, it was not a surprise to him. She had attempted it before. John, a salesman age thirty-five at the time, was left with two daughters, ages thirteen and three, and a six-year-old son.

Bob is a forty-five-year-old foreman. His wife died two years ago after suffering from multiple sclerosis for more than a decade. The last few years of her life had been especially traumatic. As she began abusing drugs to control the pain, she became verbally abusive to their two teenagers.

Sam, a thirty-seven-year-old factory worker, became a widower recently after his wife was killed in a car accident. She had been at a party with her boss, and there had been a lot of drinking. On the way home, the boss drove the car over the side of a mountain. Sam was left with responsibility for four children, two sons and two daughters, ranging in age from seven to fourteen.

Through various unfortunate circumstances, these fathers joined the ranks of more than one hundred thousand widowers raising children alone.[1] When a father begins raising his children alone following his wife's death, he is often moving into a role he is not prepared for and does not want. He not only is faced with the loss of a marriage partner, financial contributor, and homemaker, but he also has to pick up new skills and responsibilities. He is different from the divorced custodian in that he was neither seeking single parenthood nor was he seeking to take care of the children alone. He is dealing not only with these new responsibilities, but also with his and his children's pain. How does he cope? It was learned from thirty-six widowers that adapting to life after the death has not been easy. With time, though, it is something most fathers and their children manage. The fathers, in talking about the deaths of their wives, the demands of childrearing and work, starting a social life, and helping their children deal with the loss, paint a picture that is ultimately optimistic.

Dealing with Death

Widowers in the United States are more likely to be older men whose wives have died from an illness associated with age than the three younger men with children described at the beginning of this chapter. In fact, widowers with young children have become increasingly rare during the twentieth century. Before that, maternal mortality because of childbirth was a common event, leaving the father not only with children to raise but also a farm or business to run without his wife's help. Because of recent medical advances and social changes, divorced fathers with custody are ten times more prevalent than widowers. Even though divorced fathers are more common, more rituals exist to help widowers. Funerals are one way of officially saying goodbye, for example. Assisted by a mortician and a clergyman, the bereaved are led through steps that many have walked before. A period of mourning follows, during which one accepts visits from friends and relatives, prepared dinners, and donations in the deceased's honor. These steps can play an important part in beginning the grieving process and moving the family toward resolution.

One way to think about the grieving process is to look at the stages the bereaved may pass through in an attempt to accept the loss and move on with life. Elizabeth Kubler-Ross identifies these stages as:

1. Denial—when the fact of the death (or the impending death) is not accepted;

2. Anger—when one feels rage at the thought of the death;

3. Bargaining—when there is an attempt to strike a deal with God to forestall the death or bring back the living;

4. Depression—when the sadness of the loss sets in; and

5. Acceptance—the final stage, when one is actively coping with the death.[2]

Passing through the first four stages is necessary, according to Kubler-Ross, before one can move to the point of acceptance, which she sees as the goal of grieving. It is important to point out that a widower dealing with the loss or impending loss does not necessarily have to pass through these stages before accepting the death. Author T.A. Rando prefers to think in phases, not believing it is necessary for everyone to follow the same path. She believes people may go through one phase and come back to it at a later time. She characterizes three broad phases of normal grief reaction as follows:

1. Avoidance. The mourner is dazed, confused, and numb. As recognition of the death seeps in, denial takes over. This is seen as beneficial at the time, a way of dealing with the pain. Avoidance helps the person through the funeral and is marked by a separation of the emotion from the event.

2. Confrontation. The mourner begins to experience the shock of the loss. The pain of the loss hits home and a wealth of suppressed emotions comes to the fore. Extremes of emotion are felt and there may be a sense of panic about having to handle things alone. Reactions of anger and guilt are common—anger at the loss and guilt if the relationship was ambivalent at the time of death. The mourner may also experience depression and despair, irritability, anxiety, and tension.

3. Reestablishment. The mourner begins letting go of the pain and moves toward a healthy return to life. The pain is not forgotten but is placed in a context that permits the person's life to go on. Success at this stage comes and goes and may be marked by old feelings of depression or anger. Reentry into the world may be accompanied by feelings of guilt in that the deceased is now being left behind.[3]

In general, experts believe that full recovery from grief is a very long process that may never completely occur. Rather, there is a gradual reentry into life if people are able to work through their feelings at their own pace.[4] Reactions to death vary tremendously, with few patterns seen as unhealthy. People cope with death in very different ways. The father who does not seem to mourn a great deal is not necessarily uncaring. He is just reacting in a different way than a father who dissolves in tears at the drop of a hat. Mourning may continue for a long time without being pathological. Accepting a wide range of reactions to the mourning process is an important part of dealing with the whole experience.

Aside from stages or phases of grieving, a widower with children has to confront a number of specifics immediately, or within the first few months after the death of the mother. Legal and financial issues must be settled.[5] If a will exists it must be executed. Any monies that have been set aside through annuity plans, IRAs, life insurance policies, etc., have to be taken care of. Property settlements may have to be made and outstanding debts that exist in the wife's name have to be rearranged.

The reactions of others must be handled. At the time of a death, people are often unsure how to behave. They worry they may say the wrong thing and thus say nothing at all.[6] Offering assistance with child care, cooking, and cleaning for a short period of time following a death is quite common. With a father, though, it can take on a new dimension, as these are often activities with which he has had little prior experience. Sometimes the opportunity for the father to learn how to do these things is denied him by his own sense of shock and disbelief.

Dealing with the children is of primary importance. The loss they are experiencing is easily as great as the father's. Because the father is also trying to cope with the death, it may be particularly difficult for him to provide the children with the attention they need. It is not uncommon for parents, when asked about their children's behavior during the first few weeks following the death of the other parent, to say that they do not know, do not remember, or were "too out of it to help the kids."

Children have an easier time understanding death the older

they are.[7] The magical thinking that comes with television where people are killed and reappear on the same program or on different programs can be terribly confusing when trying to apply that to one's own parent. They can even believe that they were somehow responsible for the death. A child who once screamed at a mother that he wished she were dead is paralyzed with fear that his saying it made it come true. Older children can have similar fantasies and often return to an earlier stage of development when confronted with death. The surviving parent has to be careful to not assume that only the youngest children in the family need special care. Each child has needs no matter how strong a particular child may appear.

Vague explanations of death, rather than helping the children, sometimes can hinder their ability to understand and cope. Consider the young child who is told that "Mommy died in her sleep," "God took Mommy," or "Mommy died after being sick." Now think about what the child has learned from that about sleep, God, and being ill.[8] Despite the tremendous loss the father is feeling, he needs to tackle some key issues immediately. The first step is dealing with the children. Explaining death to a child, particularly when it is a parent who has died, is a very difficult task. Some suggestions are:

1. Explain the death in a way that is age appropriate.

2. Be clear about the cause of death and be complete in giving the information.

3. Accept whatever reaction the children have to the death—this may range from disbelief, to deep depression, to complete denial where the child seems initially unaffected and wants to go to school the same day.

4. Let the child decide if he or she wants to go to the funeral. In helping the child weigh the decision, consider the age of the child and what you think the tone of the funeral will be.

5. Be honest with your children about your own feelings. It is okay for them to see you cry and to hear that you are sad. It is not a weakness to show your sadness.

6. Talk about the death when your child wants to.
7. Your child will need your reassurance. He or she will ask for it in many small ways, sometimes with words, sometimes with actions.

After a period of mourning, reentering the social scene is an important step. There seems to be a generally accepted period of mourning that lasts from either six months to one year following a spouse's death. This period varies based on one's own experiences with death and one's culture. Following that time period, reentry is necessary for the well-being of both the father and the children. It is not easy, though, and is affected strongly by the relationship the father had with his wife. Whether it was positive or negative, the type of relationship they had leaves a definite imprint. For example, if the father had a very strong marriage he may be reluctant to get involved again with someone who will not be able to replace his wife. On the other hand, a good marital relationship can encourage him. With a positive view toward women and intimacy, he may be eager to begin socializing.

The research on widowers tends to describe them as having an initially more difficult adjustment than the divorced father. Given the fact that many widowers were in satisfactory marriages, as compared with the divorced fathers, this would be expected. It has also been found that the more preparation the father had for the death, the easier the adjustment.[9] The research also indicates that widowers receive more support from others than do divorced fathers.[10] As mentioned earlier, when there has been a death, people are bound to react sympathetically. After a divorce, questions of blame and failure are more likely. In addition, the family is more likely to pull together after a death than after a divorce. The children seem more willing to help out and the father is more willing to ask for and accept help. After a divorce, the father is likely to feel guilt and not want to burden the children. The view of the absent mother is quite different, too. Idealization of the mother by both the father and the children is more common after death than after divorce.[11]

The Thirty-six Fathers

The widowers were slightly older, with an average age of forty-five, than the divorced fathers discussed elsewhere in this book.[12] At the time of their wife's death, they had been married from between five and twenty-six years. The interviews took place an average of four years after they had been widowed, making them a group with single parenting experience. Their children ranged in age from three to the mid-twenties, with a fairly even distribution of girls and boys. Three fathers, one of whom already had custody, were divorced at the time of the death. The marriages of the other fathers were not all made in Heaven. Like any other group of marriages, some were happy and others were not.

CIRCUMSTANCES OF THE DEATH

The wives died from a variety of causes. The most common reasons were suicide, cancer, and other lingering illnesses. Accidental deaths, such as car accidents and freak injuries around the house, were also mentioned. Half the fathers had some time to prepare for the death. John, the father whose wife committed suicide, said she had suffered from a long history of mental illness that included occasional hospitalizations. Previous suicide attempts with drug overdoses had been thwarted at the last moment. With each attempt and with increasingly erratic behavior, the children had grown wary of their mother. Even though she remained an important person in their lives, they had begun to gravitate toward John for their nurturing. When she finally succeeded in killing herself with a sleeping pill overdose, it was John who discovered her. John was faced with having to discuss two difficult issues with the children: the loss of their mother and the reason for that loss. John told them exactly what had happened. He wanted them to hear it from him rather than from anyone else. He believed in this way he had the most control over the information. "I had actually practiced in my mind even before she died how I was going to tell them. It was still horrendous to have to do it." His oldest daughter, thirteen, was the most upset. The younger children had a difficult time understanding the meaning of the death. This confusion is common among young children in general, as the stories provided by other fathers will show. While being honest with the children worked out as well as could be expected, it did result in some embarrassing moments. When an adult would ask the three-year-old what happened to her mother, she would answer, "She killed herself." An awkward silence usually followed.

The suicide has been hard for other family members to accept also. John's in-laws are not forthcoming when asked how their daughter died. They report that she was murdered.

In thinking about how he handled the children immediately after the death, John has one regret: not taking them to the funeral. The children, even years later, lament to him that they did not have a formal opportunity to say goodbye.

Bob's experience was quite different from John's. His wife was diagnosed as having multiple sclerosis shortly after their second child was born. A long ordeal began that was typical of the course the disease takes—loss of muscle coordination, bladder and bowel control problems, pain, and eventual confinement to a wheelchair and then to bed. After being medicated with increasingly strong drugs, she eventually became addicted and developed a secondary alcohol habit. The combination of depression and anger from having multiple sclerosis capped off by her addictions made her impossible to live with. She became verbally abusive to Bob and their children. The more they retreated from her the more abusive she became. The children stopped bringing friends over to the house and spent as much time away as they could. As in John's family, Bob's children also gravitated toward him for support. He became accustomed to running the household and taking care of an invalid. When she finally died, it was a blessing for everyone. She had not wanted a wake or a funeral and her wishes were respected. Bob and the children felt they had already gone through a wake in the months before she died. Her body was donated to science at her request.

Sam was the least prepared. It had never occurred to him that he would have to raise his children alone. His marriage was stable and happy. Both he and his wife worked outside the home so when she was killed in the car accident he "lost it all. She meant everything to me and also helped pay the bills. With my job being an hour's drive each way I needed her to keep my life and the kids' life together."

Sam was given the bad news during an early morning visit from a state trooper. He decided to tell only his twelve-year-old daughter and inform the younger children when they came home from school in the afternoon. That would have given him a chance to consider how to explain the death to the children he believed would be the most traumatized. But Sam's conversation was overheard by another child and soon everyone knew. "It was impossible to keep it a secret," he said. All four children decided to go to school anyway. "School was a place where they had good relationships with teachers and friends who could help them with the death," Sam said.

They all attended the funeral. He showed them where the accident had taken place. He made every effort to have them understand what had happened. "They did real well, but I noticed recently as I was looking over a picture taken at the funeral, that no one was smiling."

Other fathers handled the deaths differently. Pete, an electrical engineer living in Ohio, had custody of the children when his ex-wife died from a freak accident in the bathtub. "My daughter was very upset but did not go to the funeral, which was in New Jersey. I offered to send her. My son never really knew her and was more upset because we were upset." Another father, whose wife died of cancer, did not take his daughter to the funeral. He said, "She was only two then and would not have understood what was happening. A lot of our family was dying at that time, too—my mother, her grandparents. I thought enough was enough."

Joe's children were five and eight when their mother died from a brain tumor. Joe had prided himself in understanding his children's emotions, but he was struck by what he saw as his own ineptitude in handling them at the time of crisis: "I was kind of oblivious to their reaction because I was so out of it. My parents took over and they said the children were doing crazy things at the time. I was just paralyzed. My daughter was more verbal. She kept asking why Mommy was sick. My son (the five-year-old) is more of an observer. I talked to the children when my daughter confronted me and I told them what little I knew." Both children went to the funeral and were out of school for about a week.

Marty's family had prepared themselves for the death in advance. His wife died after a lingering case of leukemia that was hastened by a blood clot caused by a rollerskating fall. "The children were stoic about it," Marty said. "My teenage daughter became a little lady overnight and helped out at the viewing by greeting everybody. My younger daughter sat and watched TV."

Fred's children reacted much more emotionally. "It was weird. At the funeral, the little one (age six) didn't cry at all. And then, later in bed with me patting her back she sobbed for a long time. I was dumbstruck. It made my skin crawl. But I guess when kids cry about that stuff adults feel better. The oldest two were also weird. They were hers from a previous marriage. I had tried to adopt them during the marriage but their grandparents wouldn't allow it so my wife hadn't pushed it. They had no idea how to react but were initially very emotional. I am still close to them now and my stepdaughter wants me to walk down the aisle with her at her wedding."

From these fathers' stories we can see that the reactions of the children can vary greatly. People cope with death in different ways. Whatever approach a family member takes can be adaptive. In addition, we see that children in the same family can have quite different reactions.

Running the Household and Working

The demands of running the house remain after the wife's death. Some men had been involved in the cooking, cleaning, and laundry during the marriage, particularly those whose wives died after a lengthy illness. Other fathers had left these chores to their wives. Paul, whose wife was killed, sought immediate assistance. "When my wife died she left me with three children to raise. I've had twelve housekeepers in two years. The children ran roughshod all over them. Thankfully, I now have an elderly housekeeper who is proving to be adequate." Not everyone can afford nor wants to have a housekeeper in their family. In fact,

Paul and John were the only two of the thirty-six who were employing housekeepers when they were interviewed. Paul's is a live-in and John's works on a part-time basis. John, who was making a good income when his wife died, hoped to provide as much continuity in his children's lives as possible. He initially hired a housekeeper who would arrive at seven in the morning and stay until five in the evening, to cover for him during his long commute to work. "It would have been nearly impossible for me to continue at my job without someone there for as many hours as she was there." With the children now older, a housekeeper is needed only from 7 A.M. to 10 A.M.

With so few housekeepers being employed among this group, the chores are usually completed by either the father alone, the children alone, or the father and children together. With few exceptions, children age ten or older were helping out with the housekeeping. They were most likely to be assisting with cleaning and laundry and least likely to be doing the cooking. The fathers appear to be as likely to get help from a son as from a daughter, supporting the previous research that showed that children were willing to pitch in and help the widower. One father complained about having to shop, though. "With my work schedule," he said, "the only time to shop is Friday night and that's the most crowded time."

Working and balancing the demands of the home were not easy for this group of fathers. Fourteen of the thirty-six said they found it very difficult, eighteen somewhat difficult, and only four not at all difficult. The ones who found it the easiest were self-employed. The fathers had to undergo a whole range of job changes—reducing travel, changing hours, bringing work home, arriving late and leaving early, and so on. Eight of the fathers reported quitting, being fired, or being laid off because of the demands of single parenting.

Some fathers worry about their contributions at work. Sam, for instance, feels he has not been pulling his weight. Even though everyone at work has been supportive of him, his own expectations for his performance are not being met. This is not uncommon for men who work full time and take care of the children. Something has to give. For Sam it is his work performance. Raised like so many other men who define their competence as men through their competence at work, Sam has had to readjust his view of himself and he is not happy about it.

Bosses vary in their support of the widower. Most, though, when they learn that an employee's wife has died, allow a certain degree of flexibility for at least a few months. All of them, except for instances where fathers were fired, were described by the fathers as being at least somewhat supportive. One father, though, complained of the usual single-parent difficulties with working full time. "If the kids are sick, I have a real problem. I have to get my mother-in-law to help out. Sometimes my daughter calls me at work and it tears me up I can't be at home with her. It all is depressing sometimes. You have home and work and the kid. There is no time for fun." Another said, "I guess they understand me at work. But my boss gives me work to take home at night. He says I can do it while I babysit."

Dating

One of the hardest areas for these fathers was rekindling a social life. When a loved one has died, finding someone new is often a seemingly impossible task. Each father approaches dating in his own way, usually waiting an appropriate amount of time before stepping back into the social scene. If the children object strenuously to his dating, and see it as trying to replace their mother, the father may hesitate before initiating dating. Under these circumstances, dating can become an emotion-laden event, one where the father's struggle for independence is marred by the children's need to hold on to the past.

By four years after the death of the wife, almost everyone in the survey had begun to date. But satisfaction with their social lives varied. Nearly half the fathers were dating at least once a week, with another quarter dating at least once every other week. The remainder dated rarely or never. Despite the level of social activity, satisfaction with their social lives was mixed. Only a third said they were satisfied, with the rest being "mixed" or unsatisfied. Some of the possible reasons for their dissatisfaction have been discussed in chapter 7. But the father's fears about reentering the social scene, fears about sexual performance, lack of finances, still being in love with the deceased, the children's objections, confusion about what the father wants in a woman, and an inability to bring dates home all can make the experience less than something out of a fairy tale.

For example, John eased into dating slowly. He began going out six months after his wife died, at first dating only people he knew. He considered them "safe." Essentially, he believed they would feel sorry for him and not place demands on him for emotional or sexual intimacy. After a year, he began broadening his horizons and dating people who were not aware of his situation. These women would be more likely to see him as an equal. Then, he said, he began to feel driven and tried to cram in as much socializing as he could. He also set a timetable for himself. "I decided I would wait three years after her death and then remarry. Well, that date has come and gone and I'm still single. I guess I'm getting used to it."

Bob was flattered by the attention he got from women when he joined Parents Without Partners and liked the experience of socializing with a group rather than on a one-to-one basis. Socializing for Bob came to include square dancing. Unable to touch his wife for years because of the pain she felt from her illness, he found touching a woman during a dance to be an overwhelmingly moving experience. He now square dances four times a week. Even though Bob feels comfortable touching women at a dance, he is not prepared for a more intimate experience. Having a woman spend the night with him is completely out of the question. "My children and I are not ready for that. Maybe when they have left home."

Sam began dating after six months, but only occasionally. Because he still misses his wife, dating is something he does not relish. Living in a small town, he is not optimistic about the prospects of meeting someone new. Usually, he just socializes with his children. They either go out alone or with another family.

Other fathers talked of having flashbacks about their wives when they thought of dating. When one father went out, he kept envisioning his wife in a certain bathrobe she liked to wear. Those flashbacks were the beginning of a difficult period for him. He subsequently became increasingly depressed and even suicidal before going to a counselor for help.

Another father said dating reminded him of "necking when I was in high school. Only when I kissed the date I would flash on my wife. It was real weird at first." His daughter made it more stressful for him by actively objecting to his dating. One time she ran in-between him and his date and said, 'Watch out. My daddy likes to tickle.' His women friends would complain that she was hostile to them on the phone. She would demand to know who was calling. She would then sit there and time him with a stop watch when he was telephoning.

Joe, when asked about his dating experiences, exclaimed, "I could write a book about that! At the beginning, it was very hard. My first two dates were disasters. I didn't know how to act and all I did was talk about my wife. It made my dates uncomfortable. As I dated more, I saw it was a totally different world. One woman whose house I went to for dinner began kissing and hugging me as soon as I got in the door. I had to do a lot of learning quickly. But in general, single women were very understanding. The kids had a tough time at first. My son would ask questions like, 'Is she going to be my new mommy?' Or they would be quick to comment and say, 'She's a loser.' Or one of them would come down with a stomachache just before I went out. Sometimes, though, they were very perceptive and would pick up on something about a date long before I would."

As mentioned, comments from children about their father's dates are not unusual. One father said he was being encouraged by his daughter to date and that she rated the women. As the only female in the home, she was hoping her father would remarry quickly. Another father said his daughter wanted him to remarry because she needed someone who could properly do her hair.

Socializing remains one of the most difficult areas for all single fathers, whether widowed or divorced. Yet going out is necessary if the father is to begin a new life. Dating sends an important message to the children that life goes on. Realizing the children are sensitive to the father's dating and handling that sensitivity with care can make the father's socializing more enjoyable for everyone.

Raising the Children

As the children are struggling to get over the pain of the death, the single father has to establish a new relationship with them to replace the one that existed when the children's mother was alive. Unlike the divorced father, the widowed father does not have to contend with another parent's interfering with the raising of the children or with visitation or custody battles. But he also does not have the parenting support (the time off and financial and emotional assistance) that follows the more amicable custody arrangements. Helping a child deal with the death of a parent has to be the most difficult experience a parent ever undertakes. Death brings a final separation. It can be dealt with but it takes time, support, and understanding.

While the widower helps his children adjust to the death of their mother, the children often try to help the father, too. Sensing his enormous needs, perhaps more acutely than their own if they are in a stage of denial, they may pull together to take care of Dad. He becomes their focus and their own mourning can be delayed. This might be especially true if the oldest is a daughter. Trying to fill the shoes left empty by her mother, a daughter may take over many of the typically female functions in the family. She becomes a parental child. This may not always be a problem and can help the family through a difficult period. But the daughter must return at some point to a more appropriate position with her own peer group. If not, difficulties can arise and the pursuit of a normal childhood may be denied.

In John's case, a problem arose with his daughter. When his wife first died, he dedicated a large amount of time to trying to meet the physical demands of raising two young children, to the detriment, he feels, of his oldest daughter. She was turning sixteen and had needs he did not understand. He feels his lack of involvement with her created adjustment problems that would not have existed had he handled things differently. With no attention from her father and no role to play initially in the family, she naturally fell into a caretaker position. She tried to take charge of housekeeping even though a housekeeper had been hired. A succession of housekeepers quit because of her interference. John tried to intervene by encouraging her to spend time with her friends. But lacking the attention she needed from her family, she clung tightly to her newfound position.

Dating became an issue. He would stay out until 3 A.M., yet set an 11 P.M. curfew for her. He would comment on the company she kept only to hear similar remarks about his dates. In an escalating battle of wills the tension smoldered. When he was at work she would call to talk to him for hours, yet sit in her room refusing to communicate when he was home. John valued the telephone talks because they were his most meaningful conversations with her, but he also worried about the time he lost at his job.

By the time she reached nineteen (after three years of strain), things began to work themselves out. She entered a commuter college and was establishing a life of her own. John had had time to get over the death. With the help of family counseling, they have now established more of an adult relationship and have come to enjoy each other's company.

The next-oldest child has done well in school despite John's feeling he failed as a disciplinarian. "I was afraid of their feeling not loved and I needed them to be friends with me. As I developed adult friends, I needed them less as friends and could be their father. My youngest is also doing well in school now."

Bob has had it much easier. With time to prepare for his wife's death, he was able to establish a good relationship with both of his children. He is proud to say he has heard his children's friends are envious of the relationship they have with their father.

Sam described a pattern that was similar to John's. The oldest daughter assumed the mother's role, but relinquished it when he was home. At fourteen she was cooking for the younger three children while Sam was at work. But when he returned, she scampered off to be with her friends.

Many fathers have difficulty discussing the death with the children. They tend to believe that if they discuss the death once or twice and give the children the opportunity to share their feelings, there is no need to discuss it further. They see handling the death to be similar to handling other tasks—once you do it, it is taken care of and does not have to be done again. Some fathers, though, realize that the death needs to be discussed on an ongoing basis. As children grow, their perception of their mother's life and death will change. They may see a movie or hear a friend talk about someone dying and will need to discuss it again. In addition, the children may not deal with the death directly but may show feelings about it in other ways—like crying an un-usual amount when a pet dies. To some extent, that child may also be crying for her mother.

Some fathers approach the issue of the death periodically through family rituals. One father explained, "I wouldn't say we talk about it a lot but when we do things and it reminds us of her, we'll talk about it. We do remember the dates of her birth and death but don't really do much else anymore. We have a new life now (three years after the death)."

Joe, as a way of keeping their mother's spirit alive, began giving his children some of her things when the children got a little older. One daughter received a signed Bible that had been a favorite of her mother's. On holidays they place flowers at her grave. "We talk about her once a week. Something will come up or they'll see something of hers and ask me about it. But I put away photographs of her after a while. I didn't want the place to become a mausoleum."

For another father, the memory is very much alive. "We talk about her almost every day. I have a picture of her in the bed-room and I'll go in there to see it as a constant reminder of her. Thinking about her makes me feel good."

Other Experiences

One of the patterns seen among the fathers was delayed bereave-ment. The period of time immediately following the death is filled with a great deal of activity. Funeral arrangements have to be made, friends and family visit, new work and school schedules have to be worked out, and so on. Once the flurry of the first six months ceases, schedules have been worked out, attention from others has ceased, and things have returned to a new sense of normality, a low period can set in. With all distractions gone, this is when fathers experience the most depression. At this time the true impact of the loss of a wife and mother hits. Thus if a father is asked two months after the death how he is doing, he may honestly answer that he is doing well. Four months later that may not be the case. Sometimes this low period is sparked by the start of socialization and the flooding of memories that accom-panies it.

Not all fathers go through this setback. Some may experience a more gradual progression to a healthy adjustment and a readiness to pick up their lives again. Whatever course bereavement takes, it is important to remember that grief does not have to necessarily be resolved within any preconceived time period. There is nothing wrong with the father who grieves longer or in a different way than someone else.

The support of others can help the father in this process. Many fathers reported in-laws, parents, and friends as being helpful with the children and with making funeral arrangements. The fathers do receive a great deal of positive feedback. One father said, "Most people give me compliments, that really makes me feel good." Another said, "When it first happened, people gave me sympathy and they were not sure if I could handle it. My wife's sister started dividing up my kids, saying they would each take one, and I put the kibosh on that. I think her sisters were feeling bad for me and were doubtful I could raise all of them, but I said from the very beginning they were going to stay with me and we were going to be a family. My parents were very supportive."

Joe found that while his family was supportive, his in-laws were less available. "I've had to make the effort to stay in touch with them and they only live a mile away. I don't know how to talk to them about their daughter dying. It is not something we talk about."

Sometimes just being a single parent causes problems for the widowers. They get "tarred" by the same brush that often affects other parents raising children alone. Mack, a mechanic earning twenty-five thousand dollars a year and raising two children, six and twenty, had problems renting. "After we moved to Oregon it took me five months to get someone who would rent to me. The same thing happened when I moved to Ohio. They come up with all these reasons like they don't want children or I'm not qualified to pay this much rent. I had to buy something in one city just to have a place to live. Finally I moved again and talked myself into a rental. The landlord told me later why I was a risk. He was wondering at first what I would do with the kids while I was at work. He said he thought I was going to leave them to run around alone and get into trouble. Now he says I'm the best tenant he has."

Some Fatherly Advice

All these fathers advocate getting involved in activities after the death of a spouse. "Staying inside and feeling sorry for yourself never helped anything," John says. Getting together with other single parents, especially widows and widowers, has been helpful to many fathers both in giving them information and in providing an atmosphere where they can feel open.

Bob suggests that single parents try not to become their children's peers. He credits his good relationship with his children to remaining in the father role and not trying to become too involved in their activities. Bob's attempt to *not* become too involved in activities with his children stands in contrast to what most fathers suggest. But it is important to remember that Bob's situation, with his wife dying after a lingering illness, permitted him to take a very active role with his children for years. For the father who left much of the caretaking of the children to the wife, involvement in activities with the children becomes a new way to get to know them. But a balance must be struck in which the children's needs do not control the father's life. Sam and John feel that a good parent-child relationship is based in part on the father's meeting his own needs first. If he is content with himself, then he can be a better parent.

Reaching out to support systems is at the core of the fathers' coping abilities. But it is not always easy for men to reach out or to accept help. John says this reluctance made it especially rough for him. "I tried to do everything on my own and show I could make it. I couldn't." Now when help is offered he jumps at it and does not feel like a failure because he has accepted it. He also does not believe that it takes much to help him. "The help I appreciate the most is a cup of coffee. If someone wants to help, offer coffee."

Other fathers list a variety of helpful hints: "Shouldn't be too concerned about what other people think." "Use common sense rather than secondhand advice." "You better expect to invest every minute of every day as a parent because it can send you into a tailspin. I've taken a course in parenting but so much of it you learn along the way. I talk to my mom and sisters about a lot of things. You have to add all of this onto a full-time job and a house. There really isn't any book to tell you how to do it." "Get involved with your kids in things they enjoy. I bought a boat for everyone to share and that has been a godsend. We are together and we are doing something fun."

Joe suggests "taking the time out to make a list of what you want to accomplish in raising the kids by yourself. Hopefully the values you choose will be good ones. Then go ahead and do it. Try to make life as normal for yourself as possible by doing as many things as a two-parent family would do."

Becoming a widower is probably the hardest thing a father will ever have to do. It is not an insurmountable task, though. With time, attention to the children, self-understanding, and reaching out to others, most fathers will maintain their families and grow from the experience.

Things to Remember If You Are a Widower

1. Talk to your children directly about the death (or the impending death). Address whatever fears they have. They may wonder if the same thing that killed their mother will also kill them or you.

2. Give yourself permission to grieve at your own pace.

3. Remember that while experts believe mourning may never be completely resolved, you must work to get on with your life.

4. Expect a down period six months to a year following the death and do not take it as a setback if it happens.

5. Socialization and dating are normal parts of life and need to begin at some point. This is important for you and the children.

6. Expect socialization and dating to be uncomfortable and frightening. You are probably out of practice.

7. Consider joining a self-help group for single parents.

8. If you continue to be depressed for a long time or believe

you are having difficulty in mourning, seek professional help. Seeking help is a healthy way of taking care of yourself.

9. Rely on friends and family for a while. That is what they are there for.

10. Some people may not know how to react to you or may not know what to say when they hear your wife died. Do not take their discomfort as a statement about you as a person.

11. Talk to your children periodically about their mother. Look for indirect ways that they may be thinking about her or talking about her and ask them if they want to talk about her. Listen carefully to what they are saying *and* doing. Anniversaries of important dates, birthdays, and holidays are particularly poignant times.

12. Idealization of a deceased parent is common. When it prevents the children or you from accepting new people into your life, it can become a problem.

13. Spend time with your children but do it in a balanced way. Do not feel that you have to drop everything in your life until your children are old enough to leave home.

14. Learn about normal development in children so that you know what to expect at different ages.

15. Accept whatever reactions your children have to the death. Do not try and force them to deal with it in a certain way.

16. Accept and like yourself without trying to become a superdad.

17. Check other chapters in this book for other suggestions about living alone with your children.

12

Twenty-five Years Later:
The Story of One Family

THIS chapter is the story of one family, taken from interviews with a father and the four children he raised. Unlike all the other fathers discussed in this book, where there are children eighteen years old or younger, this father gained custody of his children almost twenty-five years ago. He and the children, who are now adults, talk about their experiences growing up as well as their current feelings about marriage, relationships, and childrearing. They also candidly discuss the differences between being raised by their father and by their mother. The father gives his impressions of his failed marriage, how he gained custody, and what life was like for him raising four children when single fathers were much rarer than now.

The interviews with the family members took place over a five year span, beginning in 1984.* Four of the five family members were personally interviewed, and the fifth was interviewed by telephone and through written correspondence. The three sons were interviewed together. The family members could talk off the record if they wanted to give me specific background information about a situation without having the information included in the chapter. The mother was approached but refused to be interviewed. When Susan, the oldest child, found out her

---

*The bulk of the chapter centers on the family at that time. It is from their perspective in 1984 that we begin, nearly 20 years after the custody arrangement was made. When this book was being written, I reinterviewed Peter to learn how the family had changed. This was placed after the previous conclusion to give a sense of change.

mother had refused to take part in the interviews, she told me: "I knew Mom wouldn't agree to talk to you. I'm sorry for you because she is so neat. But Mom's basic feeling is that it wouldn't help us kids, so why bother? I hope you can understand that instinct in her. It's very basic to who she is."

Trying to weave five people's lives into a coherent story has proved difficult. There are different impressions of major family events. Harsh, angry feelings are expressed, as well as warm, happy ones. Their stories aptly illustrate how one family grew up. As such, they provide a framework for understanding the families currently being raised by a father. At the time of the interview, the youngest child, Keith, had just graduated from college, signaling an end to the parents' responsibility for their children. It was a fitting time to ask the family to reflect on growing up with a single father.

The Family

Peter and Gail, both fiftyish, are the father and mother. Peter runs an art gallery. Gail is a newspaper reporter, an occupation she has held since 1953, when they were married. The children are Susan, now twenty-eight; Barry, twenty-six; Vince, twenty-five; and Keith, twenty-three. The four children live in three different cities; two of the children live near their mother, and none lives near Peter. The three oldest are successfully employed in a variety of professions; Keith is just entering the job market. At the time of this writing, both Susan and Vince, who are married, report serious problems in their relationships, and both are either going through a trial separation or actively seeking a divorce.

THE FAMILY BEFORE THE DIVORCE, THE DIVORCE ITSELF, AND CUSTODY

One thing that Peter said attracted him to Gail was that she was "pretty sexy." There was also an "opposites" attraction. He saw Gail as being spontaneous and very lively, while viewing himself as sober and somewhat reserved. Both of them worked at the beginning of the marriage. Gail would take time off from work with the birth of each child but, because of the nature of her work as a reporter, was able to return to work on a part-time basis very soon afterward. After their last child, Keith, was born, she returned to work full time. A housekeeper was hired to take care of the children and the home. The family lived near a major eastern city.

According to Peter, as Gail became more successful in her work, she began spending more and more time away from home in pursuit of stories. Sometimes she had to do her interviews at night. Peter felt the housework and child care were falling increasingly on him. He resented the extra responsibility and resented the fact that she was not home much with him or the children. Her investment in her work rather than in the home and the marriage became one of a number of major stumbling blocks in the marriage. In the last year they were together, tempers flared. During one particularly bad fight, Peter says, he hit Gail for the first and only time in the marriage. Gail ran crying into a back room of the house and shut the door. Shortly thereafter, Peter and Gail separated, and she took the children.

(As will be seen throughout this chapter, Peter's memories can be quite different from those of the children. Children sometimes forget certain events and may overdramatize the particulars of others. This can also be true for adults.)

The three sons, who were between four and eight when their parents split up, do not remember much about life with both parents. The two oldest boys do recall their parents fighting occasionally and the hitting incident just described. They report that their father was always accusing their mother of not fulfilling her motherly duties and that one time, during a fight, she scratched his face after he accused her of having an affair. When Peter left the house for his own apartment, Barry, then eight, was told by Gail that the reason for the breakup was that his parents did not love each other anymore. Vince, who was one year younger, was told that he was too young to know. Looking back, the three sons are still unsure of the reason for the divorce. They have suspicions about what was going on but no clear idea. Susan also does not know of any specific reason. She does remember her parents constantly reassuring the children that although they did not love each other, they both loved them.

During the year they lived with their mother, their old house was sold and they moved to a smaller home. Peter used to see the children on the weekends. He found being a noncustodial father hard, even though he was on good terms with Gail. He says: "Basically, she was a very good mother and we agreed on most things. Everything was done amicably. I had not really considered taking the children. I stayed very involved with the children. But I found it difficult to have to plan weekends, and she resented my spending time at their house, so I had to take the children away from there. It was a problem to spend time with them and it was a problem to entertain them." During this period, Peter says he was making weekly support payments. By all accounts, Peter was a very involved noncustodial parent.

WHY PETER GAINED CUSTODY

Not only do the memories of adults and children differ, so too do the stories given by divorced spouses as to what has happened. In this situation, Peter is speaking for himself; the children are relating what they remember and also what they heard from Gail.

After the children lived with Gail for a year, Peter gained custody. The reasons for this vary depending on who is telling the story. Peter says Gail was having a hard time handling the children, especially the three boys. She went to a lawyer to get help in giving custody to Peter for a year, at which point she wanted to get the children back again. Peter agreed to take the children but said he would not give them back after a year. He felt having the children shuffled from house to house was not in their best interests. Peter said he was happy to gain custody of the children, although he had never really given much thought to what it entailed. It had never occurred to him to pursue custody actively before Gail relinquished it, although Peter remembers wanting the children because he was unhappy with the way the housekeepers Gail hired took care of them.

The children have a different version of what happened during the time they were living with their mother. Although they do not recall many details of their living situation, the sons believe they went to live with their father because he was not making support payments and their mother could not afford to raise them.

Susan, after speaking with Gail, also gives a different account from that given by her father. She says her father was not paying child support and that he took custody of the children in part because he was about to remarry and Gail thought two parents were better than one, and in part because he was unhappy with the way they were being raised. Financial problems brought on by Peter's lack of consistent support payments were also plaguing Gail. Susan adds that after Peter had custody for a year, he wanted to give the children back to Gail, who refused, saying it would not be good for the children to go back and forth.

The children do not recall anything traumatic about the actual switch from one house to the next. They say that one day their parents told them to pack their things to go live with Dad. Susan says: "It occurs to me how flexible we all were. I don't remember being sad at the move. I've always been close to Dad and I was thrilled to be back in the city [where he lived]." At the time, the children were between four and nine years old. Looking back on that time, Susan says: "I do know how much pain she went through having to give up her babies. Mom used to do wonderful things like rock us to sleep, all four of us stretched out on her bed. And she used to wake us up in the morning with a special song that we still remember. It was incredible to me how much energy she put into mothering us."

Life with Dad

Peter says the first thing he did when he got custody was hire a housekeeper. She became the first of a stream of housekeepers who were to play an important part in how the children were raised until Keith reached high school. Peter says that having someone there was a big help to him. The children remember spending a great deal of time with housekeepers. When they were young, this meant that neither the children nor Peter had to deal with the drudgery of housework, which would become a major bone of contention when the children were older.

MONEY

Money was a recurring problem for the family. During that time, Peter's art gallery business was up and down, which meant the family's income also fluctuated. The lack of consistent income over the years left the children with the impression that life was full of great financial uncertainty. According to Peter, Gail would buy them clothes and toys but never sent child-support payments to him. The children remember her giving them all the things that their dad could not afford. When Peter's business was going well, there would be a celebratory mood in the home, followed by periods of belt-tightening.

Other memories concerning money stand out for the children. Vince remembers seeing his father crying one day because of problems with his business. Barry and Keith remember that when things were bad financially, their father's temper flared more quickly. Vince said, looking back on that time: "Finances really put the screws to Dad. Mom did not feel financial pressures and he did, so he screamed more."

SOCIAL LIFE

All the children were popular when growing up. They never felt singled out because they were being raised by a single father. In fact, they said many people did not seem to know they were living with their father. When teachers mentioned a special project that the children were supposed to work on with their mothers, the children made a mental adjustment to asking their father for help or would go to Gail, who, by the children's account, remained very involved with them.

Many of their friends were also products of single-parent families, and this may have eased the transition for them. Vince felt there must have been some common bond that attracted him to the children in these families.

The family moved many times during those years but always stayed in the same school district, so the children's friends remained the same. The reason for the frequent moves was that they lived in rentals because Peter could not afford to buy a house. The constancy of the neighborhood was calculated by Peter to make it easier for the children.

There were bittersweet experiences, also. The children sometimes felt more appreciated by their friends' parents than by their own. Barry and Vince were good athletes; after sporting events, which the children remember Peter rarely attending, the boys would get a great deal of attention at their friends' houses but little at their own. This attention helped to sustain them but made them resentful of their own home life.

A different set of circumstances also drove them to friends' homes. The boys in particular remember there never being much food in the house, especially the kind of junk food children thrive on. They would go to their friends' homes for all the goodies they could not find in their own cupboards.

As already discussed, the memories of children and parents often differ. So do the perspectives they bring to situations that arise. What the children understood about Peter's need to socialize comes from a child's perspective. Adults see these needs in another light. To the children, Peter's dating took him away from them; to Peter it was a necessity.

Peter's social life was very active. Peter explained to the children that they would have to understand his need to socialize and that his life could not totally revolve around them. Peter says there was rivalry at times between the women he dated and his children, but he never felt his social life was handicapped by being a single parent. Some women were turned off by his having children; others were drawn to him because his parenthood made him a more attractive potential husband.

During the time the children were growing up, Peter remembers spending occasional nights out with women. Women were more likely to spend the night with him, usually coming after the children were asleep and leaving early in the morning before they woke up. Peter did not feel the children were bothered too much by his dating.

The children, however, remember being upset by their father's dating. Susan says: "I was jealous of the women Dad dated. And I think they were jealous of the relationship he had with me." Barry remembers being put to bed and then seeing Peter leave. Vince once walked in on Peter when he and a date were lounging in bed. Vince thought nothing of it at the time. All the children feel their father was a better parent when he was not dating because then he had more time for them.

One year after Peter began raising the children, he married a woman named Lisa, whom he had been dating for a while. Peter had reservations about the marriage, thinking she did not fully understand what she was letting herself in for with four children, but she pushed for it. She made no real attempt to parent the children after she moved in. One reason she did not try was that she was small, and most of the children were physically as big as she was. Another is that she did not have what Peter describes as a "maternal instinct"—a characteristic that Peter points out was notably lacking in all his wives.

One year later the marriage ended. Peter says Lisa asked for a divorce because she was frustrated with him. Vince and Barry remember Lisa's leaving. She came out to the porch where they were sitting and started to cry. She told them she was leaving, that she loved them, but that she just could not live with their father. She has had no contact with the family since them.

HOUSEKEEPING

Sometimes children in one-parent families are called on to do more around the home than they did when both parents were in the home. In this family, as in many others, the assumption of new responsibilities for Peter and the children led to problems. At times an oldest daughter is singled out as the father's confidant.

As the children got older, they began taking care of themselves with the help of Susan and Barry. A housekeeper was no longer needed. Peter says the decision not to continue to hire one was based on the children's age, the expense, and the difficulty in getting a good housekeeper.

Without a housekeeper, the work that had been done by someone else fell to Peter and the four children. Sometimes Peter would be traveling and would leave the children on their own. Keith describes an evening routine of Peter being out, Susan cooking, and Barry going around and locking up the doors and windows. In addition to the housework, which the children shared with Peter, at early ages they made their own lunches, much to the amazement of their friends.

Susan felt that although she did the same amount of housework as the other children, she shouldered more of the emotional burden in the home. She said she played the role of the wife every day when Peter came home. She would ask him how his day had gone and talk with him about his relationships and the family's financial situation. This began when she was fourteen. This was also the age at which she ran away from home. "I was frustrated. I was feeling pressure at home from all the emotional responsibility. I ran away for a few days and then came back home. Dad never said anything about my being gone. It was like, 'Well, you've been gone and now you are back.' But even then, whenever we kids did something like that, we would call our mother and check in with her."

Without a housekeeper, the door was also open to a long series of battles over housework. The children say their father would come home from work and say, "I work all day and should not have to come home and clean this house, too." The children say that Peter would resent Barry and Vince going to sports team practices because it meant they could not help out with the cleaning. They recall constant battling and screaming over the housework and being hit occasionally if it was not done. They feel they were given too much responsibility at the time and, in turn, not enough restrictions on their behavior. They were allowed to come and go as they pleased when they were growing up—a situation that made them, by their own description, "viciously independent."

Peter agrees that housework was a problem for the family. He feels he made a particular point of not putting too much pressure on Susan to take care of the younger boys. He wonders if he should have put more pressure on them to assume responsibility. He says he was home a good deal of the time and, if he had to travel, it was for no more than a week at a time.

The children recall one time in particular when he was away for a few nights and left twenty dollars on the table for them to use for food. A big fight erupted over how the money should be spent.

FATHER-CHILDREN RELATIONSHIP

A theme discussed in chapters 5 and 13 and repeated here is the difference in the nature of the relationship that sometimes develops between fathers and sons and fathers and daughters. The three sons differ from Susan in the feelings they hold toward Peter. In turn, the way the sons feel about Gail is also different than what Susan feels.

Vince and Keith said they were afraid of their father's temper. Keith said: "When things were bad, he was on us. We caught it. He slapped us a lot. He was unpredictable and would explode. But he would calm down immediately and everything would be okay right after that." Vince felt Peter picked on him especially: "He never gave us support. He deals with us now better as friends than he did when we were growing up. One time when he was picking on me a lot, I was twelve at the time, I decided to run away. Keith came too, and we rode our bicycles twenty-five miles to Mom's house. Only she wasn't home that weekend. So we stayed there alone." While Vince and Keith were upset and scared by Peter's yelling, Barry was able to immunize himself against it: "I did not let it bother me at all. I learned to ignore it."

Keith reported that after his siblings had grown up and left the house, his relationship with his father hit a particularly bad period. He remembers Peter being after him to do the housework and their having a fight during which Keith threatened Peter with a screwdriver. Keith said that after that point he got along much better with his father.

Vince believes Peter may have felt uncomfortable in his role as father. There were times when they felt he did not know what to do with them, and this made things awkward for everyone. Barry remembers his father sitting down with him to discuss sex: "I had learned all about it from the kids in school, and when Dad sat down with me to discuss it, I said I knew about it already. He seemed very relieved."

Susan reports a much different relationship with her father: "I've always been very close to my dad. Mom says it has been that way since I was born. Dad and I have some very similar outlooks on life. I've always made a special time to be with him and felt a lot of love from him. He was very involved in my life. We shared many of the same interests. I remember times in my life when I was hurting and he was there. But I also see that his relationship to me, as both parent and a person, was very different than the relationships he had with my brothers. They are much more angry."

The children feel that Peter's work was his salvation. It was what saved him from having to spend too much time at home in a role in which they feel he ultimately was uncomfortable.

Peter says that although he did find single parenting harder than he had anticipated, he enjoyed it. He realizes there were difficult times between him and the children, especially his sons. He says he had definite ideas about how things should be done around the home and admits to having a temper. His temper may have affected how well he got along with the children as they were growing up. He feels he spent an adequate amount of time with his children, however, given the circumstances of his work, and remembers attending many school functions in which they were involved.

When the three oldest children had left home for college, Peter married Helen, his third wife. Peter and Helen are currently separated. She did not play an important part in their upbringing but now, since she and Peter have separated, remains in contact with most of the children. She even attended Keith's college graduation. Like Gail and Lisa, Helen is described as having few motherly attributes.

Whereas the children saw Peter as begging for his freedom from them, he saw himself as trying in many different ways to get along with the four children while also trying to run a tight ship. There were many happy times, too. Both the children and Peter have fond memories of meals around the dinner table, and of trips to the beach. They did then and still do find Peter a fascinating person to talk with. Even though Peter did not have a fondness for sports in common with his sons ("They must have gotten their athletic ability from their mother," he jokes), the sons tell of having an especially good time building things with Peter at home. Working on a project with their father took on a special importance for them because it was something they could all share.

GAIL AND THE CHILDREN

The three sons took a protective stance concerning their mother. During the time the children were living with Peter, Gail, according to the children, was playing a very important part in their lives. Not only were they visiting her an average of once a week, but she was giving them a great deal of emotional support. Vince said that Gail, who lived in a series of apartments, always picked a place to live where there would be an extra room to sleep in and a swimming pool or a basketball court nearby. Barry said that even though she did not live with them, he always knew she would be there if they needed her. "We knew we were a priority in her life," he said. Keith said: "She was there when we felt lonely, sad, or beaten up on. We could call her." Susan adds that their mother was the key parent for her brothers, whereas her father was the key parent for her.

Susan's relationship with her mother when the children were younger was different: "I was the only person who really rejected Mom. My brothers, especially Vince and Barry, never did that. Sometimes I think this is also the reason Dad felt so comfortable with me. I think I really felt deserted by her. But I also saw to it that we did not speak. There was about a year and a half when I refused to have anything to do with her. She'd call and I wouldn't talk to her if I answered the phone. So you see, in a way, Dad had me all to himself. And I was pleased as peaches to be the apple of his eye."

As Susan grew up, their relationship changed. "It's easier for me to discuss my relationship with Mom as it is now. When I turned nineteen it was as if there was this sudden desire to get to know and understand this lady, and we've been very close ever since. As I've gotten older it is now Mom who I turn to for emotional guidance and assistance. We talk at least once a week. We share some crazy times laughing. It's been just a joy for us to grow closer and closer."

Sometimes if there were fights in the house and Keith was feeling overwhelmed by his older siblings, he would call Gail and she would mediate over the phone, talking first to one child and then to the other. Peter, out shopping for art, was often unreachable at those times. It was also Gail who attended sports events at school and gave support where the sons felt Peter offered very little. Occasionally she would come to school conferences, too.

Although the children loved the attention they got when they went to their mother's (she would cook special meals for them and buy them clothes), they also were aware that she was spoiling them. Like their father, she did not put many restrictions on them. Vince perhaps depended on her the most. During his junior and senior years in high school, he spoke with her on the phone every day. He would call her each morning to wake her up for work: "If I did not call her, she would get up late."

The children are happy their parents have stayed on such good terms. They feel they reaped the benefits. For seven years after the breakup the whole family continued to get together for Christmas. Gail and Peter, along with Peter's third wife, Helen, attended Keith's college graduation. As well as they got along, the children are aware that things are better than if they stayed together. "They are such opposites," Keith says. "I would rather have the family we have now where everyone gets along. We have the best of both worlds. They made a good team, but I am glad they did not stay together. They did not love each other, and it worked out better for all of us."

Peter has a different view of the relationship between Gail and the children. He does not think she was a very involved parent: "She would see them on the weekends, but I always thought she was breezing in and out and trying to fit them into her life. She never offered to take them for any length of time. One time I called her and said: 'Look, I have to get away for a vacation for a week. Would you please take them?' She was happy to do it but she never offered on her own. She almost never made any attempt to regain custody of them." Because of what he perceived as her lack of concern about the children, he seldom consulted her about decisions affecting them and handled them on his own.

The Children as Adults

The children, having described their experiences growing up, were asked to talk about how they see their lives now. They were asked about their views on being raised by their father, marriage, and having children. They were also questioned about their apparent protectiveness toward their mother.

The sons, for different reasons, feel sorry for both their parents. They feel their mother, who never remarried, sacrificed everything for them. They see her as the victim in the relationship between her and their father. It is this perception of her as a victim that may cause them to be protective of her now. There is no such protectiveness evident when they talk about their father. They feel sorry for their father because of the awkwardness they think he felt as a father and because they think he now feels guilty about not spending more time with them when they were younger.

Susan has no such feelings of remorse for either parent, but she is more content with her own situation. (One of the more interesting points that came out of the interviews is that, despite some of the anger the sons in particular feel for their father, both they and Susan are glad they lived with him rather than with Gail.)

The children were asked to reflect on whether they felt there was anything different about being raised by a father than by a mother and whether this had any effect on them now as adults. This is a difficult issue because the way that one is parented is idiosyncratic to the personalities of the father and mother and to other facets of the home situation. Also complicating this question is the fact that the children were not isolated from their mother while they were growing up.

Vince said that one of the differences in being raised by a father was that they turned out to be stronger people, more independent: "We grew up faster." Keith states: "We all benefited from living with him. Mothers are so damn protective. We were exposed to things that a lot of kids were not exposed to. We were better off without her, but we knew she was on call. Dad either taught us or forced us to have responsibility. We are all very commonsensical. From our first bicycle on, we have learned how to raise money and go out and do our own things so we can survive, and we have gained a lot from that which could be due directly or indirectly to Dad."

One exchange between the sons further brought out some of the issues they were feeling about being raised by their father and not their mother, and the impact it had on them. Barry said: "Glad we weren't raised by her. She would have spoiled us. It was nice to go there and be spoiled, but it turned out better being raised by Dad." Keith responded to this, "I don't know if we had lived there full time if she would have spoiled us." Vince added: "She didn't really have the chance to spoil us. She had us three months out of twenty-five years."

Barry looked at his brothers for a moment and said: "We are all viciously independent. With relationships, I have had a hard time. I am very selfish because I am used to getting my own way, because we always got our way. There was no one to tell us otherwise." Vince agreed with this: "Yeah, we all have built cubicles around ourselves, whether it be for protection or because we've had to. Almost to the point of being selfish like Dad. Because we have had so little, we are reluctant to relinquish what we have. So we're selfish."

"Do I wish Mom raised me instead of Dad? This is a funny question," Susan wrote, "and one that I have talked a lot about over the years. Mom would have been a lot stricter with me than Dad. Dad basically gave me free rein. But I was never in need of a lot of supervision and restrictions. I don't know how I would have turned out with Mom. I know when it comes to the custody issue, I wouldn't break up my children, but I would agree to let my husband raise them if he could do a better job of it. But I have this very keen desire to have children one day."

Susan, in a separate conversation, echoed this theme of independence: "I'm probably more independent and self-sufficient because of all the love I have gotten from him." She adds that it has had a positive effect on her relationships with other people: "An interesting thing has resulted from the [pending] divorce [between Susan and her husband]. I place such a strong emphasis on honesty and friendship from men, I've never really learned how to play games. Some men find this disarming. Men and I are equals and allowed to have the same or more similar roles in a relationship. This has caused a problem sometimes."

The sons also hold a view of women that reflects a great deal of respect for their equality. Keith says: "I see them as equal but think our peers do not. They have had two-parent families and have seen mothers in a certain way, and I think we see them in a more up-to-date way than they do." Vince, who is currently separated from his wife, agrees that women should be equal but admits to trying to get out of sharing the housework in his own marriage.

Vince wonders whether seeing his father always acting so protectively of his own feelings has affected his relationship with his wife. He finds it difficult to share his time with her in a way that may be similar to the difficulty Peter had in sharing with them. Keith reiterates the feelings of Barry and Vince but adds a dimension that is similar to that mentioned by many children of divorce: "We never had parents who showed affection for each other so it's hard to know how to do it now. I also feel there is this box that I have built around me. It is like the song 'Cat's Cradle,' where the father sees his son has grown up just like him and does not want to see him. It scares me to think I will be selfish like him. Kids like to be held and told they are loved and stuff like that."

Barry, hearing this reference to the song, said: "I am scared I am going to grow up like him, being selfish with my own children. I don't want to have kids." Keith also worries about how he will react with his children and wonders when he will be ready for childrearing: "What scares me is that I have seen so many families so neat and tight and think that is great. I don't have anything to give me guidelines. But I am hoping some day. . . ." Vince, because he is married, has given the most consideration to parenting. He feels good about the prospect of being a father: "I want to take my kids and do the opposite of what I got." Not having felt much support from his father, he wants to make sure his children get it from him.

Susan is the most optimistic about marriage: "Marriage is very important to me. Inside me I have this very basic belief that life is fair, and that even though this [marriage] did not work out, the next one will and I am not afraid to push forward."

Peter has been affected by his relationships with his children over the years. Not only has he become a lot more relaxed with them, he has moved increasingly into the role of friend rather than parent. He has become a lot more affectionate physically. Vince notes: "He recently has been very demonstrative and has done hugging and kissing in the last few years. For a long time there was no contact, but there is now. It makes me feel better. I like it." Peter believes he has done as good a job raising his children as was possible, and he is proud of them.

The children also talk about how well they have all turned out. Vince says how he is happily puzzled that, with all they went through, none of them got in trouble with the law or became involved with drugs. He and his siblings all echoed the belief that the family, despite various problems, has turned out well.

Susan, ever the optimist, said: "I only feel blessed for the relationships I have with both of my parents. They were always there when I needed them in very different periods of my life. And now that I'm away, our relationships have even gotten stronger."

Conclusions (1984)

The family is in a period of transition. The last child has finished college, and both parents can let go of a little more of their parenting responsibilities. The children now describe relations with their parents ranging from tolerant to very warm. Their personal lives reflect some failure and concern about future relationships. The sons worry about their ability to have adequate relationships with women. Yet they take pride in having turned out well. Their fears about how they will handle the future are on their mind, but at the same time they believe in themselves.

In other ways the family's situation is similar to that of many of the single fathers who took part in the survey. The family's fluctuating income was a recurring problem. Housekeepers could be afforded, but other amenities often could not. Peter's work schedule sometimes made family routines difficult to follow. As in many single-parent families, the children may have "grown up a little faster" because of the responsibility they all had. They became "viciously independent," perhaps at too early an age.

There is a general consensus among the children that being raised by a father fostered this independence, that mothers protect children more and spoil them. Their father had a more analytical or commonsensical approach that is a reflection of the way many men approach situations. In this sense, what these children had growing up is different than if they had been raised by their mother. What they will teach their own children, if they have them, will probably be different, too. Barry, Vince, and Keith want their children to have a better experience than they had. Susan hopes she can have as good a relationship with her children as she has with her parents.

Five Years Later

In 1989, five years after the initial interview, Peter was recontacted and interviewed about his children. He is still running an art gallery and experiencing the ups and downs that are so common in that business. He has developed a serious relationship with a single mother who raised her three daughters alone and he expects to marry her in the near future. Susan and Vince, both of whom were undergoing marital difficulties in 1984, have divorced and remarried. Susan, now thirty-three, is the happy mother of a daughter and wants to have a second child. Peter says, "She loves mothering, loves being home, and is in no hurry to get back to work." Vince, thirty, has been remarried for a year and is also interested in having children. Barry, thirty-one, and Keith, twenty-eight, are both successful in their careers and are involved to varying degrees in relationships with women.

The three sons have lived near each other and in the same area as their mother, Gail, for over five years. The proximity to Gail was important to them when they were in their twenties, but as their careers progress, this closeness is threatened. Keith is about to be transferred to the midwest and Vince may move away also. Thus the family, as commonly happens when the next generation is upwardly mobile, is spreading further apart.

Peter says he, like all parents, wishes he had more contact with his children. They speak occasionally on the phone and were together as a family in the sons' part of the country over Christmas. He visited Gail then, also. "We had a pleasant time together," he said. "I think as a family we've been very fortunate. There always seems to be a problem or conflict to solve in other families, while nothing serious has come up in ours. Things are going quite well."

For Peter and the children, as probably with all families, there was ambivalence and questioning about the past and the experiences they had. With more time and greater maturity, some of the self-doubts about the past have receded. The apparent successes of the family members have helped them achieve a greater sense of well-being. Confidence in the future continues to grow. In many ways, this family may represent what the experiences of the other families in this book will be in the future. And that future is a hopeful one.

13

What Every Father Should Know about His Children

with Risa Garon

PARENTING is not an easy task. It was not easy when there were two parents in the home and is likely to be much harder when you are doing it alone. In most single-parent families, when the mother moves out it means a loss of daily support and advice. It also means you no longer have the time off from the children that her presence was providing. You, like many other single parents, most likely have your hands full. Gaining an understanding of your children can go a long way toward helping them and you adjust to the divorce process and to life in the single-parent family.

At the time of separation, most parents are bombarded with so many concerns that they may tell their children about the divorce in a perfunctory manner without focusing on the children's feelings and concerns. They may also, without being aware of it, discourage the children from sharing their feelings in the belief that talking about these feelings will be painful for them. This conveys to the children that it is not okay to have feelings about this major family change. Parents may believe that because their children do not have visible symptoms or problems, there is no reason to discuss the divorce. Yet experts who have worked with families of divorce agree that children experience a grief process similar to the parents' grief experience. Your children probably are experiencing some of the feelings of loss and anger that you feel or felt. Just as you need to work to resolve these feelings, they do, too. To optimize your children's growth in healthy ways, consider the following short-term and long-term goals for them:

1. Help your children understand that they did not cause a marital separation;

2. Help your children maintain a loving relationship with each parent;

3. Help your children to feel capable of having their own loving relationships in the future;

4. Help your children resolve the anger around the divorce and disengage from ongoing parental conflict.

Help Your Children with Their Feelings

Common feelings in addition to anger and loss are shame, loneliness, relief, sadness, anxiety, and ambivalence. Often children experience a variety of seemingly contradictory feelings. A child may be happy and relieved to be with her father but feel lonely for her mother and cry for her at night. Try and accept whatever your child is feeling. There are no right or wrong feelings. You can set a positive tone by sharing and conveying a message that it is okay for parents and children to have uncomfortable feelings and to talk about them. Acceptance of feelings different from yours as a parent is crucial in sharing and developing trust with children. Beginning this process may seem awkward and risky but it can establish a method of healthy communication between parents and children.

UNDERSTANDING THE LOSS

One of the most common feelings we have seen in children after a separation or divorce is loss. Similar to feelings involved with death, children adjusting to parental separation experience the loss of a parent, the loss of time with both parents, and the loss of an image of family. Some children will handle the loss by denying it: they may keep it to themselves for a long time; they may make up stories about what their "family" (with both parents still together) did over the weekend; they may fantasize that a parent has returned. Try not to take their denial personally. They are not denying you as their parent but rather the pain of the situation. Younger children may develop physical symptoms, while older children may misbehave in school to get both parents working together. There are the classic stories of children who become ill, notice their separated parents are joined together in concern over them (perhaps for the first time in months), and remain ill to keep their parents together. Parents can help reduce this attempt to get them back together by explaining the reasons behind the divorce. When done appropriately, this can establish a realistic base and give the children understanding and reassurance about the change. Without badmouthing each other, parents can explain the reason for the marriage ending. Children have the opportunity to understand aspects of their parents' personalities and situations they were not previously aware of. This can help the children realize they were not responsible for the breakup. It can also, where appropriate, place the possibility for reconciliation in a realistic context. We acknowledge, of course, that parents do reconcile. That is why parents need to share aspects of the separation with their children that are realistic and are put in terms that children their age can understand. Whether you are discussing reconciliation or a permanent separation, being realistic prevents your children from feeling a false sense of hope.

Sometimes children's feelings of loss remain with them. Despite the growing number and visibility of single-parent families, many children still feel "it's not the same" as an intact family. One boy said he likes his girlfriend's family more than his own because hers is a "normal family with a father and mother." Many children lose not only their intact family but extended family as well, such as grandparents, aunts, uncles, and cousins. It is very helpful when parents can acknowledge the pain or loss their children feel.

Parents and children can cope with their feelings of loss in positive ways. They can foster a unique identity for their single-parent family by making a fresh start in how they think of themselves. For example, new rituals or customs can be established. Perhaps the children can cook dinner every Sunday night or plan the menu. Maybe you and the children can do something with another family once a week or have a time after dinner to sit together and read or play a game. Most children need structure and routine to feel secure and part of a family. Having children take part in establishing a routine appropriate to their age can add a sense of permanence and hopeful expectation that a random day-by-day schedule cannot provide.

WORKING WITH ANGER

Anger is difficult for most people to express and resolve. In many situations in which anger is expressed, there is an accompanying feeling of hurt or disappointment. Rather than expressing their feelings directly, children sometimes contain them until something sets them off. By that time those feelings have built up and are expressed in explosive terms, or rage. A teenage girl was scheduled to have dinner and spend the evening with her mother. Even though she felt very pressured, with two exams and a paper due the following day, she decided she would still keep the date. She planned to explain her predicament over dinner, cutting short their time together while still being able to have half of the visit. Disaster struck. Her mother blew up and yelled, "You don't care about me and you never call anymore except when you want something." The girl, feeling the same hurt as her mother, ran out in a rage. Discussing her feelings with her mother later, the mother was able to say that she felt hurt that her daughter did not seem to want to spend much time with her. Hearing her daughter's response about the pressure of school, she was able to see this was not a deliberate withdrawal on her daughter's part, but reflected the behavior of a normal adolescent. For each of them, their sense of being misunderstood had been building for months. Because their feelings had not been talked about as they occurred in specific situations, they were expressed inappropriately.

Many parental behaviors can fuel a child's anger. In fact, the list is quite long. One parent's leaving the home, having an affair, being an alcoholic, working too hard, neglecting the other parent, and so on are all behaviors that upset children. Specific divorce issues that exacerbate children's anger are feeling embarrassed by the divorce, having two sets of homes, two sets of rules, and having to travel back and forth, being exposed to ongoing parental conflict, undergoing financial changes, being split up from a sibling, dealing with a parent's new spouse, boyfriend, or child, and losing the idealized sense of family.

When children do not have a vehicle through which to express their anger directly, they may internalize it and feel depressed—powerless that they cannot effect any change in their lives. They may become physically symptomatic with headaches and stomachaches and ulcers. They may displace their anger onto their siblings, peers and, yes, maybe even you! They may get into a lot more fights and start running with the "wrong set" of friends. They may experiment increasingly with sex, alcohol, or drugs.

Parents wonder what to do if children express anger toward the other parent. We encourage reality testing—do not deny the problem and feelings but do not pour gasoline on them, either. Check out the problem in a nonjudgmental way. If what your child says is accurate, she or he has a need to be understood and respected by you and may need adult help.

A factor related to your children's expression of anger is how they perceive your handling your own anger. Many children complain that their parents will not "let them be mad," but yet the parents can be angry and take it out on the children. Your being able to express anger openly and appropriately allowing your children to do the same can be helpful.

The more closely you are in touch with your own anger and can express it in various degrees from slight annoyance to rage, the better model you will be for their handling anger in healthy ways. If you can state that you are angry, what factors are contributing to your anger, and what you need to do to resolve it, you are well on your way to providing that healthy model. You are also allowing your children to be angry and to express it. This is different from parents and children kicking in doors, or screaming four-letter words at each other and running away.

Recognize, though, that it is probably difficult for you as a parent to be the recipient of your children's anger, especially if it is inappropriately expressed. Sometimes, parents and children need a cooling-off period before they can be civil with each other. At a calm time, parents and children can discuss healthy ways to resolve their intense feelings of anger in order to communicate feelings to each other.

How can you set an example? For instance, if you are angry that your children were late and did not call you, tell them: "I am angry that you didn't call me when you knew you'd be late," or "I was hurt because you were inconsiderate," rather than burying your feelings. At the same time, do not give them the message that their behavior can control your feelings to a great extent. You must take that responsibility on yourself. Engage in physical exercise if you need to rid yourself of tension. That can help you think and express yourself clearly. Time outs are crucial for survival. When children and parents say they are too angry to talk, call a truce. Send the children (or yourself) to another room and state that you will resume your discussion when there is less tension.

When Children Worry

Children have many worries about their own and their parents' lives. After a divorce, they usually hear vague discussions about money, college, child support, sale of homes, and so on. They worry about not having enough money for their needs and they worry about the safety and security of their parents. Afraid to share their fears with parents, children often worry about the death of the parent they live with and what will happen to them in the future, particularly if they don't have a close relationship with the other parent. When such eventualities are spelled out in the form of wills and/or divorce decrees, it is important to inform children and discuss their feelings and concerns. You may even possibly alter what has been agreed upon by you and their mother if the children raise grave concerns about those decisions.

Usually, children and adults can work through the more acute process of the divorce within two years. Although this may seem like two hundred years, time not only heals wounds but allows you to develop your new family unit. While the adjustment to divorce is a continuing process, there is usually a time when parents and children accept their new family structure. Children begin to feel secure again. They fantasize less about parents being together. Fathers and children establish rituals, have shared jokes, ways of doing things, favorite places and new people in their lives. Children are able to focus on their own tasks—school, friends, and activities—and the divorce is no longer foremost in their minds. It helps to remember that adjusting to separation and divorce is an ongoing process. If parents and children can understand that it is appropriate and normal to continue to ask questions and raise concerns about the divorce, they will feel more comfortable sharing with each other. Sharing feelings without being judged or considered abnormal can serve as a wonderful example for parents and children to communicate about other matters as well.

KEEPING CHILDREN OUT OF THE MIDDLE

Parents remain parents to their children forever. Although children may leave home, there are still weddings and births and graduations, and other decisions and events that may call for both parents' involvement with their children and each other. One of the most important achievements parents can work toward is getting along with each other to be effective parents to their children. Research on the significance of this relationship clearly emphasizes the *damage* that is done when parents do not get along and continue to put the children in the middle. Children talk about how hurt they feel when a parent badmouths the other parent in front of them. It is important to understand that children have a sense of loyalty to each parent and feel caught when that loyalty is threatened.

There is a distinction that needs to be made concerning comments a parent might make about the other parent. To discuss negative feelings and opinions about the mother is badmouthing. "Your mother is a no-good alcoholic" is an example. Commenting on the behavior of a parent to protect and help your child understand that parent's problems is not badmouthing.

"I'm concerned about your driving in the car with your mother when you tell me she's drinking," is exercising parental responsibility. (With young children you must step in here and prevent it.)

Parents can serve as sounding boards for their children's expressions about their other parent. "It sounds like the visit was really hard because Mom didn't play with you," can help the children ventilate as well as explore ways to express their feelings directly to that other parent. "What can you say to Mom the next time you're together?" helps children see that they have choices.

Sometimes children need confirmation that the other parent has problems and/or has trouble being an effective parent. Parents feel ambivalent because they want their children to have loving relationships with the other parent, yet feel a need to protect them from being hurt by that parent. The hurt can stem from a missed visit or from physical or emotional abuse by the other parent. Permitting children to explore their feelings and concerns is a key to the solution. How do they feel about the other parent? What would they like to do about visits? Parents may "push" the children into loving the other parent when children do not have loving feelings or need time to work through their hurt and anger. One fourteen-year-old youngster we worked with did not like going to his father's new apartment. It hurt him too much because it reminded him of his father's leaving. He would go there for dinner but it took him years before he'd sleep over. If his mom had pushed him, he would have been very upset. Another sixteen-year-old girl refused to see her mother because her behavior toward her was so inconsistent. "I feel like I'm on the end of a yo-yo and if I'm not perfect, she'll destroy me with negative criticism!"

Children feel extremely torn and tense when they are subjected to continued arguing between parents. "I thought they got divorced to stop all this arguing," children frequently tell us. Children become fearful and angry, and worry about the safety of their parents and themselves. It is important to remember that as parents you're providing coping models for your children. It would be helpful if children were not around when you talked or argued with their mother. Children sometimes blame themselves if they are named during arguments and they need reassurance that they do not cause personal conflict.

One winter, a nine-year-old living with his mother talked about how he was a messenger for his parents. His mother told him to tell his father to take him to the mall for boots. The father told him to tell his mother he would not buy boots when he was paying such large child-support bills. The father refused to buy the boots; the child was anxious the whole weekend with him because he feared that his mother would be mad at him. These conflicts become burdens to children and prevent them from feeling at ease with either parent. They need to focus on their own appropriate age-related tasks rather than assuming adult responsibilities.

Parents also may make their children detectives to keep informed about court hearings, new relationships, and the other parent's social and financial life ("Is Dad dating anyone new?" "Does Mom have any new furniture?") When parents tell their children specifically not to tell the other parent about a piece of information, children feel very conflicted. They would prefer not having to be responsible for that request.

Again, as the custodial parent, you can help your children by talking to them, encouraging them to express their feelings to their other parent, remaining neutral when possible, and supporting your children as the behavior and situations with the other parent indicate. This places them in control of situations and can further help reduce their worrying. It also permits them the chance to establish loving relationships with both parents, which can serve as models for their establishing relationships with other people as they become adults.

At times, of course, giving children more control is not needed. There is not one divorced parent who has not talked about being manipulated by the children. Children may be the ones pitting one parent against the other and avoiding responsibility for their behavior. All children, regardless of their family situations, will try to "put one over" on a parent to get their way. Having divorced parents makes it easier. "Well, if I were with Mommy, she'd let me." (When, in fact, Mom said *no* yesterday!) Especially when you are trying to establish a closer relationship with your children and want things to go well with their mother, it is hard to accept that they may have reasons for not wanting things to go well. One way of dealing with this is to find out what is at the root of this behavior. Does the child want to live somewhere else? Is there too much or not enough visitation? Does the child want more freedom? Communicating with your ex-wife about it can help to short-circuit attempts to have parents disagree.

Finally, you may discover after long, hard work on your relationship with your children that they want to go live with their mother. It is natural to feel devastated by this but important to give your children the opportunity to try. Experts in the field see this as an attempt on the child's part to try one last time to have a close relationship with the other parent and/or put closure on that relationship before they become adults. You will need to be ready to "catch" your children if there are problems with the new living situation and the children want to return. Discuss this in advance. Decide how long your child can try living with his or her mother. Try to remain flexible, while not giving the message that your child can come and go. Use this as an opportunity to teach your child how to handle relationships responsibly and to understand that he or she has an impact on other people.

To further help you understand your children, we would like to present the results of a survey conducted among young adults who had spent some or all of their childhood living alone with their father.[1] These adult children ranged in age from eighteen to twenty-six, had an average age of twenty, and, with the exception of two, were either employed or in college. The majority of them (nineteen) were female and they came from nineteen different states. They had lived with their father an average of seven years, with the range being from one to sixteen years.

Twenty-six Young Adults Discuss Their Experiences Being Raised by Dad

"I would like to say that not every parent is like my father. He is a very patient and understanding man. Now that I am older, I feel that my father and I have developed a wonderful relationship. I can discuss everyday problems that I face, such as men, sex, school, money, friends, and drugs. I enjoyed the way I was brought up. Every family has benefits and problems just as we did."

Those are the words of Jane, an eighteen-year-old who spent thirteen years of her childhood being raised by her father. She and her brother were abandoned by their mother when both were quite young and they have not seen her for years. Jane, currently a college student living at home, feels optimistic about her future. It has not been easy, though. The teen years were marked by conflict around her smoking and drinking and the family's financial problems. Well aware of the struggles fathers have in raising children alone, she offers the following advice: "Be easy on your father, because it is twice the work for him to understand you as it is for a mother. Discuss your feelings and problems with him. If you don't feel comfortable doing that, talk to a friend or seek counseling."

Jane is fairly typical of the young adults who responded in the study. Common conflicts in their teen years revolved around curfews, money, smoking cigarettes, drugs, drinking, the types of friends the teen associated with, and household responsibilities—not that different from most teens!

A twenty-year-old named Ali complained about the chores she was given when she first began living with her father. He gained custody four years ago after her mother, who had a series of mental breakdowns, moved out of state. Immediately she was given responsibility for the home and her twelve-year-old sister. She believed her biggest conflict with her father revolved around the home. "He wanted a housekeeper, not a *very* active sixteen-year-old." The household responsibilities were just one sign of problems that were brewing in other parts of their relationship. "He had trouble understanding the emotions of a teenage girl. His temper flared and I would often end up crying." Her mother was no help to her. "There was a great loss of closeness between us. She said we weren't close because my father brainwashed me. But she had a breakdown and left me—I never left her."

As a young adult Ali has a somewhat cynical view of the experience. "I learned how to deal with men living with my father. I'm not disillusioned by them now as many of my college friends are." Yet Ali also is aware of the pressures her father was under. She gives the following advice: "Try to be understanding—they are going through a rough period as well."

COMMON THEMES IN THE TEEN YEARS

The teen years are frequently difficult regardless of whether a teen is living with one parent or two. We wondered what conflicts these young adults had had during those years. Sometimes the question was avoided and an angry response given instead. One twenty-year-old young man who had a very difficult time living with his father replied, "We never talked about problems—I never could talk to him. He was never wrong." When his parents split up, he was seventeen. The only reason he stayed with his father was to finish high school in his home town, because his mother had moved. Later he softened slightly and, when asked if there was anything good about having lived with his father, answered, "I matured a lot faster and learned the values of life faster. In a sense, I don't regret living with him."

Not everyone had problems during the teen years having to do specifically with the father-child relationship. Sue, twenty-one years old, answered, "There were never really any struggles. I was really just angry at the divorce situation—not at my father or mother." She had been living with her father since she was fifteen. Sue chose to live with him because he was staying in the home and because she got along with him better than with her mother. A college student who now lives in a dormitory, she spends free weekends split between her parents. Things were not always smooth between Sue and her mother, though. "I was very angry that she left my father. I did not speak to her or her new husband for a year after the divorce. Now we get along much better."

Difficulties in working out a relationship with the noncustodial mother were common. The most frequent complaints were that these young adults felt uncomfortable with her because of anger they felt toward her, because of her drinking, and because of the men she was seeing. The following are examples that were given: "I didn't see her—I had inner conflicts about her, though." "I didn't like to go to her house because of her boy-friend." "I was very angry with her that she had abandoned me." "Alcohol (hers)."

When Teenage Daughters Are Raised by a Father

To some extent, being raised by a father was problematic for daughters. Half the females, when asked what was the most difficult aspect about being raised by a father, gave answers that indicated that, because they were female, they did not feel understood. None of the sons gave this response. This sheds further light on the finding presented in chapter 5—that the fathers expressed the greatest satisfaction raising preadolescent daughters. It may be that with adolescence, some of the comfort that existed between father and daughter gets replaced by increasing discomfort. The daughters here mentioned that they did not feel they could talk to their fathers about "female things" and that a "man would not understand" some of the feelings they needed to talk about. One twenty-five-year-old said, "In my house, there were all boys so I was in all male surroundings. I found it hard to develop feminine traits, like nurturing and hugging." Another female said it was difficult to talk to her father because, "I was very shy about my period and not being able to talk with him about sex." Finally, one young adult spoke of the confusion she had in maintaining boundaries between herself and her father. She and her two younger siblings moved in with their father when she was fourteen. They were living with him because her mother "wanted other things than three children and a husband and he loved us very much." She became overly attached to him and found separation at the age of nineteen to be tough. "I have become too dependent on him and now he doesn't have any time for me." In a similar vein, a few daughters complained that they were being pushed into the mother's role in the home, a role they usually did not want and one that sons were not pushed into.

Some of the feelings these daughters express are signs of miscommunication and the normal tension that can develop between a father and daughter. Part of growing up is reaching the stage of identifying with your own sex. As part of this stage, young men and women feel more comfortable talking about certain issues with same-sex adults. The responses of these daughters should not be taken to mean that they would have preferred living with their mothers—in many cases the daughters chose the father. A different set of feelings might have emerged if they had been living with their mother. Rather, it points out the need for fathers raising daughters to be acutely aware of their needs when they reach puberty.

At the same time, the daughters accrued benefits from being raised by their fathers. Some said they became more independent and had a better understanding of men. Others said they learned about "male things" like cars and machinery that they felt they would not have learned from their mothers.

Sons complained also about having to babysit and take on more responsibility. Only one of the eight sons, though, said he felt he could not talk about his feelings with his father. Either there is an easier flow of communication between father and son or sons do not have the desire to talk about their feelings with their parents to the same extent daughters do.

Their Self-esteem and Their Own Marriages

How have these children of single fathers fared? Without a comparison group of other young adults who were raised by a single mother or by both parents, definitive conclusions cannot be made. This group does provide us with a snapshot that is similar to the pictures provided by other researchers[2] studying young adults raised by their mother—most are doing satisfactorily, though a distinct minority are having problems. Almost two-thirds were content with themselves and a slightly higher number were optimistic about their having a successful marriage. About one-third feel uncomfortable with themselves and slightly less than one-third are pessimistic about their own marriage. Given that these are children of divorce, and that divorce does put children at risk, we could argue that this is not a surprising number. Whether living with a father mitigates or worsens the young adult's outlook cannot be responsibly concluded from the limited survey information. We can say that many children who live with their father while growing up emerge into young adulthood feeling comfortable with themselves and optimistic about the future.

An interesting finding did emerge concerning self-esteem. Daughters who reported that they felt comfortable talking with their father about their feelings at the age of sixteen were more likely to say they were content as a young adult than daughters who said they could not talk to their fathers about their feelings when they were sixteen. One possible message that emerges from this for fathers is that if you work on communication with your teenage daughter, it may pay off for her as a young adult.

Young Adults' Advice for Other Children

Children have a part in making things better in your family. You do not carry all of the responsibility. Many of the young adults offer advice to others living with their father. Not only can you learn from these suggestions, but also you may want to share them with the teenagers or older children living in your home.

The first words of wisdom come from a twenty-year-old college student who lived with her father for fifteen years:

"Dad is taking on two traditional roles, the provider and the nurturer. Remember that all men may have been raised to suppress the 'emotional' side—be sure to seek out nurturing from another source if he is unable to give it to you. You may have to take on additional responsibilities, like helping out around the house. It's okay to learn how to cook and clean up after yourself but *girls,* never assume the surrogate wife or mother role. You could become confused or resentful of this responsibility. Keep it a father-daughter relationship. In addition, do not play matchmaker. It is Dad's job, not yours, to find another mate. Be sure to talk about your sadness or anger because if you don't, the feeling may come out in negative ways. Try to remember the main purpose of parenting is to raise children who are happy with themselves and are capable of surviving when the parent is gone. Stay optimistic. Remember you are going to have your own life one day and hopefully your dad will be a positive part of it. Finally, be sure to tell Dad when he is doing a good job. Let him know you love and appreciate him."

Others said, "Keep communications open—talk about things that are important to you."

"Sit and talk. Make him understand if you think he is wrong—don't let him think he's never wrong."

"Spend as much time as possible with him."

"Get on his good side fast."

"It's tough at times but if your father is like mine it is all worth it."

"Even though it is tough talking to a man about personal things that you need your mother for, do it anyway because it will make you closer."

"Be supportive and very understanding. Don't get discouraged by stressful situations. It will work out!"

"A new situation always takes time. Do not expect too much in the beginning. Stay open to him and tell him how you feel while trying to understand what he is feeling."

"Still keep in touch with your mother."

"If you can be the best you can be you will learn to do things yourself. Gain satisfaction from your personal triumphs—then you won't miss so much the encouragement given by two people (your parents). You won't need it so much because you'll be happy with yourself."

"Be patient. Single fathers have a tough job. As a child you don't realize how hard their job is."

When Therapy is Needed

It is not unusual for parents to realize that professional assistance may be needed to help their children cope with the divorce. Sometimes a father may come to that conclusion on his own, sometimes a child may ask for it, and sometimes another adult, perhaps a schoolteacher, will suggest that the child could benefit from seeing a therapist. This does not mean you have failed as a parent. It does not mean the child is "crazy" or is going to have a problem with relationships for the rest of his life.

Rather, it may be helpful to see your child, and it may apply to yourself, as having difficulty with the transition to the single-parent family. People often get stuck trying to adapt to changes. Seeking professional help at those critical times is one way of dealing with those changes. If you, as a father, can view a therapist as an ally in promoting positive relationships between family members, then therapy can become a time for growth.

When seeking help, you need to view yourself as a consumer of services and shop around for a therapist with whom you and your children will feel comfortable. You can obtain the names of therapists (usually social workers, psychologists, counselors, or psychiatrists) from friends, pediatricians, guidance counselors, and legal professionals. Before you begin calling different therapists find out from your insurance company (if applicable) how much they will reimburse you for individual, family, and group psychotherapy.

Some questions you can ask the therapists are:

1. What experience have they had working with children from divorced families?

2. Does the therapist communicate with the parents and share how the children are doing?

3. If appropriate, does the therapist do family therapy? A therapist who has experience in working with families of divorce will understand how important it is to consider the whole family and not just focus on the child. Because the child is affected by the other family members, it is advisable for those members to be included in some stage of the treatment process.

4. In addition, will the therapist use individual or group treatment? (Peer counseling can be especially effective.)

5. Will the therapist communicate with the school and the child's other parent? If so, what are the procedures and what would you as the father like the school to know?

It is important that you tell your children they are going for counseling. You should also explain when and why. Children complain bitterly when they are not informed in advance and are just deposited at a therapist's door. The need for treatment should be presented in an honest and positive way. Cite positive examples of how your child is coping. Explain the need for the child to have someone outside the family to talk with and that you are willing to be involved. You may also express your concern about your child's negative behaviors and desire to have them resolve particular problems.

As is common, some children will balk at going to therapy. You may have to be firm in having them go and help them overcome their stereotypes of people who see therapists. Your child may say, "I don't need a shrink," or "I'm not crazy." They need reassurance from you that they do not belong in either of these categories. In being firm about their going for help, you can offer them a say in who they will eventually see. You could give them two people to interview, for example, and have them decide who they want to work with. This is also the opportunity to explain about confidentiality and to stress the positive elements of the relationship they will be able to build with the therapist.

Changes Children Make in Therapy

Therapy for your child may mean that he or she undergoes some changes that ultimately will be positive. At the same time, do not expect overnight miracles. The therapy process can take a long time. One of the most significant changes that occurs in treatment is that your child may begin expressing feelings more. For example, many children say that they kept their feelings inside because they did not want to hurt their parents, did not know what they were feeling, or were afraid they would fall apart if they expressed their pain, hurt, anger, or sadness. When children are given an opportunity to express feelings to a therapist, they may come out in a flood that can continue at home. Many of those feelings may be hard for you to hear.

As these feelings start coming out, one danger is that you may believe that the therapist is siding with the child against you. This is especially true if your child says, "My counselor said I should tell you how I feel." Before concluding the therapist is encouraging disrespect of authority, contact the therapist to get his or her exact point of view. For you, listening and responding to your child's feelings may be very painful, particularly when issues are being raised that you have not yet resolved for yourself. You may learn that you have to change, too. Those changes are easier to accept if you have the knowledge that all families, regardless of structure, have problems and that it is a sign of strength, not weakness, if the family members are willing to work on them.

Confidentiality in treatment is a very sticky issue. Children should not have to tell their parents what they tell a therapist. Therapy needs to be viewed by the child as a safe place to talk about themselves and their feelings for both parents. Sometimes parents, in wanting to know how their child is doing, will ask how a treatment session went. They will get upset when the child rebuffs them with a vague answer or tells them it is none of their business. Parents may suspect the child is keeping something from them, that therapy is not helping them, or that the therapist and child are colluding. Those concerns should be discussed with the therapist but the parent must remember that a confidential relationship is very important to the child's progress. It may also help the child to separate himself or herself from the parents' conflicts by drawing a protective boundary the parents cannot cross.

One of the most telling signs that therapy is helping is when children can speak for themselves, be assertive, and disengage from their parents' conflicts. They may state that they feel caught in the middle of those conflicts. You may hear your children say they have other plans and cannot do something with you. Or they may make different requests of you than they had before. When the children no longer feel responsible for your feelings and those of your ex-wife, you can breathe a sigh of relief that they are going on with their lives in healthy ways. Each family has to encourage autonomy and when children, especially teens, begin to break away, it is often a healthy sign.

To conclude this chapter, we would like to offer specific suggestions for ways fathers can work on some of the issues that we have discussed in this chapter. As with any suggestions, you should modify them to meet the specific needs of your family.

Specific Suggestions

NETWORKING

Many parenting tasks are learned behaviors that parents need to acquire and practice. Some men, because of their conditioning, believe that they should know everything and not ask for help. When a father realizes he does *not* have to know everything about parenting, he is taking an important first step in being able to receive help, support, and information. Networking is reaching out to others to learn from them and to teach them. It is the process of building up a team of people on whom you can come to rely. No one is formally taught to be a parent and it is crucial that fathers view learning from others (as well as teaching others) as part of effective parenting. Fathers can be like an octopus reaching out to as many resources within the community as possible to gather information, meet people, find pleasurable family activities, and locate other families in similar situations. In these ways, the father begins to build a new sense of community and of family.

Helpful courses on parenting abound at community colleges. Adult education programs have classes in parent-child communication and some school systems have resources for parents (books, tapes, classes) at their media centers. Most communities have single-parent organizations, which is one way of meeting single parents and finding out what is available in the community. Parents Without Partners and SWORD (Separated, Widowed, or Divorced) are organizations that have discussion groups, guest speakers and a variety of social events throughout the year. Other community resources, such as community mental health centers, social services, and the Bureau of Mental Health can serve as additional sources of help and support.

One important reason to participate in networking is that it provides alternative models of the family. Children and adults who are adjusting to divorce often feel a loss of family. To branch out and include other families gives a message of hope to children that life goes on, that they will not be isolated, and that there will still be pleasurable times. Some single-parent families plan holidays together. In one particular men's group at Christmas time, some fathers were talking about how they were going to miss the traditional family gathering. Other men pointed out that in their families, although there were the usual activities of trimming the tree and decorating the house, a true sense of connection was missing. Some of the fathers decided to begin new traditions, one of them being getting together with their children for a holiday meal. Each family would bring a dish to share and rotate houses from year to year.

Creating a new extended family through networking helps in other ways. Fathers may want their children to continue to participate in certain activities but be unable to take time from work to transport them there. Parents may be able to start a car pool so that they can help parents handle the competing demands. When the father has to leave town on business or for personal reasons, the network can provide child-care assistance.

A school can be a wonderful networking source. For many families the school has provided a sense of consistency, stability, and caring during a time of family upheaval. A teacher can be an ally to parent and child when informed about a student's home situation. School counselors can recommend various counseling services and coordinate professionals in the school and other agencies to enhance family and individual functioning.

Explaining Divorce to Children

1. Give children some time before the actual physical separation occurs. You can help prepare the children for this and be around to answer their questions. Don't make it too long because children may get too anxious and be unsure about the time.

2. When possible, explain the pending separation and/or divorce in a clear manner *together*. Each parent needs to speak for himself or herself. Set up agreed-upon rules beforehand. Speak about yourself, your feelings, and your perspective without bad-mouthing your spouse.

3. Reassure the children of your love for them and intention to remain actively involved with them.

4. Give your permission for the children to have loving relationships with the other parent.

5. Don't be afraid to share your own feelings. It can set the stage for open communication between fathers and their children.

6. Modify what you say based on children's ages. Understand that younger children need concrete examples to help them understand. A middle- and high-school-aged youngster can see more of the mutuality of relationships and understand a more abstract explanation. For example: "Your mom and I have not been getting along for some time. We have had happy times together in our marriage, such as (give examples). But there are so many differences and most of all, we don't have the same loving feelings for each other anymore. I wanted Mom to be home and thought she could be happy. She says she has felt like a prisoner and wants to work and do a lot of things outside the home."

"We love you very much and are sorry if we are hurting you with this decision. We will each see you (for younger children be very concrete) every Sunday. It is not your fault that we are not happy together. We need to try to work our problems out. Mom is going to move ___date___ . Her new home is at ___address___ . We thought you'd like to see it and help set up where you'll sleep."

"You can ask us questions now and later. We know there will be lots of questions as time goes on. I feel very sad. I'm concerned about how you are feeling."

Remember that discussing the reasons for the divorce and that the child is not responsible for it have to be done repeatedly. Your seven-year-old may have one understanding of divorce but then, three years later, after hearing about a friend's parents' divorce, may believe something entirely different.

How Parents and Children Can Express Anger

1. "I'm too angry to talk to you right now. I need to cool off for a while before I'm ready to talk."

2. "I feel really upset when you speak badly about Mom/ Dad. I love her/him and it hurts me when you speak like that."

3. "I'm angry because I try so hard to help you and you didn't say thank you and you yelled at me."

4. "I feel bad when you return from Mom's house and go right up to your room. I know it's hard for you to switch houses,

but when you start slamming doors and refuse to talk to me for the whole night, I feel hurt and angry. I would like to be able to talk about ways you can come home without our feeling upset with each other."

5. "When I come home after being with Mom, I feel confused. I feel sad because I get used to being with her and I miss her. I know you're real glad to see me and I don't want to hurt your feelings, but I don't feel happy. Sometimes I'm angry because I wish this whole divorce didn't occur."

6. In addition, physical activities can help get anger out so it's not taken out on each other:

- punching bags
- walking, jogging, sports
- writing letters
- punching pillow

Brainstorming Ways of Coping with Children's Return Home after Visitation with Their Mother

1. Children agree to say hello and go right up to their room for an hour or however long they need to readjust before reentering family.

2. Children talk with Dad about their angry, confused, alone feelings.

3. Children have some shared activity they and family enjoy doing together when they come home.

4. If needed, Dad can coach the child on how to avoid getting involved in parental conflicts that may arise as a result of the visit.

Raising Teenage Daughters

1. Listen to them and be aware that they may feel uncomfortable being raised by a father. This feeling of discomfort may have nothing to do with you personally but rather is reflective of the situation you are in.

2. Do not make them feel like they should take the place of the mother. Encourage them to get involved in teenage activities.

3. Have information about female development available for you and your daughters to read. This will build your understanding of what she is going through.

4. Do not be offended if your daughter seeks out other females or her mother to talk to. Consider encouraging this kind of contact just as you would want your son to have contact with supportive adult males if you were not available.

General Suggestions

1. Your children need unconditional love. This means hugging them, being affectionate, saying you care or love them, spending time with them. This is loving children simply because they are your children—not because they've achieved something.

2. You need to believe in yourself as a parent and develop a set of values, beliefs, and practices as a parent that can be adapted to your children's personality, age, and stage of development as well as your own life situation. If you truly know your children and are an involved parent, trust your gut instincts and feelings.

3. Reach out to other parents in reciprocal ways. Do not isolate yourself, then feel like a failure because your children are having difficulty and you think you're a failure as a parent. As one parent helps you in certain ways (such as suggesting how to organize homework time), you can offer help to that same parent in other ways.

4. Listen carefully to your children. If you speak to each other often and have an honest relationship, your children, through their behavior and words, will let you know how you are doing as a parent.

5. Set limits for your children so they are clear about what the rules are in your house. Try and make the rules in your house and their mother's house consistent.

6. Don't make your children your whole life. Making time for yourself and seeing friends is a healthy example for your children that life can go on.

7. Be available to your children as they go through the grief

process of the separation and divorce (if they are coming to live with you after living with their mother for a few years you will have to help them deal with the separation from her). The more you are there to support them through this, the healthier the adjustment they'll make. It will take about two years for the initial impact of divorce to be resolved but expect ongoing concerns related to divorce as children get older and are at different levels of emotional and intellectual functioning.

8. Your children will need their grandparents. Reach out to your parents, and, when appropriate, your ex-wife's parents. Reassure the older generation that they can maintain their relationship with your children.

9. You can model healthy coping! How you communicate, express feelings, resolve problems, and use resources set an example for your children to follow. The more you reinforce them for positive actions, the more they will behave in desired ways.

10. Be tuned in to them. Ask questions that help them talk about their feelings. When they are sharing their feelings, they need an empathic statement from you and acceptance. For example, such an empathic statement could be, "It sounds like this is a really rough time for you. I feel sad that you are so unhappy." Here you are not only empathic, you are providing a model that sharing feelings is important. When they are hesitant to express feelings, try to understand why. Are they afraid of your response? What do they think will happen if they express their feelings? Children fear hurting or angering a parent. You can be helpful in demonstrating that you are emotionally strong enough to work through the feelings you have when your children communicate to you.

11. Do not expect to solve all your children's problems. It helps to realize that most often, with unconditional love and support, your children will have high enough self-esteem to learn to solve problems. As you feel good about your parenting and credit yourself for the hard work involved, think about what you are doing for your children!

12. Do not believe that everything that is happening to you and your child is because you are living in a single-parent family. Parents in two-parent families also struggle.

13. Remember to keep your children out of any ongoing

conflict between you and your ex-wife. This is often difficult but is vitally important to their establishing a sense of themselves and a smoother relationship with both of you.

14. Strike a balance where you recognize, on the one hand, that you and your children are going through a transitional period where a certain amount of stress is normal. At the same time, be aware that your position as a single father is unique and may require innovative coping responses.

15. Think about the messages you received about being a man and a father as you were growing up. Ask yourself if these messages are relevant today.

Conclusion

Children who experience divorce can grow in constructive ways if given the chance to resolve divorce-related concerns. They and their parents can learn to share feelings and communicate more effectively with each other, in some cases better than they did before the divorce. Children of divorce tend to become more independent and learn to use outside resources at earlier ages than their peers. It has been said they grow up a little faster.

Therapy can help when children and parents have a difficult time adjusting to divorce. How long children are in therapy varies according to age, the reason for the therapy, and the personalities of the children and parents involved.

In your toughest moments with your children, try to remember they want to have a close relationship with you, please you, and be loved and accepted by you. While you, in turn, may need to give more, it is hoped you have felt the joy of being there for them. Remember, too, to give yourself a "pat on the back" for being an active and caring parent.

When you make family living a mutual process, with each member willing to accept responsibility for making the family work, and you view and trust your family in a positive way, you will have a greater likelihood of shared success.

14

The Future of Single Fathering

Pᴿᴏꜰᴇꜱꜱɪᴏɴᴀʟ musicians often go through a period in their training when they have to be coached in how to make their instrument a part of them. For many, it does not come naturally. It is only when the conversion is made from the musician experiencing the instrument as existing outside of himself or herself to its existing within the musician that the marriage of musician and instrument is consummated. The violin, for example, is first viewed as a piece of wood, well-polished and lightweight, with four finely tuned strings, that has the capacity for producing beautiful music. With patience, understanding, and hard work, the instrument that once lay alone in its case becomes an extension of the expert musician. It is incorporated into the musician's personality so that when it is played, instrument and musician are working as one.

Many fathers are like the novice musician. They feel initially uncomfortable with their children, but learn, with patience, understanding, and hard work, to make the children a part of themselves.

By the time you have read this far in the book you have learned three important things about being a single father with custody:

1. It is not easy.
2. Many fathers, even without preparation, are parenting successfully.
3. It can be a very rewarding experience.

Throughout this book I have tried to point out the difficulties and joys of fathering alone, how to cope with those difficulties, and how to get the most from the joys. Understanding what the typical father goes through, whether following a divorce or death, is vital to dealing with this family arrangement. Raising kids alone means an incredible time commitment and personal sacrifice. With the end of his marriage (or the death of his wife), a man's world is turned upside down. Once he has his children on his own, he is forced to deal with a new crop of issues that he may never have considered. Little in his background or upbringing prepare him for being the primary caretaker of his children. It sends him down a track few fathers have traveled. Yet here he is, out of deep concern for his children and a commitment to parenting, trying to juggle a number of balls at once. For example, managing the household, dealing with work, establishing a social life, handling the children's emotional needs, and resolving a relationship with the ex-wife all have to be maintained in a symmetry that permits none to crash to the ground. At the same time, the father is weighed down by his own feelings about the loss of the marriage and the pain of loneliness. Juggling these often competing issues, even for the most skilled (male or female), is treacherous.

Single parenting is not for every father. A few regret having the responsibility and wish it could be shifted to someone else. Most men, though, are happy the children are with them. They believe things are working out for the best for everyone involved. Whether or not they initially fought for their children, they want their situation to continue. They have discovered a new side of themselves, an enhanced capacity for love and caring. Once they have experienced it, they never want to give it up.

The commitment demonstrated by these fathers is testimony to the level of commitment men are capable of. Men have often been accused of being passengers on the emotional boat rides life provides. Believed to be incapable of caring as deeply about relationships as women and painted as distant fathers, men are excluded, and exclude themselves, from many opportunities for closeness. Yet the fathers in this book are, for the most part, men who are willing to get close, who want a hands-on approach, and who are capable of giving more than they thought.

Fathers and Mothers over Time

This level of commitment is partially demonstrated by the fact that most fathers do not give up custody once they have it. Two follow-up studies, one of fathers with custody who were recontacted three years after initially being interviewed and one of mothers without custody who were reached five years after initial contact,[1] found that most custody arrangements that go to the father remain essentially intact. Only one in twelve of the fathers, an average of seven years after first getting custody, no longer had it. Noncustodial mothers reported regaining custody slightly more often.

What about other aspects of the father's life over time? The fathers who remained single tended to report a decline in how they rated themselves as a parent. This was surprising. But, when thinking about it, this finding fits in with a developmental change going on in the family—the children growing older. After a number of years, the fathers were predominantly raising teenagers by that point, who, as was shown in chapter 5, are more taxing than younger children. Over time, the fathers may also have acquired a more realistic appraisal of the demands of parenting. This decline in self-rating appears to have been an isolated one. No other areas relating to the father's appraisal of himself or his situation (for example, his social life or his work demands) declined, with the exception of the rate of visitation by the ex-wife.[2] The children's satisfactory progress also remained in place and most fathers were optimistic about the future. Clearly, parenting for these fathers remains a viable lifestyle even as the years go on.

Of course, fathers do not always stay single. About two fathers in five had remarried within a seven-year period, usually choosing women who also were raising children. Among those who remained single, the sentiments about remarriage were mixed. Some longed for a new wife, both to help out and as a companion. Others were staunch bachelors, determined to avoid marriage vows at least until the children were older, if not forever. It was interesting to learn from the fathers who had remarried that they tended to be more involved in housekeeping with their new wives than they had in their previous marriages. Perhaps raising children alone in the interim had raised their awareness of the importance of sharing these chores!

Most (92 percent) of the mothers without custody who were recontacted were still single. Satisfaction with their current lives is quite high: almost three-quarters said things had worked out for the best for them and their children. Comfort for these mothers definitely increases over time. Those raising younger children particularly report feeling an improvement, including greater ease in being able to tell other people that they are non-custodial, something that is very difficult at first for this population. Visitation between the mother and her children, as corroborated by the fathers, was reported to have first declined. Yet it was found that once the children reached young adulthood, contact increased. This can be encouraging news for those espousing greater involvement between the child and the noncustodial parent. It most likely occurs at young adulthood because it is at that stage that children realize the importance of staying in touch with both their parents. Issues of child support and visitation are also no longer controlled by the courts or the custodial parent. Thus potential stumbling blocks to visitation are removed as the child reaches maturity.

The Future

Any look at the future must carry a few predictions about general trends. Three are offered here that are believed to affect solo parenting in the 1990s:

1. The number of single fathers with sole or joint custody will continue to grow. Even though the divorce rate peaked in the early 1980s, the trend toward fathers' seeking custody and mothers' feeling increasingly comfortable relinquishing it has been established. There is no indication that fathers are going to lose interest in raising their children after a marital breakup.

2. Children are going to find adjusting to this child-care arrangement increasingly easy. As the sheer numbers of children of divorce and of children living with their fathers increase, these youngsters will feel more accepted. More of those peers

will have experienced the same thing. Also, parents, through newspapers, TV shows, books, and magazines are gaining a greater understanding of the effect of divorce and what can be done to minimize its impact.

This prediction is not to say that divorce will ever be easy for the children. The pain from such a breakup is one of the greatest they will suffer. Yet as it becomes more common and as people have a greater understanding of how to deal with it, it becomes less problematic than it was for previous generations.

3. Fathering alone is *not* going to get markedly easier for fathers in general than it is already. The daddy track will continue. The interviews do not indicate that public opinion of these men is any more accepting than it had been, that it is changing swiftly, or that conditions at work are any more responsive. While parenting for fathers in the 1990s may be easier in terms of dealing with the children and with the court systems, continued difficulty at work and the lack of social satisfaction discussed in the preface would tend to balance things out. This is not to say that fathers cannot or should not parent alone. It is to caution that broad changes in the community to accommodate fathers are not likely to be forthcoming.

What can make fathering alone easier for fathers and their children? One expert suggests we think of custody not in terms of ownership of the children, but in terms of residence.[3] It is not that the children belong to one parent or the other, but that they live with one parent while remaining a part of both parents' lives. Thinking this way can help parents forge a stronger tie. The more parents can work together the easier it will be for the children. Children go through a number of "crises" as they grow up—puberty, first loves, the demands of school and making friends, etc.—that can make certain stages of childhood particularly demanding. Divorced parents must work to minimize those difficulties by consulting each other, keeping each other informed, and not being defensive or negative. Regardless of where the children live, reconceptualizing the "ownership" of the children can help.

Listen carefully to what your children say and give them the time they need. Do not involve them in your conflicts with their mother. As is outlined in the previous chapter, parents must be responsive to what the separation from the mother, whether it is caused by divorce or death, means to the children and accept the feelings they express about it.

If you need help, seek out the counsel of others. Learn what your legal rights are. When appropriate, try to make your place of work more responsive to your situation. Join groups for single parents, read books, and go for therapy if that is needed. It is no disgrace to ask for or receive help. Admitting you can benefit from others is a sign of strength. Ignoring a problem, or actively running from it, will not make it go away or make your family life any easier.

Understand that remarriage, if you are interested in it, may not happen quickly. Many fathers are single again for a number of years, while some never remarry. Do not rush into a new relationship just so your children can have a mother. That will not work out for you or them.

Finally, remember that solo parenting is possible. If you are fathering alone or considering it, you do not have to subscribe to the myths that men should not or cannot parent on their own. The stories of the fathers in this book are testimony to the rewarding possibilities that exist for you.

Appendix A: The Surveys

THE data for this book were gathered through two methods. First, using the same method employed for the 1982 survey (Greif 1985a), a 104-item questionnaire was published in the membership magazine of Parents Without Partners (PWP), *The Single Parent*, in October 1987. PWP is the largest self-help group for single parents in the United States, with more than 160,000 members at the time the questionnaire appeared. Divorced or separated fathers raising children alone most of the time were asked to complete the questionnaire and fold it into a postage-guaranteed mailer for return to me. I received more than twelve hundred returns over the next six months. Only fathers whose children lived with them for an average of at least five nights a week were included. Fathers whose children were with them less often were considered to have an arrangement that more closely resembled joint custody and were excluded for later use. The findings from that sample appear in chapter 10. Fathers whose wives had died also were excluded from the original data base. Their stories appear in chapter 11. Ninety-five percent of those in the main study of divorced and separated fathers had their children with them at least six nights a week—that is, the vast majority of the time. After removing questionnaires with incomplete or logically inconsistent responses, 933 usable questionnaires remained.

An exact return rate is difficult to calculate. PWP does not keep records on the sex or custodial status of its members. Drawing from a 1986 membership poll of two hundred randomly selected members, and allowing for variations between that data and this survey, magazines that were never delivered, and questionnaires that potentially were never seen, the return rate can conservatively be estimated at 20 percent but may be higher.

A second method, not attempted in 1982, was also used to

gain a sample. Graduate students from the University of Maryland School of Social Work were sent to counties in the Baltimore, Washington, and Philadelphia metropolitan areas to obtain names of custodial fathers from court records. These fathers were then sent a questionnaire and a cover letter requesting their participation. This approach yielded a return rate of almost 10 percent. These responses were combined with those of a few fathers who were not PWP members but had acquired the questionnaire from a friend or source who was a member. The second method resulted in a sample of 199. To establish the efficacy of combining the two samples, PWP members were compared with non-PWP members on a variety of demographic variables. Significant differences were found in only two areas, neither of which had been previously found to affect outcome, so the two samples were combined, resulting in a total data base by March 1988 of 1,132.

Since the publication of the survey and up to this book's publication, graduate students have conducted more than 250 in-depth telephone interviews with a randomly selected group of fathers. These interviews, which at times lasted over an hour, have provided a great deal of information about the experiences of the fathers that could not be captured by a questionnaire. The interviews also provided a cross-check on the questionnaire data. Many of the stories gained from the fathers have been included in the book.

The limitations of these approaches are important to note. The 1988 surveys are based on self-selected samples; that is, we are only learning about fathers who choose to tell us about themselves. No clear information is available about fathers who choose not to respond. Thus we do not know if we are hearing from the fathers who are doing well or those that are having the most difficulty. No systematic observation of these fathers was undertaken by an objective observer to learn how they are parenting. In addition, the sample is drawn from a self-help group and the court system. Fathers who do not join PWP and who have not had their cases processed by the courts that were sampled are not tapped. It is problematic, then, to generalize the findings from these fathers to all fathers with custody. At the same time, the large sample allows for a great wealth and variety of information to be gathered from fathers from many different walks of life. It also permits for the application of more sophisticated statistical tests than could be attempted with a smaller sample. While the statistical tests are not reported in the book, they are available elsewhere, as noted in the bibliography. Combined with the 1982 survey of 1,136 fathers and noting the limitations, these surveys provide the best source of data currently available on this population.

The thinking that goes into this book has also been augmented by research a coauthor and I undertook that eventually became *Mothers without Custody* (Greif and Pabst 1988). Based on interviews and questionnaire returns from 517 noncustodial mothers, that book provides an important counterpoint to the perspective offered by the custodial fathers. Where it is believed important to offer the other side of the coin, reference will be made to the research on mothers. In completing that book, forty-seven fathers without custody were sampled. In addition, 150 mothers with custody had been studied when the first survey of single fathers was conducted. Adding these samples together with the widowers and the fathers with joint custody, information has been gained over a seven-year period from more than three thousand single parents in a wealth of custody arrangements. Work that builds on the surveys of fathers has also been undertaken in other countries by John Wilson at the School of Social Work, Philip Institute of Technology in Melbourne, Australia; Tony Ralph and Val Brown in Davenport, Tasmania (available from the Tasmanian State Institute of Technology); and Michael Hardey at the University of Surrey in England.

Profile of the Fathers

The fathers in this book tend to be white and middle-class with an average income of $33,400, and a median income of $30,000. According to the Census Bureau, they are earning a few thousand dollars a year more than the typical white male householder in the United States with no wife present. The fathers have a range of occupations, from blue collar to professional. Most have completed at least some years of college, though one in four holds no more than a high school education. Half the fathers are Protestant, 25 percent are Catholic, and the rest either expressed no preference (17 percent), are Jewish (3 percent), or identify with other religions (5 percent). Most have only been married once and are currently divorced rather than separated. Nearly two-thirds live within fifty miles of their ex-wives, with one-half living no more than twenty miles away. Respondents come from forty-eight states and Canada, with more than half the states having at least ten respondents. The ten states with the most respondents are (in descending order): California, Maryland, Ohio, Pennsylvania, New York, Michigan, Texas, New Jersey, Florida, and Illinois.

Marriages have lasted an average of twelve years, with the fathers having sole custody for about four years at the time of the survey. Most fathers gained custody at the time of the breakup. They are raising between one and two children on average, with the oldest child having a mean age of thirteen. Sixteen percent (293) of the 1,851 children age eighteen and younger being raised by the fathers are six and younger. Forty-two percent of the fathers are raising only boys, 31 percent are raising boys and girls, and 27 percent are raising only girls. When a father is not raising all his children, those children living elsewhere are more apt to be female than male by a 3-to-2 ratio. About one father in seven is raising at least three children alone.

The term "custody" is used throughout to refer to the children's living with the father the vast majority of the time. It does not necessarily mean that the arrangement has been legalized, though 87 percent of the fathers have been to court for that purpose.

It should be noted that all identifying information about the fathers has been changed to conceal their identities.

Appendix B: Where to Go for Help

Fathers' Advocacy Information Resource, 1 Northeast 10th St., Milford, DE 19963. (800) 722-FAIR.

Men's Rights, Inc., P.O. Box 163180, Sacramento, CA 95816. (916) 484-7333.

Mothers Without Custody, P.O. Box 56762, Houston, TX 77256-6762. (713) 840-1622.

National Coalition of Free Men, P.O. Box 129, Manhasset, NY 11030. (516) 482-6378.

National Congress for Men, 2020 Pennsylvania Ave., NW, Suite 277, Washington, DC 20006. (202) FATHERS; Electronic Bulletin Board (602) 840-4752 (300-2400 Baud).

National Council for Children's Rights, 2001 O St., NW, Washington, DC 20036. (202) 547-6227.

National Center for Missing and Exploited Children, Suite 600, 1835 K St., NW, Washington, DC 20006. (800) 843-5678.

National Organization for Changing Men, 794 Penn Ave., Pittsburgh, PA 15221. (412) 371-8007.

Office for Child Support Enforcement and Reference Center, 6110 Executive Blvd., Rockville, MD 20852.

Parents Without Partners, 8807 Colesville Rd., Silver Spring, MD 20910. (301) 588-9354.

Thanks to Ginnie Nuta and Jack Kammer for their suggestions.

Widowed Persons Service, American Association of Retired Persons, 1909 K St., NW, Washington, DC 20049. (202) 872-2400.

Look for Local Chapters Of:

Fathers United for Equal Rights

SWORD (Separated, Widowed, or Divorced)

Single-parent groups meeting in churches, synagogues, mental health centers, schools, hospitals, etc.

Stepfamily Association of America

Notes

Chapter 1

1. U.S. Department of Commerce (1988).
2. Orthner, Brown, and Ferguson (1976); Greif (1985a).
3. Derdeyn (1976).
4. Rotundo (1985).
5. U.S. Department of Commerce (1987).
6. Schwartz (1989). After this book was published, Ball (1989) published an article under a similar title.

Chapter 3

1. Glenn and Kramer (1987).
2. Personal communication with Ob/Gyn Clinic, Johns Hopkins University, May 1989, and personal communication with Judith Fortier, University of Maryland Baltimore County, Aug. 7, 1989.
3. Greif and Pabst (1988).
4. Greif and Pabst (1988).
5. Albrecht and Kunz (1980).
6. Greif and Pabst (1988).
7. Albrecht and Kunz (1980) cite a higher number of fathers who gave these reasons.
8. Greif and Pabst (1988).

Chapter 4

1. Pleck and Corfman (1979); Maret and Finlay (1984).
2. Blumstein and Schwartz (1983, 144–145).
3. Burros (1988).
4. Blank (1984).
5. Special thanks to Risa Garon for many of the suggestions included in this chapter.

Chapter 5

1. Hudson's (1982) Index of Parental Attitudes (IPA) was used to measure the father's relationship with his children. This scale consists of twenty-five statements with which the father is asked to state his level of agreement. Statements include, "My child(ren) gets on my nerves," "I get along well with my child(ren)," and so forth. Scores range from a low of zero to a high of one hundred, with a clinical cutting score of thirty. Anyone scoring thirty or higher is considered to have a clinically significant problem in their relationships with their children. The IPA has strong internal-consistency reliability and discriminates well among groups of clients in therapy who were judged to have problems with their children. For the current sample, strong internal consistency was found. The scale mean for the entire sample was 13.3, with a standard deviation of 9.8. This suggests a very favorable rating by the fathers of their level of contentment with their relationship with their children.
2. Clarke-Stewart (1977); Lynn (1974).
3. Rutter (1972); Lamb and Lamb (1976); Levine (1976); Parke and Sarovin (1976).
4. Clarke-Stewart (1977, 21).
5. Ambert (1982).
6. Santrock and Warshak (1979). Some recent research also suggests that fathers experience a decrease in self-esteem as they become more involved parents. Hawkins and Belsky (1989).
7. DeMaris and Greif (1989).

Chapter 6

1. Pleck (1989).

Chapter 7

1. Greif (1987b).

Chapter 8

1. All information on mothers without custody is taken from Greif and Pabst (1988).
2. Ibid.
3. Ibid.
4. See Greif and Pabst (1988, 235–250) for more information on this family.
5. Greif and DeMaris (in press [b]).

Chapter 9

1. Polikoff (1982); Woods, Been, and Schulman (1982).
2. Greif and DeMaris (in press [a]).
3. Johnston and Campbell (1988).
4. Nuta (1986).
5. Greif and Pabst (1988).
6. See Greif and Pabst (1988) for more on reasons mothers do not pay.

Chapter 10

1. Schulman (1985).
2. Gardner (1978).
3. Forty-four fathers who completed the questionnaire for the sole custodian study were classified as involved in joint physical custody. Twelve of the fathers were telephoned for in-depth interviews. The definition of joint custody used here dealt solely with the number of overnights on the average the mother spent with the child per month. As the number of overnights spent by the mother with the children was established at eight or fewer for the father to be considered a sole custodian, nine to twenty-two was the number of overnights the mother and child would have to have together for the father to be a joint custodian. The average number of nights for the group was thirteen. The typical pattern for these joint custodial fathers was that they had the children four nights a week while the mother had them three nights a week. As it is believed to be slightly more common for joint custody mothers to have more overnights with the children, this group of fathers may not be typical of all joint custody fathers. In addition, the limitations mentioned on page 228 about being able to generalize these findings to other fathers would also apply to this group.

Chapter 11

1. U.S. Department of Commerce (1986).
2. Kubler-Ross (1969).
3. Rando (1984).
4. Adair (1986).
5. Ibid.
6. Ibid.
7. Hormann (1983); Jackson (1965).
8. Adair (1986).
9. Gasser and Taylor (1976); Carey (1977).
10. Greif (1983); Greif (1986b).
11. Burgess (1985).

12. The sample was gained from fathers who returned the questionnaire seeking information on divorced and separated fathers with custody. Since they were widowers, they were excluded from the initial analysis. Some fathers indicated they completed the questionnaire because they wanted the plight of the widower to be known. Twelve fathers were interviewed in-depth by telephone.

Chapter 13

1. In an attempt to learn more about the children's experiences growing up with their father, seventy-six fathers who had children eighteen and older were telephoned and asked if a questionnaire could be sent to that young adult. All fathers agreed and provided an address to which the questionnaires were mailed. Twenty-six usable questionnaires (34 percent) were returned and provide the basis for what we believe is the first look at this large a sample of young adults who had been raised by a single father.
2. Wallerstein and Blakeslee (1989).

Chapter 14

1. The information for this section is discussed in greater depth in Greif (1987b) and Greif and Emad (1989).
2. In Greif (1987b) the involvement of the ex-wife was shown to have increased according to one measure. A five-year follow-up was conducted with the same sample two years later, at which point the first measure no longer showed significance. Thus, it is generally believed, as was confirmed by Greif and Emad (1989), that the visitation of the mother does not increase and may decrease, at least for a number of years following the father's gaining custody.
3. Kaslow (1989).

References

Adair, C. 1986. Beyond grief. *The Single Parent,* 24(4), 24–27.

Albrecht, S.L., and Kunz, P.R. 1980. The decision to divorce: A social exchange perspective. *Journal of Divorce,* 2, 319–337.

Ambert, A.-M. 1982. Differences in children's behavior toward custodial mothers and fathers. *Journal of Marriage and the Family,* 44, 73–86.

Ball, A.L. 1989. The Daddy Track. *New York,* Oct. 23, 52–60.

Blank, H. 1984. Testimony of the Children's Defense Fund before the Subcommittee on Elementary, Secondary, and Vocational Education of the Educational and Labor Committee, April 30.

Blumstein, P., and Schwartz, P. 1983. *American couples.* New York: William Morrow.

Burgess, J.K. 1985. Widowers as fathers. In *Dimensions of fatherhood,* S.M.H. Hanson and F.W. Bozett, editors. Beverly Hills: Sage Publications.

Burros, M. 1988. Women: Out of the house but not out of the kitchen. *New York Times,* Feb. 24, pp. A1 and C10.

Carey, R.G. 1977. The widowed: A year later. *Journal of Counseling Psychology,* 24, 125–131.

Clarke-Stewart, A. 1977. *Childcare in the family.* New York: Academic Press.

DeMaris, A., and Greif, G.L. 1989. The influence of family structure on parent-child relationships in single father households. Unpublished manuscript.

Derdeyn, A.P. 1976. Child custody contests in historical perspective. *American Journal of Psychiatry,* 11, 1369–75.

Gardner, R.A. 1978. Social, legal, and therapeutic changes that should lessen the traumatic effects of divorce on children. *Journal of the American Academy of Psychoanalysis,* 6: 231–247.

Gasser, R.D., and Taylor, C.M. 1976. Role adjustment of single parent fathers with dependent children. *The Family Coordinator,* 25, 397–401.

Glenn, N.B., and Kramer, K.B. 1987. The marriages and divorces of the children of divorce. *Journal of Marriage and the Family,* 49, 811–825.

Greif, G.L. 1983. Widowers. *The Single Parent,* 26(7), 29–32.

———. 1985a. *Single fathers.* Lexington, MA: Lexington Books.

———. 1985b. Single fathers rearing children. *Journal of Marriage and the Family,* 47, 185–191.

———. 1985c. Practice with single fathers. *Social Work in Education,* 7, 231–243.

———. 1985d. Children and housework in the single father family. *Family Relations,* 34, 353–357.

————. 1986a. Clinical practice with the single father: A structural approach. *International Journal of Family Psychiatry*, 7, 261–275.

————. 1986b. The special problems of the widower. In *Re-Searching Death: Selected essays in death education and counseling*, R.A. Pacholski, editor. Lakewood, OH: Forum for death education and counseling.

————. 1987a. Mothers without custody. *Social Work*, 32, 11–17.

————. 1987b. A longitudinal examination of single custodial fathers: Implications for treatment. *American Journal of Family*, 15, 253–260.

————. 1989a. Split custody: A beginning understanding. *Journal of Divorce*, 13, 130–140.

————. 1989b. Single fathers with custody. *Family Therapy Networker*, November–December, 38–39.

————. 1989c. British and American fathers: A brief comparison. *The Single Parent*, 32(6), 15, 46.

Greif, G.L., and DeMaris, A. 1989. Dads raising kids: A new survey. *The Single Parent*, 32(1): 12–14, 45.

————. In press (a). Single fathers in contested custody suits. *Journal of Psychiatry and Law*.

————. In press (b). Single fathers who experience discomfort when sole custodians. *Families in Society*.

Greif, G.L., and Emad, F. 1989. A longitudinal examination of mothers without custody: Implications for treatment. *American Journal of Family Therapy*, 17, 155–163.

Greif, G.L., and Pabst, M. 1988. *Mothers without custody*. Lexington, MA: Lexington Books.

Greif, G.L., and Zuravin, S. 1989. Natural fathers: A placement resource for abused and neglected children? *Child Welfare*, 58, 479–490.

Hawkins, A.J., and Belsky, J. 1989. The role of father involvement in personality change in men across the transition to parenthood. *Family Relations*, 38, 378–384.

Hormann, E. 1983. Explaining death to children. *The Single Parent*, 26(9), 25–27.

Hudson, W. 1982. *The clinical measurement package: A field manual*. Chicago: The Dorsey Press.

Jackson, E. 1965. *Telling a child about death*. New York: Hawthorn.

Johnston, J.R., and Campbell, L.E. 1988. *Impasses of divorce*. New York: The Free Press.

Kaslow, F. 1989. Family law issues in family therapy practice. *American Journal of Family Therapy*, 17, 155.

Kitson, G.C., Lopata, H.Z., Holmes, W.M., and Meyering, S.M. 1980. Divorcees and widows: Similarities and differences. *American Journal of Orthopsychiatry*, 50, 291–301.

Kubler-Ross, E. 1969. *On death and dying*. New York: Macmillan.

Lamb, M.E., and Lamb, J. 1976. The nature and importance of the father-infant relationship. *The Family Coordinator*, 25, 379–385.

Levine, J. 1976. *Who will raise the children?* New York: Bantam Books.

Lynn, D.B. 1974. *The father: His role in child development*. Monterey, CA: Brooks Cole.

Maret, E., and Finlay, B. 1984. The distribution of household labor among women in dual-earner families. *Journal of Marriage and the Family*, 46, 357–364.

Nuta, V.R. 1986. Emotional aspects of child support enforcement. *Family Relations*, 35, 177–181.

Orthner, D., Brown, T., and Ferguson, D. 1976. Single-parent fatherhood: An emerging lifestyle. *The Family Coordinator*, 25, 429–437.

Parke, R., and Sarovin, D.B. 1976. The father's role in infancy: A reevaluation. *The Family Coordinator*, 25, 365–371.

Pleck, J. 1989. Family-supportive employer policies and men's participation. Paper presented to Committee on Women's Employment and Related Social Issues, National Research Council, Washington, D.C., March 20–21.

Pleck, J., and Corfman, E. 1979. Married men: Work and family. In *Families today*, Vol. 1, E. Corfman, editor. Washington, D.C.: U.S. Department of Health, Education, and Welfare.

Polikoff, N. 1982. Why are mothers losing: A brief analysis of criteria used in child custody determinations. *Women's Rights Reporter*, 7, 235–243.

Rando, T.A. 1984. *Grief, dying, and death: Clinical interventions for caregivers.* Champaign, IL: Research Press Co.

Rotundo, E.A. 1985. American fatherhood. *American Behavioral Scientist*, 29, 7–25.

Rutter, M. 1972. *Maternal deprivation reassessed.* Baltimore: Penguin.

Santrock, J.W., and Warshak, R. 1979. Father custody and social development in boys and girls. *Journal of Social Issues*, 35, 112–125.

Schulman, J. 1985. Who's looking after the children? *Family Advocate*, 5(2): 31–37, 43–44.

Schwartz, F.N. 1989. Management women and the new facts of life. *Harvard Business Review*, 89, 65–76.

Silverman, P. 1987. In search of new selves: Accommodating to widowhood. In *Families in transition: Primary prevention programs that work*, L.A. Bond and B.M. Wagner, editors. Beverly Hills: Sage.

Terkel, S. 1974. *Working.* New York: Pantheon.

U.S. Department of Commerce, Bureau of the Census. 1986. Household and family characteristics: March 1985. Series P-20, No. 411. Washington, D.C.: Government Printing Office.

———. 1987. Households, families, marital status, and living arrangements: March 1987 (Advance report). Series P-20, No. 417. Washington, D.C.: Government Printing Office.

———. 1988. Marital status and living arrangements: March 1987. Series P-20, No. 423. Washington, D.C.: Government Printing Office.

Wallerstein, J., and Blakeslee, S. 1989. *Second chances: Men, women, and children a decade after divorce.* New York: Ticknor and Fields.

Woods, L., Been, V., and Schulman, J. 1982. The use of sex and economic discriminatory criteria in child custody awards. Paper published by the National Center on Women and Family Law, Inc.

Index

About the Author

G EOFFREY L. GREIF received his doctorate from the Columbia University School of Social Work. He has written more than thirty articles on single parents and is the author of *Single Fathers* and the co-author of *Mothers without Custody,* both published by Lexington Books. His work has been widely cited in professional literature, newspapers, and magazines, and on television and radio. He serves on the International Professional Advisory Board of Parents Without Partners and is contributing editor to *The Single Parent* magazine. He is currently associate professor at the University of Maryland at Baltimore School of Social Work.

Contributor Risa Garon, LCSW, is a certified family life educator and a diplomate in social work. She is director of the Family Life Center's Children of Separation and Divorce Project in Columbia, Maryland.

DATE DUE